Protecting Your Children from
SEXUAL PREDATORS

Also by Leigh Baker

When Your Child's Been Abused:
A Parent's Handbook

Protecting Your Children from

SEXUAL PREDATORS

LEIGH BAKER, PSY.D.

ST. MARTIN'S PRESS ⋈ NEW YORK

PROTECTING YOUR CHILDREN FROM SEXUAL PREDATORS. Copyright © 2002 by Leigh Baker, Psy.D. All rights reserved. Printed in the United States of America. No part of this book may be used or reproduced in any manner whatsoever without written permission except in the case of brief quotations embodied in critical articles or reviews. For information, address St. Martin's Press, 175 Fifth Avenue, New York, NY 10010.

www.stmartins.com

Book design by Ellen Cipriano

Library of Congress Cataloging-in-Publication Data
Baker, Leigh.
    Protecting your children from sexual predators / Leigh Baker.—1st ed,
      p. cm.
    ISBN 0-312-27215-4
      1. Child sexual abuse—Prevention. 2. Child molesters—Psychology. 3. Child molesters—
Identification. I. Title.
    HV6570 .B35 2002
    649'.4—dc21   2001048875

First Edition: April 2002

10 9 8 7 6 5 4 3 2 1

*This book is dedicated to
the two most important people in my life,
my children, David and Jessica.*

Contents

Acknowledgments

I'd like to begin by acknowledging the courageous victims and their families I have treated throughout the years. By sharing their pain and witnessing their triumph over tragedy, I was given inspiration for this book.

The preparations to write set the stage for the daunting task ahead. Therefore a very special thanks goes to Danny Padnick for offering your home, your heart, and your loyalty to me during those first laborious months.

My wonderfully talented son, David Baker, helped me every step of the way. From researching the first ideas to reading my final drafts, your insight and creativity are greatly appreciated. To Jessica Baker, my spirited and gifted daughter, your remarkable ability to help me clarify, simplify, and organize my writing was invaluable.

Next, I would like to thank my literary agent, Craig Nelson. I appreciate your calmness throughout my emotional storms and your helpful feedback that kept me on course. To my editors at St. Martin's Press, Lara Asher and Joe Cleemann, I offer my gratitude for your praise, your enthusiasm, and your encouragement every step of the way.

I want to acknowledge the competent work of my research assistant, Carol A. Retseck. You juggled the demanding work of a deputy district attorney while completing research that was so essential to this book.

I would also like to thank all of the professionals who opened their doors to me for an interview. Your information was so helpful in writing this book. A special note of appreciation goes to two well-respected and caring professionals, Dr. Mickey Wright, who has specialized in sex offender treatment for over twenty years, and Debbie Crapeau, who works with sex offenders at the Resource Center for High Risk Youth in Denver. I learned a great deal from working with the two of you. Thank you for always opening your doors when I knocked. A special note of gratitude goes to Gail Ryan, who reviewed some of my material and helped me formulate essential ideas in the book. To G. Thomas O'Malley III, a fellow author and loyal friend, your spirit and confidence guided me throughout. I thank you for your help in reading my manuscript.

Thank you, Jerry Katz, for coming through at the very end. Your caring and friendship helped me through the tough times, and your dedication to this book came at just the right time.

Working on this book periodically drained my emotional reserve, and during those times, certain individuals paid the price. I would like to acknowledge the patience, encouragement, and the loyalty of my dedicated doctoral students and the staff at the Trauma Treatment Center of Colorado. A special thanks to Jody Cleveland for your support and interest in my work. And finally, a declaration of appreciation goes to Lindsey Linford, not only for reading the first few chapters and giving me valuable feedback, but also for listening to my endless literary aches and pains.

Author's Note

With few and obvious exceptions, like Megan Kanka, the names and identifying characteristics of the sexual predators, their victims, and the families
involved have all been changed; many are composites of the hundreds of
cases I have encountered. This book is for informational purposes and is
not intended to take the place of legal or medical advice from a trained
professional. The fact that an organization or web site is listed in this book
as a potential source of information does not mean that the author or
publisher endorses any of the information it may provide or recommendations it may make. Further, readers should be advised that web sites
offered as sources for information may have changed since this was written.

Preface

Child abuse is not an uncommon phenomenon. The media familiarize us daily with images of physical and sexual violence against children. Talk show hosts, newspaper reporters, and radio personalities gather experts, victims, and perpetrators to discuss this deadly disease that kills more children each year than floods, fires, earthquakes, and other natural disasters. Through the journalist's lens, we have seen the victim's face awash with tears and looked into the eyes of an angry predator being led up the stairs of the courthouse.

Has all this exposure made us immune to the reality of child sexual abuse? Do we tend to see the carefully executed montage of images that is flashed on our television screen as an authentic representation of child abuse, or do we transfer this into a file labeled "entertainment" so that it can be stored away with those titillating Sunday movie specials? When we are inundated with exposure to sex and violence, we slowly become invulnerable to its impact and incredulous about its existence.

We live in a paradoxical society that has the capability of capitalizing on violence while simultaneously launching a campaign against its spread. Thus, along with the discovery that sexual abuse has media value, a crusade against child maltreatment has emerged. This campaign has been vocal and prolific in spreading information about child sexual abuse. Celebrity spokespeople such as Oprah Winfrey, Roseanne Barr, and Marilyn Van Derbur-Atler, former Miss America of 1958, have spoken out against child sexual abuse. With their status and self-revelations, they have added critical armaments to fortify the fight against this ominous foe.

The data collected in the 1998 publication by the National Clearing-house on Child Abuse and Neglect spoke to the relative success of our nation's battle against child abuse. In 1990, approximately 2.3 children in a thousand were abused. In 1998, that figure decreased to 1.6. (These figures include all forms of abuse: physical, emotional, and sexual.) Yet while this decrease is encouraging, the fact remains that in 1998 over 1 million cases of child sexual assault were reported.

The fight against child abuse has taught parents to empower their children with lessons on "good and bad touch," "being able to say no," and "how to avoid strangers." And while this has resulted in a lower degree of sexual assault in school-age children, it has not proven effective in pro-tecting the very young. According to the 1998 report from the National Clearinghouse, the highest rate of child sexual abuse occurred in the infant-to-three age group. In fact, this was the only age group that showed an increase in sexual abuse, and it suggests that preschoolers may not be benefiting from the same lessons we teach school-age children.

Very young children are not capable of protecting themselves despite the lessons they may have received from parents; therefore this age group is the most vulnerable to predators. Thus parents must assume full respon-sibility for protecting those children who might not be able to convey in words what has happened to them.

For over fifteen years I have witnessed a march of child survivors passing through the doors of my practice and seen the profound emo-tional, physical, and spiritual damage that occurs as a result of sexual abuse. I was hopeful that by treating the symptoms of abuse in the safe confines of the playroom, these young victims could heal. And many of them did recover and go on to live productive and fulfilling lives. How-ever, as time wore on and a steady stream of child victims continued to flow into my clinic, I often asked myself, "Why is this virus of abuse continuing to spread?"

Throughout years of watching this abominable scourge devastate the lives of children, I have come to believe that curing those left in its wake is only one part of the solution. Once a child is abused, the damage is done, and the experience becomes an integral part of the victim's psycho-logical makeup. Preventing this beast from finding its way into the shelters of our homes should therefore be our primary focus.

So what methods can we use to keep our children safe and prevent a predator from gaining access to them? Most of us have already taught our children the basics of safety and have fortified our homes with burglar alarms, high fences, and electronic devices that can detect unwanted visitors. Yet predators continue to find their way into the sanctum of our homes. What more can we do?

The problem lies in our inability to detect the predator before he or she is allowed access to our children. We may invite the adolescent next door to come over and watch our children while we enjoy an evening on the town. We may allow Aunt Susie to take our young son on an overnight camping trip. Or we may bring our daughter to the orthodontist who appears to be "overly affectionate" with his adolescent patients. However, if we know more about the characteristics of predators and how to detect their path of seduction, we might be better equipped to determine if the adolescent baby-sitter, "Aunt Susie," or the friendly dentist poses a threat to our children.

Animals rely on smell, sound, and vision to help them sense danger, but what do humans have to signal imminent peril? We have our intuition, which helps guide us through unknown territory. Our intuition or "gut level" feelings, as they are often called, are our internal "red flags"; and are similar to the instinctual senses animals use to warn them of danger. As humans, we have the distinguished benefit of accumulated knowledge to guide us through the often precipitous road of survival. Therefore, if we can assess how and why danger may occur, we can choose to alter our course before tragedy strikes.

Our knowledge of predators is a critical tool in preventing the spread of sexual abuse. Psychologists, sociologists, and law-enforcement officials have provided us with vital information about the personalities and behaviors of sexual predators. Unfortunately, as noted previously, much of this information has been exploited for the purpose of entertainment as it is sifted down to the public through shocking stories of child abduction, serial killers, and sadistic sexual crimes.

Initially, the horrific images on our television screen immobilize us with fear for the safety of our children. But by the time our favorite evening host flashes his endearing smile on the screen and distracts us with his political humor and quick-witted celebrity interviews, we are lulled back into a false sense of security. We believe that the evil we have just seen is merely another form of entertainment, and therefore we often miss the critical information we need to prevent predators from crossing our children's paths. When we ignore the fluff of the dramatic and look at the hard facts beneath the media glitter, what does the raw data of statistical research tell us about predators?

From the most recent report published by the National Clearinghouse on Child Abuse and Neglect, we know that most predators are not complete strangers to their victims. Whether they are a family member, step-parent, counselor, coach, or teacher, in *nine out of ten cases of child sexual abuse, the predator is someone known to the child.* Therefore, while "stay away from strangers" has proved to be a wise adage, it does not help children avoid the dangerous snares of those predators who don familiar faces.

Figures collected from the National Clearinghouse also warn us that most predators are men, and that a male parent figure is the most common child sexual predator. Nonfamilial males make up the second largest group, followed by male relatives. Further, statistics tell us that the home is not always the safest place to be. Three out of four child sexual abuse cases occur in the home of the child or the home of the molester.

However, child sexual predators are not always men. As we begin to break through the barrier of social denial and cultural stereotypes that promote females as defenseless and sexually nonaggressive, we discover that women *are* capable of sexual abuse. In fact, according to the 1999 Federal publication *Child Maltreatment,* published by the U.S. Department of Health and Human Services, females are responsible for approximately 11 percent of sexual abuse committed on children. And, as you will learn, this figure is likely a low estimate.

L et's review what we know about predators up to this point. They can be either male or female — although it is more likely that they will be male — and they often already know and have access to your child. We also know from FBI profiles that the average child sexual predator is "a white male in his early thirties, who is employed and has a moderate level of education." This is not surprising since so many U.S. citizens fall into this category. Yet it does serve to remind us that predators don't have to be unsavory characters that lurk in the darkened corners of inner-city squalor. They can appear as ordinary as the boy who bags your groceries or as seemingly devoted as the religious youth counselor who teaches Bible studies to your children.

Yet the information you have been given so far about predators is not sufficient to protect your children. You must also be aware of how predators behave, what signs they give of their abusive intent, and the personality characteristics they share. You must become familiar with their patterns of seduction and the psychological ploys they will use to disguise themselves as "harmless" individuals. Armed with this type of knowledge, you will be in a better position to prevent them from gaining access to your children.

Sexual abuse has transformed itself in the twenty-first century. As society has spread its technological wings and taken flight, the germs of sexual abuse have adapted for survival. As we find more ways to inoculate our children against abuse, this tenacious disease has mutated to stronger and more virulent forms. For example, sexual predators have adapted to the Internet as they slink through cyberspace in search of prey. New prevention programs have arisen to address this type of sex abuse, and parents need to learn how to utilize these protective measures in order to block the channels through which these cyberpredators travel.

It is the intent of this book to awaken those parents who are falsely lulled into believing their children are safe and to uncover the sobering reality that predators can be found anywhere. It is only through your skills in detecting them in the midst of the suburbs, classrooms, churches, day-care centers, and doctors' offices that will determine whether your child can be kept safe from abuse.

Some of the prescriptions offered in this book for protecting your children will be familiar to you. You may feel that you already know what steps to take to hire a baby-sitter, and you do not let your children wander unsupervised throughout the neighborhood. However, when the strains of running a household, working full time, and caring for the emotional and physical needs of others necessitate cutting corners, we may loosen our grip on the fundamental ways in which we take care of our children. Some of us have even allowed the adolescent we barely know to watch our kids because the regular sitter was busy. And how many of us have taken the time out of our hectic days to accompany our son to the neighborhood greenbelt to meet his new friends? And what about those times when we are too busy reviewing the notes for a morning meeting to monitor the information our teenager is accessing on the Internet? We know what behaviors are expected of us, but there are times when we simply forget. If reading this book reminds you that daily supervision and monitoring are essential in protecting your children from harm, then it has served its purpose.

•   •   •

By teaching parents how to defend their homes against predatory assailants, it is not my intention to create widespread panic. Rather, I envision parents establishing a greater sense of security and safety in their homes with the knowledge gained from this book. Despite how alarming and frightening the statistics and the stories may seem, they can be used to fortify you with the strength, courage, and the intellectual ammunition to protect your children from harm.

The people you will meet in this book are based on my interviews with professionals, sexual predators, victims, and my own case studies. All names and identifying information have been changed, and many are composites.

As you meet the people in this book, you may recognize one of your child's neighbors, baby-sitters, pastors, teachers, or Boy Scout leaders reflected in some of these characters. Shed the fictitious name, remove the character from the setting, and place this person squarely in front of you. Access the Sex Offender Registry, talk openly to your child, and interview this person yourself. Check off the number of warning signs that you can detect, and make it known to everyone involved that you and your child have an understanding and a communication that crosses the borders of all other relationships. In doing so, you will forewarn this person that you are educated and armed with the knowledge and resources to protect your child from sexual abuse.

Protecting Your Children from
SEXUAL PREDATORS

Introduction

Sue sits alone on a wooden bench in the police station. She holds a Styrofoam cup filled with coffee as she anxiously stares at the clock on the wall. Fifteen minutes have passed since her daughter went into the interview room with Detective Robert Perry and the social worker. Sue pictures ten-year-old Jennifer sitting, frightened and ashamed, opposite two adults as she answers their probing questions about Max. Sue bends her head down in sadness as the steam of the coffee mixes with her tears. Her seemingly happy life had been shattered just twenty-four hours ago when Jennifer told Sue that Max had molested her. How could Max, the man she'd once trusted, adored, and married, have hurt her little girl in such a horrible way? Sue leans her head against the back of the bench; but as she closes her eyes to rest, the vivid details come flooding back.

Just yesterday morning, while driving Jennifer to school, Sue had excitedly told her daughter about their plans for a family ski vacation. As Sue described the new condo they'd rented at the base of the mountain, she noticed that Jennifer remained quiet. Sue glanced over at Jennifer, who sat in the car with her fists clenched tightly in her lap. "What's wrong, honey? You don't seem happy that we're going skiing."

"I don't want to go, Mom. I want to stay home," Jennifer replied, as they'd approached the front of the school. Sue turned to her daughter. "Jennifer, you love skiing, and we will all be together. Why don't you want to go?" It was then that Jennifer uttered those tragic words, words that would echo in Sue's mind long after they were spoken. "Max touched my privates. I don't like him anymore. I'm not going."

Sue was shocked as she sat with her hands gripping the steering wheel. What had Jennifer just said? Could it be true? Could Max have done such a horrible thing to Jennifer? With the engine still running, Sue reached over to embrace her daughter. Jennifer collapsed into her mother's arms and began to cry, "I don't want to go to school today." Sue turned the car around and in silence returned home.

At the kitchen table, sitting over mugs of hot chocolate, they talked about Max. Jennifer sobbed uncontrollably as she told her mother how Max had assaulted her. "Mommy, when we came back from our summer trip in the mountains, Max came into my room one night. He was acting funny. He pulled my nightgown up and touched me all over. He kept coming into my room at night, and sometimes I would pretend I was sleeping. I cried when he touched me, but he told me to stop. He said that it was our secret, and I shouldn't tell you because you would be mad. He said if I told anyone, the police would come and take me away."

Sue became enraged. She wanted to call Max right at that moment and confront him but something stopped her; she needed more time to think. Sue suggested that Jennifer take a nap. While tucking Jennifer into bed, Sue reassured her that Max's threats were untrue. "You did the right thing by telling me, Jen, and those kinds of things should never be kept a secret. Max is the bad one. You did not do anything wrong, and he lied to you; no one will take you away."

Jennifer hugged her stuffed animal as she pleaded, "I don't want Max to come back here, Mom. Please make him go away." Sue reassured Jennifer that Max would not return and that she was safe. Jennifer, comforted by her mother's words, quickly fell into a deep sleep.

Sue was also tired but she knew sleep would not come. Instead, she wandered aimlessly around the suburban home that she and Max had bought last year. She ran her hands over the soft fabric of Max's favorite chair, straightened out the pillows on the couch, and eventually climbed the stairs to their bedroom. She glanced over at the dresser filled with framed photos and saw their wedding picture taken just two years ago. She and Max looked so happy. Over on the nightstand, there was a photograph of Sue, Max, and Jennifer standing proudly on top of a mountain they'd climbed that summer. Max was in the middle with his arms around Sue and Jennifer as he smiled proudly at the camera. Could the Max in this picture be the same man who had attacked her daughter? Anger engulfed her as she slammed the picture down, shattering the glass.

Sue once again thought of phoning Max. She pictured Max sitting behind his wide oak desk closing financial deals over the speakerphone while keying memos into his computer. Sue had to admit to herself that she was frightened of how he would react when he was confronted with Jennifer's accusations.

Instead, Sue decided to call Jennifer's pediatrician for advice. The nurse asked Sue to bring Jennifer into the office that afternoon. When the pediatrician came to the waiting room after examining and talking to Jennifer, he informed Sue that he was calling in a report of sexual abuse to social services. A dam broke inside of Sue as the tears spilled down her face. She was so ashamed. How could she have allowed this to happen? Why hadn't she known about Max before he'd had the chance to hurt her little girl?

Later that day a social worker came to the house to talk to Jennifer and Sue. Her questions to Sue only reinforced the sense of guilt that was building inside her. "Where were you when the abuse occurred?" "Why didn't Jennifer tell you after the first time it happened?" "Did you notice anything unusual about Max's relationship with Jennifer?"

That evening, as Max prepared to leave his office, he was arrested and charged with child abuse. Max called Sue from the county jail. "What the hell is this all about, Sue? I never touched that kid, I swear." Sue told Max that she had been instructed not to talk to him about Jennifer's statements and that he was not to be allowed back in the home until this was "all settled." Max screamed into the phone, "What does that mean, Sue, *all settled?*

I didn't do anything, and I'll be damned if I'm going to be kicked out of my own home." Sue hung up the phone, exhausted from the emotional ordeal she had been through since that morning. After tossing and turning for hours, she finally fell into a troubled sleep.

In the morning she and Jennifer went to the police station for further questioning. They were greeted by the social worker and a man in street clothes who introduced himself as Detective Perry. He told them that he was the officer in charge of investigating Jennifer's case. Sue watched as her small daughter, flanked by the two towering adults, walked bravely down the hallway to the interview room.

A siren blaring loudly outside the station startles Sue back to the present. She takes a sip of the now lukewarm coffee and once again glances at the clock. An hour has elapsed, and Sue becomes worried. What if they take her daughter away from her? The social worker had clearly warned Sue that Jennifer could be removed from the home if Sue had any further contact with Max. Sue had replied with indignation, "How could you think that I would ever place Jennifer in danger?" Yet as soon as Sue said this, she realized the irony in her statement. Sue *had* allowed a man to move into their home, and this man *had* hurt her daughter.

Sue feels vulnerable and alone and wishes that someone were with her at this moment. Placing the coffee down, she sorts through a stack of brochures on the table. As she begins to read a pamphlet, Sue discovers that she and Jennifer are not alone. They have just become one of 1.2 million families who would report abuse in the year 2000. Sue has heard about child abuse through radio, newspaper, and television reports, but she'd never thought that it would happen in her family. However, as she reads on, she learns that child abuse knows no socioeconomic, religious, or ethnic distinctions.

When Sue had agreed to marry Max, she had mistakenly believed that he would add security and comfort to her home. Yet after reading about the prevalence of sexual abuse in stepfamilies, she realized that she should not have been so blindly optimistic about Max joining the family. The pamphlet quoted a study done in 1998 by the National Clearinghouse on Child Abuse and Neglect that found stepfathers *three times* more likely to sexually abuse their stepdaughters than biological fathers abuse their natural daughters.

Sue also learns that a man who has a history of sexual abuse is more likely to commit abuse again, particularly if he does not tell his partner about his past. Sue thinks about what Max has told her about his life and realizes that, despite a few details, she knows very little about his history. When she and Max were dating, he'd told Sue about his first marriage to a woman who had a little girl. He was young when they'd married and had felt a lot of pressure to financially provide for his newly acquired family. The marriage ended after a few years, and his ex-wife had moved to another state. Max never saw his stepdaughter again.

What if Max had abused this girl and that was why his marriage had ended? Could this be the reason that his family had moved away? Sue felt a sickening sense of fear tightening around her. Max had never told her about a past history of abuse. Could he have been planning to hurt her daughter all along?

Sue finishes reading the pamphlet and looks up to see Jennifer emerging from the interview. She is alarmed at how pale and withdrawn Jennifer appears. Without a word spoken between them, Sue helps Jennifer into her coat and gloves and guides her out to the car. While waiting for the engine to warm up, Sue glances at her daughter curled up in the backseat like a baby ready to take a nap. Sue remembers Jennifer as an infant, and a stab of pain pierces her heart as she realizes that the innocence of childhood has been stolen from her daughter.

That night, after Jennifer has been safely tucked into bed, Sue sits at the kitchen table and once again thinks about her daughter's abuse. Sadly, Sue's situation is not unique. In thousands of households throughout the United States, parents of abused children will spend sleepless nights alone battling with their feelings of sadness, anger, and guilt.

Eventually, the sense of hopelessness and desperation that Sue feels will diminish, but not before she and Jennifer endure many hardships. Max will be put on trial, and Sue and Jennifer will have to take the stand to testify. During this time, Sue will file for divorce, and she and Jennifer will move to a new home. They will both seek therapy to help them through their process of healing.

For a long time Sue will blame herself for "not protecting Jennifer." Many times throughout the following year, Sue will find herself telling a friend or a colleague at work, "I will never again become involved with a man. I am going to focus on Jennifer and try to be the best mother I can."

With the help of her counselor, Sue will explore her relationship with Max and discover that despite being a very good and caring mother, she had made a wrong choice about Max based on her lack of knowledge about sexual predators. Sue will acknowledge that she never willfully placed Jennifer in danger and that what happened to her daughter could have occurred to any child despite a mother's best intentions. In order to have prevented this, she needed to be more aware of how sexual predators behave and the characteristics they display.

Sue will also realize that she does not have to stay away from *all* men in order to protect Jennifer; she just has to recognize *which* men to avoid. Sue will come to understand that Max was dangerous because he was a predator.

The term *sexual predator*, when used by law enforcement and the judicial system, is, in actuality, a very serious subclassification of sexual offenders. In order for a sex offender to be classified a sexual predator, he or she must have committed a series of sexually *violent* acts. Further, most sexual predators suffer from mental disorders that increase the likelihood that they will repeatedly engage in sexually violent offenses. Therefore a relatively small percent of sex offenders are actually classified as sexual predators. However, *Merriam-Webster's Collegiate Dictionary* defines a *predator* as "one that preys, destroys, devours, plunders, or lays to waste," and I have chosen to use the classification of "predator" throughout this book to convey the detecting, stalking, and injuring strategy used by all sexual offenders, not just those the law views as violent.

Identifying a predator is not an easy task. Predators can disguise themselves in many ways. Like the wolf in *Little Red Riding Hood*, cloaked in Grandmother's clothing, a predator may appear kindly and harmless. Other predators may mask their identities by donning the costume of a "knight in shining armor," while some appear in the rags of poor unfortunate souls who were never graced by good fortune. Therefore it is important that you look at the man or woman beneath the facade before he or she is allowed access to your children.

In the first chapter, you will learn the ten basic characteristics of a predator. These will help you determine if any of the people to whom you are exposing your children are at a high risk for harming them. Characteristics such as a need for control, an inability to take responsibility for his or her actions, a low self-esteem, and a history of alcohol or drug use are just some of the warning signs that will notify you of danger.

Predators follow similar patterns of behavior as they lure their victims down the path to devastation. These behaviors can be categorized into five main stages; and if you recognize these stages, you can prevent a predator from engaging your children. In chapter 2 you will meet three preschool children and Mr. Bob, their teacher's aide. As Mr. Bob selects little Jensen for his next victim, you will have the opportunity to follow the heinous seduction of this innocent and observe the crafty maneuvers of the five stages of abuse. You will see exactly how Mr. Bob detects his next prey, approaches, gains control, and prepares Jensen before committing the sexual abuse.

Identifying the common characteristics of a predator and recognizing the five stages of abuse are important techniques in protecting your children. But remember that these predators are experts at trickery, and therefore you need to defend yourself against their deception by strengthening your own detection skills. In meeting the four different types of predators in chapter 3, you will have the opportunity to get a closer look at each type of predator and learn how his childhood set the stage for his abusive career and witness how he maneuvers his victims.

The most deceptive and beguiling of the predators is the *narcissist*. This predator is charming and smooth as he skillfully seduces his victims with his financial success, sexual prowess, and confidence. However, if you have the knowledge to detect such a fox beneath the prince's clothing, you can slam the door in his face before he ever crosses your threshold.

The *inadequate predator* appears harmless at first glance. He often presents himself as an unfortunate "victim of circumstances" since nothing has ever gone his way. He may have a history of being fired from jobs, and he is childlike in his dress and behaviors, and therefore your kids will love him. How could you know that this seemingly innocent man is capable of committing such heinous acts unless you really understand this type of predator?

A man with no conscience is dangerous because he can harm others without feeling any remorse. You will meet such a man in the *antisocial predator*. This individual, like the narcissist, can pretend to be charming, caring, and sensitive. However, antisocial individuals can pretend to be just about anyone. After meeting this predator, you will be so familiar with his act that you will be able to discern him at a glance.

Not all predators get sexual gratification from preying on children. In fact, *pedophilia*, a sexual attraction to children, is not as common among sexual predators as one would think. The narcissist and the antisocial predators usually choose children as victims, not because they are sexually attracted to them, but because children are easy targets. The *pedophile*, on the other hand, abuses children because he derives sexual gratification from them. You will have the opportunity to become familiar with such a man and therefore recognize him before he has a chance to harm your children.

Females have long been regarded in our society as the nurturers and protectors of our young. They have carried the torch of domesticity and comfort as they protect, guide, and sustain our most intimate relationships. That is why it is so difficult for most of us to comprehend the breach of tradition and fundamental values that occurs when a woman sexually abuses a child. Many feminist views espouse that women are not fundamentally sexual tormentors, and that when they do display sexual aggression it is in response to the male violence to which they have been exposed. But in chapter 4 you will see that women are capable of initiating sexual abuse, and that they do not always offend against children while under the influence of a man. You will learn what characteristics women predators share with male predators and in what ways they differ. You will also become familiar with three types of female predators and have the opportunity to travel with them as they take their young victims through the stages of abuse.

Since we tend to focus on children as the victims of sexual assault, we often ignore the startling fact that they, too, can be sexually abusive. Statistics from the U.S. Department of Justice collected from 1991–96 warn us that 40 percent of the offenders who victimized preschool children were juveniles.

Like adult perpetrators, *juvenile sexual offenders* are not all alike. While they share a number of similar characteristics, they are quite diverse. In chapter 5, you will meet some of these sexually abusive youths and observe their characteristics, behaviors, and motives for sexually abusing other children. You will learn how to use this information in selecting baby-sitters, counselors, and other adolescents who will have contact with your children.

Because childhood is a time of sexual experimentation, it may be more difficult to discern just which behaviors constitute abuse. Therefore a general guideline is provided that outlines sexual behaviors found in normal children versus those demonstrated by sexually abusive children.

Sibling sexual abuse is far more common than we would like to imagine. In fact, surveys have found that at least one out of four adults report that they were sexually abused by a sibling during childhood. The accessibility of siblings and the opportunities they are afforded for unsupervised contact increase the likelihood of sexual experimentation. However, the difference in age, size, and the power between children in a family can take sexual experimentation to a more dangerous ground. Sibling sexual abuse may be occurring right before the unseeing eyes of parents if they are not able to successfully discern what behaviors signal danger. In chapter 6, you will learn more about sibling sexual abuse and meet families who have been victimized by this trauma.

Many of the parents you will meet in this book allowed an abuser access to their children because they were unable to detect a predator. However, what if a predator you have never met comes uninvited into your home and harms your children? By traveling through the vast territory known as cyberspace, dangerous strangers may do just that. Millions of children have access to the Internet everyday, and they are all potential victims for adult predators who stalk the chat rooms of young people.

In chapter 7, you will meet a thirteen-year-old girl, Melissa, who became one such victim of Internet abuse. Without ever actually meeting her abuser in person, Melissa was lured into a cyberrelationship that progressed from virtual courtship to marriage. The end result was that Melissa, on her cyberhoneymoon, was expected to respond to explicit sexual dialogue from her cyberhusband, who in reality was a forty-nine-year-old repeat sexual offender. This chapter will teach parents about the different types of abuse that children may be exposed to on the Internet and offer suggestions on how to set limits on children's recreational use of the computer.

In chapter 8, you will learn what resources are available to you in identifying sexual predators in your community. You will discover how different laws protect the community and how the Sex Offender Registry is implemented in your state. If used properly, the registry can be helpful in uncovering who in your community has been charged with sexual abuse. However, it is important to understand how people get on this list and why a guilty man's name may not appear on the registry while an innocent man may be listed along with other convicted sex offenders.

Controversies exist as a result of public access to the Sex Offender Registry. An important concern is that knowledge of a sex offender's residence could elicit outrage and fear in a community. And without full understanding and an awareness of the issues involved in treating predators, fear and ignorance can overtake even the most well-intentioned citizen. Hate crimes have come to our attention, particularly in the last few years, as vigilante groups take matters into their own hands and express their intolerance through violence. In this manner residences and group homes where sex offenders live have become targets for hate when information about their whereabouts become public knowledge.

Some professional organizations have become vocal in their opposition to the way in which the sex offender registries are structured. They not only voice their dismay about the potential violence that could ensue when names and locations are available for public use, they are also concerned about its impact on young children who have committed a sexual offense. Children as young as ten have had their names printed on this list. Being labeled as a sexual predator at an age when a child may be too young to truly understand his or her behavior can be extremely detrimental. Labels can hold tremendous self-fulfilling powers and therefore may determine the course of a young child's life.

T he message you have received so far is perfectly clear: "Keep your children away from predators!" And as we have seen, by defining a predator as an individual who stalks, approachs, grooms, and attacks children, we have a pretty clear picture of what type of person to avoid. But is every individual who has sexually abused a child considered a predator, and furthermore will he or she always be considered dangerous? Take, for example, the man who has committed sexual abuse on a child and feels terrible guilt and remorse. He truly wishes to change and will do everything in his power to make sure he does not reoffend. Should this man be given a second chance?

In chapter 9, you will have the opportunity to sit in on a group therapy session with twelve male sex offenders. Through the group process that will be structured by two therapists, you will learn about the elements that are essential in the rehabilitation process. You will become acquainted with the basic tenets of sex offender treatment so that you can more accurately assess whether a sex offender you know continues to pose a threat to your children.

You will be introduced to Maggie, a young divorcee with two small children. She has met Brian, who disclosed to her that he had sexually molested his twelve-year-old niece and was currently in treatment. She likes Brian and wants to believe that he has changed, but she worries about the safety of her own children. You will follow Maggie and Brian from their first meeting to their final session with the therapist. And as you do, you will come to understand the necessary restrictions that need to be in place to ensure your children's safety if you decide to be in a relationship with someone who has sexually abused a child.

The final chapter offers you ways that you can put into practice what you have learned about sexual predators to further ensure the safety of your children. You will learn how to design safety plans so that your children can easily understand what behaviors are dangerous and what actions they should take when they are confronted with potential harm. You will see why establishing open and honest communication in your family is essential in detecting and preventing child sexual abuse. You will also read about behaviors that are commonly found in sexually abused children so that you can intervene as soon as possible if your child is unable to tell you in words what has occurred.

S ome of the people you will read about in this book come from actual cases I have treated in my practice. When I think about all of the individuals who have provided me with inspiration for my writing, Joannie comes to the forefront. Petite, dark-haired Joannie had the strength and determination to help her children survive sexual abuse. She remained avidly committed to the process of healing right up to the day when we said good-bye.

"I plan to become involved with child sexual abuse on a national level. I believe that we need to have an awareness of what is happening to our children," Joannie told me during our final session. It was then that I told her about my plans to write a book about sexual predators. I asked her if I could use her story in my book. She was delighted that she could help others, yet she also expressed regret. "I just wish that this book had been available to me before I met Roy. Reading this book might have saved my children and me from the pain and suffering we had to endure. Promise me that you will tell that to your readers."

I hope that this book fulfills the vow I made to Joannie many years ago. I trust that her plea can serve to motivate parents to learn more about protecting their children from predators so, unlike Joannie and her children, they will not have to suffer the devastation of child abuse.

The Ten Most Common
Characteristics of a Predator

Sylvia, a divorced mother of two teenage girls, has been dating John for over two months. John is a business executive who had previously been married. He is charming, fun, and attentive. Their relationship is in full bloom; and for the first time in many years, Sylvia is hopeful about her future.

Sylvia decided it was time to invite John over to the house to meet her daughters. Much to her disappointment, John, who was usually witty and charming, sat silent and withdrawn during dinner. He appeared uncomfortable and awkward with Sylvia's girls; and when it was time to clear the table, without offering to help, John retreated into the family room to watch television. After Sylvia and her daughters had washed the dishes, they joined John. Sylvia tried to elicit responses from him, but he continued his mute vigil in front of the television. Her daughters soon became discouraged and went to their rooms.

Sylvia was angry when she finally confronted John. "You've been quiet all evening and you ignored my daughters. What's wrong?" John reacted with noticeable anger as he raised his voice in protest. "I thought you were acting rude! I never had a chance to say one word. I felt left out, Sylvia, like I was a fifth wheel."

Without giving Sylvia time to respond, John left the house, slamming the door behind him. Long into the night, Sylvia remained awake thinking about what had happened that evening.

One question kept churning in her mind. Should she continue to see John?

◆

Beth and George have an eleven-year-old son named Josh. Josh is spending the summer at his first sleep-away camp. During parents' weekend, Beth and George meet Josh's eighteen-year-old counselor, Rick.

Rick appears to be a quiet and withdrawn adolescent boy who, despite his apparent shyness around adults, is remarkably comfortable with the younger children. The kids seem to love him; and at times, Beth and George have a hard time distinguishing Rick from the rest of the campers. The day before the parents are scheduled to leave, the counselors plan a family rafting trip. The weather is cloudy that day, and the river turbulent. When the campers and their parents disembark, shivering from the cold, they rush to their cabins for a hot shower.

Beth finishes showering early and decides to walk over to see Josh. As she rounds the bend, she can hear peals of laughter coming from Josh's cabin. Beth smiles to herself, thinking about how much fun Josh is having at camp.

When she reaches the cabin, she is astonished to see Rick and the boys hitting each other with wet towels. Some of the boys have towels around their waists, while others are running around naked. Rick is in the center of the mayhem, and the towel he had secured around his middle has just fallen down, revealing his naked buttocks. Beth is startled by what she sees and is not sure what to do. Should she stop this activity, should she report this incident to a supervisor; but more important, should she continue to leave Josh at this camp?

◆

Sally's thirteen-year-old daughter, Kim, needs braces. Sally takes Kim to Dr. Season, an orthodontist Sally has been referred to through her dental plan. At their initial meeting, Sally is impressed with how friendly and comforting Dr. Season is, particularly with Kim. On a tour of the office, Sally notices how Dr. Season greets the children with reassuring pats and hugs. One particular adolescent girl with an intricate set of headgear locked onto her teeth sits silently as Dr. Season puts his hand on her knee and asks how she is doing. Sally notices that Dr. Season's hand lingers a bit too long on the girl's leg.

After Sally and Kim leave the office, Sally is aware of a churning sensation in the pit of her stomach. She turns to Kim and asks her what she thought of Dr. Season. Kim shrugs her shoulders and replies, "He's okay. I like him, I guess." But Sally is not sure whether she should choose Dr. Season to be Kim's orthodontist.

Cindy and Justin Morgan moved into their new home two weeks ago. Their seven-year-old twin boys, Jake and Jarred, have already made many new friends. Cindy and Justin feel comfortable letting the boys ride their bikes on the cul-de-sac and play at the neighbors' homes. Most of the families have children except for elderly Mr. Rook. He has lived alone since his wife died eight years earlier, and he enjoys the company of children.

The kids in the neighborhood spend a lot of time at Mr. Rook's house because he has the latest video games and a house filled with candy and soda. However, the Morgans are becoming concerned about how much time Jake and Jarred are spending at Mr. Rook's house. Sometimes the boys come home with toys and special treats Mr. Rook has given them. Cindy and Justin had collected some of these toys and are planning to return them to Mr. Rook.

Just the other night, Cindy had questioned the boys about Mr. Rook. The twins had looked uncomfortable but reassured their mother, "Mom, he's a great guy. You should see all the stuff he has at his house. All the kids go there." Yet the Morgans continue to worry; something just doesn't feel right. Should they allow their sons to continue to spend time at Mr. Rook's house?

The situations you have just encountered are not uncommon. With subtle changes in the actors, the settings, and the dialogue, scenes of this nature occur everyday throughout the world. And while the above vignettes may appear different, they all have one thing in common: each family had come in contact with a sexual predator, an individual who had the power to devastate the lives of their children.

Sylvia, Beth and George, Sally, and the Morgans had to make a critical decision concerning the safety of their children. With limited information, they had to decide whether to allow their children to continue their relationships with individuals who had displayed questionable behavior.

Each man had manifested actions that were clear warning signs of potential danger. Charming and successful John had displayed inappropriate jealousy of Sylvia's relationship with her daughters. Shy and awkward Rick had engaged in childishly sexual behavior with his young campers. Friendly Dr. Season had made overly solicitous gestures, which included physical contact, with his teenage patients. And finally, elderly Mr. Rook had bribed children with video games and treats to come into his home.

John, Rick, Dr. Season, and Mr. Rook had displayed personality characteristics that are commonly found in predators; and unless a parent knows how to understand these behaviors, their actions can be tragically misinterpreted. For example, we have all known a "seemingly well-intentioned" individual like Dr. Season who makes others feel special and is extremely affectionate or lonely, and "sympathetic" men like Rick and Mr. Rook who appear harmless and in need of companionship. Yet upon further inspection, these men were neither sympathetic nor harmless. They did not have the best intentions for the children they were meeting, and their friendly and affectionate behaviors were manifestations of deeply disturbed personality characteristics that are most commonly found in predators.

John's unreasonable jealousy was an example of his need for complete control and to always be the center of attention. Rick's awkwardness with his peers and his regression to childlike behaviors signaled a pervasive sense of inadequacy and low self-esteem. Dr. Season's friendly pats were a sign that he felt entitled to take liberties with those who were not in a position of power, and Mr. Rook's facade of a harmless old man disguised the perverse sexual fantasies of a pedophile.

Defining common characteristics of individuals who sexually abuse children is complicated. There exists a significant percentage of people who share similar traits to the sexual predator with one exception, they do *not* sexually abuse children. So just how can parents predict whether a sexual predator is interacting with their children?

The following ten most common characteristics of predators will help you better understand and classify those behaviors that you may be observing. It will help you assess whether you should be concerned about the physically affectionate doctor you have just taken your daughter to, the overly solicitous coach who wants to spend extra time with your son, or the quiet adolescent who frequently asks to baby-sit for your toddler.

TEN MOST COMMON
CHARACTERISTICS OF A PREDATOR

The following traits can serve as a general map to guide you in identifying potentially harmful individuals:

1. Refusal to take responsibility for his or her actions and blames others or circumstances for failures
2. A sense of entitlement
3. Low self-esteem
4. A need for power and control
5. A lack of empathy
6. An inability to form intimate relationships with adults
7. A history of abuse
8. A troubled childhood
9. Deviant sexual behaviors and attitudes
10. Drug and/or alcohol abuse

Remember that each one of these characteristics alone does not necessarily define a predator. There are many individuals who manifest these traits and will never sexually abuse a child. However, the combination of these attributes and the degree to which they control a person's behavior distinguish a sexual predator from other individuals.

Next, we will take a further look at the four predators you met at the beginning of this chapter in relation to these ten common traits. Some of these traits are readily apparent in the men, while others are not. Remember that it takes time to really get to know someone. However, if you listen closely to what people say and observe carefully how they interact with others, you can assess whether or not these traits are present. Some of the information you will learn about the four predators comes from an in-depth knowledge of the individual and therefore was not readily available to the parents. However, behavior that reflects any of these traits should always be taken seriously, particularly when the safety of your child is in question.

Refusal to Take Responsibility for His or Her Actions and Blames Others or Circumstances for Failures

It is not difficult to determine if an individual is displaying this trait. If you listen closely and long enough to how people describe their lives, you can become adept at picking out those statements that clearly illustrate an inability to take personal responsibility for one's life. Many people present their lives as a series of events that unfortunately drove them to failure.

Ironically, individuals who prey on the innocence of others usually define themselves as "victims." Whether it be a terrible childhood, betrayal by a partner, or being unjustly fired from a job, they find excuses to avoid taking responsibility for their own behavior. They tend to see themselves much like helpless animals backed into a corner by a more powerful foe with only two options: curl up in defeat or retaliate. Their explanations for their misbehavior sound as if they were merely reacting to the unjust circumstances around them. Initially, their plights may appear sympathetic to the listener; however, after a while their excuses for bad behavior sound like well-rehearsed tirades against the injustices of the world.

Many predators blame a horrible childhood, an inequitable society, and the unfairness of the legal system for the conditions of their lives. Therefore when a man complains that he has not seen his children in five years because his ex-wife moved out of state and took the kids, it is important to explore this further. This may be a man who blames his estrangement from his children on his ex-wife and doesn't assume responsibility for the fact that he may have abused his spouse or his children. A convicted sex offender may state angrily that he is never allowed to see his children because of the unfair legal system that continues to put sanctions on when and how he visits his children. Once again, this is a man who is blaming the system for his alienation from his children and not assuming full responsibility for the consequences that resulted from his own actions.

Aside from those suffering from mental illnesses that seriously impair their decision making, individuals have the capacity to choose how they will conduct their lives. Psychologists recognize the importance of early childhood development and environment as providing us with an array of possibilities from which to choose. Certainly a person who was raised in an impoverished environment with abusive parents has significantly different choices than the privileged child who was lavished with love, attention, and material possessions. However, it is ultimately our free will that selects those possibilities we are faced with and makes us responsible for our own lives.

Many people spend years in therapy in order to understand the traumatic underpinnings of their childhood. But when an individual leaves the therapist's office, for the rest of the day he or she alone is responsible for deciding how to treat coworkers, friends, a loved one, and a child. People who understand this concept live more fulfilled and determined lives as compared to the shallow and limited existence of those who believe they are reined in and held hostage by forces beyond their control.

Let us now take a closer look at the four predators we met during the introduction of this chapter to see how they avoided taking responsibility for their behavior.

John sat mute and unresponsive throughout Sylvia's dinner and then stormed out of the house when she confronted him. He admitted feeling "left out" and "like a fifth wheel," and this may be understandable in light of John's first encounter with Sylvia's daughters. It is not uncommon upon an initial meeting with a girlfriend's daughters to feel somewhat awkward; however, he offered this as an excuse for his sullen silence and rude behaviors. He went even further by *blaming* Sylvia and her daughters for his behavior because they left him out of the discussion.

John did not apologize for reacting in such a childish manner and offered no reassurance that he would change his behavior. This was Sylvia's first clue that John blamed others and avoided taking personal responsibility for his actions.

Sylvia was the only one of the four parents who actually witnessed this personality characteristic in the predator. However, if we delve deeper into the other three personalities, we can find ample evidence of this destructive trait.

Dr. Season, like John, has a pattern of avoiding personal responsibility for his actions. Ten years earlier, Dr. Season had been touching, squeezing, and patting young girls in much the same manner as Sally and Kim observed. During this time, one of his adolescent patients had accused him of touching her breasts. The girl had told her parents, who'd immediately called the police to report the incident. Detectives investigated the girl's allegations, which Dr. Season had adamantly denied. Dr. Season had hired a noted defense attorney, and his case was eventually dismissed on a technicality. Unfortunately for the other adolescent girls who would continue to see him, Dr. Season never was held accountable for the pain and humiliation he had inflicted on his patient and because of this, he was allowed to continue his inappropriate fondling. To this day Dr. Season thinks of himself as "wrongly accused"; and in his mind, the dismissal of his case further justified his innocence. Dr. Season not only adamantly denied the charges, he continues to chastise the parents of the girl who'd reported the allegations to the police. He is still outraged at the victim's parents who "believed such nonsense from a kid" and blames them for all the money he had to spend on his defense.

Rick also does not take responsibility for his inappropriate sexual behaviors. Instead, he blames the taunting mockery of his peers for making him feel insignificant and lonely and is therefore in desperate need of attention and recognition. Rick had never had the opportunity to express his adolescent sexuality through typical teenage interactions, such as dating; therefore he had a reservoir of unmet needs. In truth, Rick had been severely damaged by his ostracism from his classmates; however, this cannot be used as an excuse for his actions. He has to assume responsibility for deciding to channel his anger and frustration into sexually inappropriate activities with younger boys.

And finally, Mr. Rook takes no responsibility for his sexual acts against children. If he were to be caught, his defense would be that the young boys were his friends and that they liked coming to his home because he provided them with the attention and privileges they did not receive at their own homes. He would also project some of the responsibility for the abuse on the victims themselves, claiming that they were excited and aroused by the sex games he played with them.

A Sense of Entitlement

Not only do certain individuals see themselves as victims, they go a step further. They want *compensation* for their victimization. They believe that the world owes them something in return for their pain and suffering. These individuals feel justified in their actions. They believe they have been unduly wronged, and therefore they deserve to get what they need regardless of the cost to others. They may not report income on their taxes because "the government cheats me by taking so much of my money," steal profits from their place of employment because "my boss is a thief—I never got that raise he promised me," or lie because "no one has ever believed me anyway." As you can see, a sense of entitlement is a dangerous trait because it can justify almost any behavior.

Feeling entitled can also stem from a belief that certain individuals have privileges because of their special attributes. These attributes, whether they be fabulous looks, athletic prowess, considerable wealth, or a high-ranking position in a corporation, give the "entitled ones" license to disregard others in less prestigious positions. They believe that they are beyond reproach, and that they have earned the right to lord their position over others in order to satisfy their own needs. For these types of men and women, their position of power provides them with dangerous justification for their harmful behaviors.

John is a perfect example of a man who believes that he deserves special consideration. He expects conversation to center around him, attention at all times, and other people to recognize and satisfy his needs. And when this did not happen that night at Sylvia's dinner, John had become enraged and eventually stormed out of her house.

A sense of entitlement is abundant in Dr. Season. After all, he had worked hard to become an orthodontist, and his practice was demanding. He complained to colleagues that he worked long hours; and when he got home, his reward was often screaming kids and a tired wife. He willingly shared with his golfing buddies that his wife did not care about his needs and that she was too busy shopping and playing tennis to ever realize how much he had sacrificed to finance "their good life." What Dr. Season might not tell you directly, but which is implied every time he takes advantage of his lofty position to touch one of his young patients, is that he feels entitled to get some of his physical needs met by hugging and caressing the children in his care. Dr. Season views his diploma on the wall and his letters of recommendation as testaments to his unique abilities. He believes he is special and entitled to a "few indiscretions now and then," no matter how injurious they are to the frightened young patients who sit captive in his chairs.

Low Self-Esteem

Even though a predator may appear confident, self-assured, and entitled, this is merely a facade to hide from view a weak and vulnerable sense of self. In fact, most predators feel deeply inadequate and insecure about themselves. Many of them are survivors of disturbed childhoods, where their developing sense of self was deeply marred. Throughout their lives they learned maladaptive ways to hide this sense of inadequacy by foisting upon others a controlling and belligerent persona.

An inadequate sense of self is a dangerous malady. It can cause undue rage when it is exposed, and it can severely alter the way a person perceives the actions of others. The slightest indiscretion may appear like a slap in the face to an individual who is harboring an already damaged ego. Therefore John's perception that Sylvia and her girls had ignored him all evening caused him to be angry and retaliate with sullen silence. Dr. Season, with all of his accolades and accomplishments adorning the walls of his office, still needs constant reassurance that he is attractive and acceptable for behind Dr. Season's diplomas and awards there hides a damaged self-esteem. He'd learned long ago in his childhood that the only way he could get the love and caring he desired was to "do good things." Therefore, throughout his life, his accomplishments had become mere pathways to obtaining something he'd always yearned for—unconditional love and acceptance.

The teenage counselor, Rick, is also carrying around an impaired self-esteem. Since childhood, he had not gotten along with his peers. He can still remember how he suffered shame and humiliation on the playground when he was called names and physically abused by his classmates, or the humiliation he'd endured in gym class when the captains never chose him for their teams. Years of loneliness and never feeling accepted had scarred his view of himself. The only way that he believed he could gain recognition was through the eyes of a child small enough to look up to him. Yet tragically, Rick had begun to translate his need for attention and recognition into sexual behaviors that he imposed on the vulnerable youth who depended on him. And last, Mr. Rook, who also spends most of his time with children, is a man with a seriously impaired self-esteem. As a pedophile, he has warped his sense of self into a lonely individual who lives solely to satisfy his perverse sexual desires.

A Need for Power and Control

Because many predators experience a deep sense of helplessness, they struggle for power and control throughout their lives. While a certain need for control is common in almost everyone, most adults learn to accept those situations that they can't govern. We learn early on in our lives that, in exchange for complete control, we can ultimately accomplish a great deal through our cooperation with others. We also learn that to have friends and other meaningful relationships in our lives, we must relinquish a certain amount of control. Healthy adults do not always strive to rule others; instead, they respect people's needs for autonomy and allow for the differences among them to diversify and enrich their lives.

To develop trust in one's self and in others, a child must be raised in an environment that adequately meets his or her needs. Therefore, individuals who are raised in homes that lack the consistency and nurturing needed to build this basic trust will struggle throughout their lives with issues of control. A lack of control is frightening and overwhelming for those individuals who learned early on that their environment could be an unpredictable and harmful place. Because predators harbor deep-seated insecurities about themselves and the world around them, control is the only way they can gain a foothold in the rocky terrain that characterizes their precipitous environment.

Unfortunately for those who are caught up in the quest for control, their existence becomes a never-ending struggle for power. The four predators you have already met fought all their lives for power and control.

John's need for control was illustrated in his frustration over not being able to direct the conversation between Sylvia and her daughters. The only way he could gain any control over the situation was to retreat into silence and eventually storm angrily out of Sylvia's home.

Rick, who had always felt so helpless every time a peer mocked him, struggled to counter this with a need for complete power. Through his position as a camp counselor for younger boys, Rick was finally able to have authority over others. However, his power was tragically misused as he orchestrated younger children's play into inappropriate sexual behaviors.

Like Rick, Dr. Season is a predator who uses his position of power to routinely abuse those beneath him. Consider the adolescent girl sitting supine in the dentist's chair waiting for the omniscient Dr. Season to fix her crooked teeth. This is a perfect example of the inequality of power that Dr. Season took advantage of every time he placed his hand on a teenage thigh or squeezed a young girl's knee.

Sexual behavior between an adult and a child is a clear abuse of power. Sexual behavior should never take place between an adult and a child because of the vast inequality that exists between the two. But for a predator who sees the world in terms of those who have power and those who don't, a child is merely another helpless subordinate who is at the whim of those who dominate and control him or her.

Gaining control over a child is not a difficult task for an adult. The power of an adult over a child is implicit in the disparity in their size, knowledge, and experience, as well as the role that adults have in guiding, teaching, and caring for children.

Winning a child's confidence and becoming a "trusted friend" for the purpose of luring him or her into sexually inappropriate behavior is a clear abuse of power. This is exactly what Mr. Rook did when he used the power of treats and his newest collection of video games to beguile young victims into believing that he was a harmless and friendly old man.

A Lack of Empathy

Empathy is a sophisticated social skill that requires a suspension of one's own needs and emotions to truly understand another person's feelings. It goes beyond sympathy, which, by definition, requires one to intellectually understand the feelings of another. To have empathy, a person must be able to *experience and share* in those feelings. You may sympathize with the plight of the starving children you see on the cover of your weekly news magazine, but to empathize with them would require that you draw on your own experiences in order to *feel* the desperation of hungry children.

One of the reasons that predators are able to abuse children is that they have a lack of empathy for others. Because they tend to center their world on their personal quests for power, recognition, control, and sexual gratification, they pay scant attention to the needs of others.

Many predators have not developed the essential skills that are necessary to empathize with their victims. Even though they may have experienced victimization in their own childhood, it does not act as a deterrent. Instead, they see their own suffering as unique and separate from others.

The ability to empathize begins from our earliest experiences with our caretakers. A parent who can anticipate an infant's needs and sufficiently fulfill them is giving the child his or her first lesson in empathy. As the infant grows, the parent must continue to care for the child in a manner that takes into account his or her developmental needs. Allowing the child to appropriately express feelings, respecting the child's needs, and teaching the child to respect the needs of others will provide the child with the necessary foundation for developing empathy. Yet few predators in childhood ever had the opportunity to learn about empathy. Most of them came from homes in which they themselves were treated unsympathetically and where their needs as children were routinely ignored.

A lack of empathy sets the stage for *objectification* of others. Objectification allows the predator to act out anger and sexual frustrations on others by divesting them of all feelings and needs. A predator has the dangerous ability to transform his victims into objects who exist only for his needs. Instead of a relationship with people, the predator has a pattern of admiring, obtaining, securing, and eventually destroying the objects in his life.

Empathizing with children also requires a certain degree of knowledge about child development. Child molesters tend to have little understanding of the developmental needs of children. Predators tend to see children as people who are "not fully formed" and, therefore, don't have the same feelings and needs as adults. By seeing them as less developed people, they tend to minimize the impact their abuse will have on children. A statement such as, *"Oh, they are young; they'll get over it. You should see what I had to go through as a kid,"* reflects insensitivity to the needs of children as well as ignorance about human development. Children "do not get over things" because they are young. In fact, childhood, like a newly planted sapling, is so vulnerable to its caretakers that any type of trauma can cause permanent scarring.

Since predators do not understand how children psychologically mature, they misinterpret children's behaviors and use this as justification for the abuse. An example of misinterpreting children's behaviors to rationalize abuse is the predator who stated, after his conviction for sexual assault on his four-year-old stepdaughter, *"It wasn't hurting her, she acted like it was okay, and she never told me to stop."* Not only is this man terribly mistaken about the traumatic impact that his abuse will have on his stepdaughter for years to come, but he is also misinterpreting the acquiescence of a preschool child.

Four year olds normally engage in egocentric thinking that causes them to believe that the world revolves around them, and that they are responsible for whatever happens to them. Thus, the four-year-old girl who "didn't try to stop her stepfather's abuse" was not "okay"; rather she was forced into submission because she believed she was to blame for what was happening to her.

Because predators during their early encounters with a victim can often be extremely charming, likable, and attentive, they may initially appear to be empathetic. Child molesters are experts in feigning empathy in order to get close to potential victims and their families. They will know just what children need and how to interact with them in order to gain their trust and friendship. They are also likely to spend a great deal of time getting close to the parents of their victims so that they eventually can have full access to their children.

Once again we turn to the four treacherous characters we met in the beginning of the chapter in order to assess their ability to empathize with others. John was already letting Sylvia know that he lacked the kind of empathy that was necessary to interact with teenage daughters and their mother. He saw the world through his eyes only, and he was unable to view the dinner from the perspective of Sylvia's daughters, who may have felt uncomfortable in the presence of their mother's boyfriend.

Rick, who is so caught up in his own need for approval and acceptance, is unable to understand the developmental needs of eleven-year-old boys. His romping half clad and slapping children on the buttocks does not respect the developmental needs of boys who are not yet in the throes of puberty but are nonetheless struggling with the concepts of sexuality.

And clearly, Dr. Season is not paying attention to the awkwardness and shame that his fondling has upon the pubescent girls in his office. His belief that they don't mind it because they like and trust him is a clear indication that he lacks the empathy to place himself in their position.

Finally, Mr. Rook, who is so caught up in enacting his own deviant sexual fantasies, is also not concerned with the devastation that his behaviors will have on the children he is abusing. His sexual gratification takes precedence and completely obliterates any sense of empathy for his victims.

An Inability to Form Intimate Relationships with Adults

People who sexually abuse children are often lacking in the ability to have healthy relationships with adults. Their relationships with the opposite sex are often intense, chaotic, and unstable. A large percentage of predators have a series of unsuccessful relationships that terminate after years of fighting, miscommunication, and a lack of physical intimacy. Because a predator may be unable to successfully negotiate a relationship with an adult, he or she turns to a child for a substitute.

Certain individuals, like the counselor Rick and Mr. Rook, cannot sustain fulfilling relationships with people themselves because of their sense of inadequacy, particularly when it comes to sexual intimacy. Inadequate individuals, as you will learn in chapter 3, have a long history of being unable to form healthy relationships with people their own age. As a result of their stunted emotional growth, these individuals never develop the skills necessary to negotiate a healthy adult relationship or find sexual gratification with a suitable partner. Therefore, for these individuals a child is seen, not only as a viable substitute for intimacy, but as the only resource for sexual fulfillment.

The Morgans didn't know Mr. Rook; and if they had questioned any of the other adults in the neighborhood, they would have discovered that he was an isolated man who, except for the children, kept to himself. No one had ever noticed any adult friends at his home. And if the Morgans had understood that his isolation from adults was a clear warning sign that he was singularly focused on children as a source of gratification, they would never have allowed their boys to go to his home.

A History of Abuse

Since the number-one predictor of child abuse is a history of past abuse, it is critical that you know some information about the history of the adults who are interacting with your children, particularly if their history includes domestic violence or sexual abuse. If an individual has ever been accused of sexual abuse, you should take this information seriously.

Many predators have a long history of sexual abuse before they ever come to the attention of the law. According to the National Institute of Mental Health, the average molester of girls will abuse 50 females before being caught and convicted, and the average molester of boys will victimize 150 males before being convicted.

The statistics are alarmingly higher for a pedophile, a man who derives sexual gratification from children. This type of predator will molest an average of 117 girls during his lifetime; but for pedophiles who only abuse boys, that figure rises to 280 male victims. Therefore, unless a predator is honest about his or her past history of abuse, or if the person has already been convicted as a sexual offender and you can access this information on the Sexual Offender Registry, you may never know if he or she is capable of harming your children.

Unfortunately, even if you know about legal complications in an individual's past, predators are likely to give you a skewed interpretation that will absolve them of responsibility. They may tell you that they were once arrested for domestic violence and explain the incident in the following manner: "The charges were made up, my ex-wife was crazy, she was the one who hit me, and she had the nerve to call the police. I was only defending myself."

Predators are also likely to minimize or deny past sexual abuse by offering statements such as the following: "*My girlfriend accused me of molesting her daughter, but I never did anything to that kid, I swear. I loved that little girl, and she and I were really close. I used to take her everywhere with me, and now I can't even see her. I don't know where her mother got that stuff from; I would never touch a kid.*"

Implicit in this statement is a clear danger sign that you need to take seriously. Whether or not he maintains his innocence, this person's statement lets you know that there have been allegations of sexual abuse in his past, and that he blames others for these accusations.

Despite his rude behavior, if Sylvia is considering continuing her relationship with John, she should ask him about his past. If she would, she would learn that John has been divorced twice, and that he has a young son from his second marriage who lives in another state with John's ex-wife. John does not see his son because, as he would tell Sylvia, "*My ex-wife is a control freak. She won't let me see my boy unless she or someone she knows accompanies us. I'm not going to go along with that. I love my son and I want to see him but not under those conditions. She has turned that kid against me; he doesn't even call me anymore.*" If Sylvia is smart, she would look further into the situation, for John's explanation may be a decoy that is masking a more dangerous reason for his ex-wife's refusal to let him see his son.

Rick, unbeknownst to his present employers, had been previously fired from a job that involved taking care of young children. Although no charges were ever brought up against him, a few parents complained that they felt uncomfortable with some of his behaviors with their children, and he was asked to leave.

Eight years ago, when Dr. Season's patient alleged that he had inappropriately touched her, he was at the height of his success and running a large dental clinic in the city. To avoid any further complications from the allegations against him, Dr. Season decided to close his office and relocate his practice to a small town in a different state. No one in Sally's community knew much about this friendly new orthodontist, except that Dr. Season's name was listed on a number of the dental insurance plans. Many consumers assume that if a doctor is listed on a health plan, he must be an experienced and ethical professional. This is not necessarily true. Although Dr. Season had no legal record, it did not mean that he was innocent. If Sally had the opportunity to talk to the young girl who had brought charges against him and a few other adolescents Dr. Season had treated in the past, she would have learned that Dr. Season had a pattern of inappropriately fondling young girls.

The Sex Offender Registry is a list of *convicted* sex abusers. Each state differs in the manner in which it makes this information available to the public. You will learn more about the origins and the functions of the registry and how to access it in chapter 10. If the Morgans had been aware of the registry and how to access it, they would have seen Mr. Rook's name listed there. He had been convicted of child sexual assault a number of years before. A review of the case would have informed them that for twelve years, Mr. Rook's wife, Elaine, had operated a day-care center in their home. In a well-publicized trial, Mr. Rook had been found guilty of molesting at least ten young boys during the time his wife ran the day-care center, and he was subsequently sentenced to twenty years in prison.

Mr. Rook had been a model prisoner, but unfortunately, he never received offender treatment following his incarceration. The parole board recognized his good behavior, and they offered him early release on the conditions that he never be alone with any child under the age of eighteen and that he register with the local authorities as a sex offender. Mr. Rook had endured almost twelve years in prison, and promised the parole board that he would never molest a child again. He was released back into the community. With his wife deceased and with no professional support or treatment, Mr. Rook had broken his promise, and unless the Morgans can prevent it, their twins could be his next victims.

A Troubled Childhood

We have all read accounts of the most serious sexual offenders who profess to have had a "normal" childhood. These offenders swear that their upbringings were good, that their parents were always available to them, and that they were taught the difference between right and wrong. So what went wrong? Are these men telling the truth, or are they psychologically naive individuals who have little ability to understand the developmental underpinnings of their deviant personalities? In some instances, the former is true.

Psychologists are often baffled when confronted by the incorrigibly violent offender who apparently had a normal childhood. Some offenders come from intact homes where their siblings have grown up to be well-functioning adults. Interviews with the parents confirm that although the rest of the family functioned well, the offender was always a "problem child" no matter how hard they tried to intervene. Early psychiatric histories and childhood medical records revealed that this individual was diagnosed as oppositional and defiant or with attention deficit disorder; but despite the medications prescribed or the residential treatments, hospitalizations, and special programs that he or she attended, this child's problems continued into adulthood. These are the baffling cases and the ones that defy psychology's recognition of the environment as a key element in shaping human behavior.

During the latter part of the twentieth century and into the new millennium, we have and are learning more and more about the brain, that mysterious entity within us that generates our every thought and movement. And therefore, when unexplainable cases cross our paths, such as the serial child molester who grew up in a loving home, we turn to brain physiology in order to find the answers. It is likely that within the next decade we will learn more about the origins of deviant behavior through brain research and be able to find cures for those human behaviors that cause pain and suffering to others.

But in the meantime, we have to make do with what we have learned through years of studying genetics and the environment and their impact on human behavior. It is generally agreed among mental health professionals that an individual's personality is a product of both inborn characteristics and early childhood experiences. We are profoundly affected by our earliest caretakers. The way in which we were treated and how we saw our caretakers treat each other formed indelible impressions on us that set the course for our future relationships. Behavioral scientists have demonstrated that role modeling is a very powerful way in which patterns of responses are wired into the brain. For example, it has been demonstrated that an adult who was raised in a violent environment is much more likely to respond to a frustrating experience with physical aggression than an individual who grew up in a nonviolent home.

Furthermore certain environments are toxic to children's development. Children whose parents engage in a bitter divorce, live in homes where abuse and neglect are the norm, and are exposed to substance abuse, poverty, and crime are at high risk for developing deviant behavior. Toxic childhood environments also include various forms of emotional abuse. Even though emotional abuse does not create physical scarring, it insidiously destroys a child's integrity. Name-calling and other forms of verbal abuse denigrate the child and erode self-esteem. A child being raised in an environment where his or her psychological needs are rarely met will learn to substitute anger, resentment, and fear for true intimacy.

When emotional needs are not met in an appropriate manner, a child will attempt to meet those needs in other ways, and this often results in the development of deviant behaviors. A child who is ignored may have learned early on how to manipulate parents to get the attention he or she desires. A child who has been taught that his or her feelings and desires are shameful may find devious ways in which to act out anger and frustration. As children grow, these destructive behaviors will become habitual as they shape and define their personalities.

Many predators are simply unaware of the toxic elements that existed in their childhood for they are psychologically unsophisticated. Many of these individuals have never explored their past and how it relates to their current behaviors. They may describe the alcoholic rages of a father as, "his bad mood when he would drink," and explain away the numerous beatings received from a parent as, "I got what I deserved." Therefore a male predator may not link up his own drug abuse as modeling the daily beer drinking of his father, nor the domestic violence he witnessed in his early years to the battering he now inflicts upon his wife and children. By rationalizing his parents' behaviors, he can then explain away his own transgressions without ever examining the root of deviance that had been planted years ago in his childhood.

Two major characteristics that often result from the toxic environments in which many predators were raised are the inability to deal with anger and difficulty communicating with others. Many predators were raised in an environment where there were inappropriate displays of anger. As children, predators may never have learned to effectively express their anger. Instead, they were taught that adults had the right to deal with anger by physical means, while children's anger was seen as unacceptable. Ironically, the display of anger in a child often resulted in corporal punishment, thus giving the child a confusing message about physical means as a way to handle one's anger.

Predators may express care and love for their child victims, especially when they are their own offspring; however, underlying their sexually abusive acts is a rage that has been brewing inside of them from the time they themselves were children. Sexual abuse is, by its very nature, an aggressive and angry act for it destroys the emotional and physical integrity and trust of the victim.

Haley, an insightful little girl of twelve, was hurt and confused by her father's sexual abuse. She did not understand how her own father could have done this to her, especially since he had been abused as a child. "Doesn't he know the pain and suffering it causes someone to be abused? He was abused when he was a child; how could he then do that to me?" What Haley was too young to realize was that her father's own history of abuse had left him with a reservoir of anger that lay beneath the surface and routinely rose to dangerous levels as it drowned every important relationship he had ever had, even the one with his daughter.

Predators also have a difficult time communicating with others. They learned early on in their childhood that expressing their needs, desires, and feelings was dangerous and often resulted in retaliatory behaviors from their parents. They were often shamed into hiding their feelings of fear and vulnerability, and were harshly punished when they demonstrated anger and frustration. In dysfunctional home environments, communication between family members is often distorted, cryptic, and ineffective. Children from these environments learn that important issues are never discussed openly and that resolution to problems is often resolved by a sudden slap across the face, a harsh command, or utter silence. It is no wonder that predators talk about their inability to communicate their feelings. They have a lifetime of stored up emotions that they were never able to sort out and share with others; therefore, they choose to act them out in destructive ways.

To combat the effects of a troubled childhood, many psychologists prescribe insight-oriented therapy. However, predators are often naive, psychologically unsophisticated, and lack insight, and thus are poor candidates for this type of treatment. Jesse, a sixty-two-year-old man who was a repeat child molester, talked about the ineffective treatment he had received after his first conviction. "I was forty-two at the time of my arrest; and because it was my first conviction, I got a lighter sentence. I was court ordered to attend therapy after six months of incarceration. I was sent to a psychiatrist who had me lie on his couch twice a week and talk about my father. It was interesting, but it did not give me the tools I needed to stop my behaviors."

However, if exposed to the proper therapeutic setting, many predators experience a revelation when they begin to learn how their childhood relates to their current behaviors. Let us take a look at Ron, a thirty-five-year-old real estate broker who was convicted of sexually abusing his eleven-year-old stepdaughter. Because this was his first offense, Ron was given a lighter jail sentence; and once he was released on probation, he was ordered to attend an offenders' treatment program. Ron would eventually learn a great deal from the program. However, initially, he was only able to mimic the insights he was being taught about predators. It would take him time to be able to gain the psychological sophistication sufficient to truly understand his inner dynamics.

In therapy, Ron explored his childhood history. His father had been abusive, and he had treated members in the family like objects to gratify his own needs. Prior to therapy, Ron had always looked up to his father as a strong-willed and independent man who had made his own way in the world. Ron had never had the opportunity to examine his own fears and anger at his father and understand the impact that this abusive man had had on Ron's own behaviors as a husband and father.

Ron also explored his own sexual history, which supplied him with the origins of his sexual fantasies. When Ron was only ten, an adolescent male baby-sitter had molested him. He'd never told anyone of this, yet the stimulation that was created by this premature exposure to sexuality lay buried beneath layers of shame and guilt. Ron had never given any credence to the fact that this incident had affected him so deeply; he truly believed that it had happened long ago and had no impact on his current behavior.

Talking to Ron, following eighteen months of offender treatment, he offered the following comments: *"When I was growing up, no one ever taught me about myself. No one ever paid attention to feelings and why people acted the way they did. We never discussed those types of things in my family, and I never learned how to express my feelings. I knew how a carburetor worked and how to rewire the speakers to my stereo but I never thought about how my mind operated. It's funny to think about, but we don't come with an operator's manual. We just have to wing it unless we break down and need to be bailed out by someone who understands why we can no longer function and how to fix us."*

Deviant Sexual Behaviors and Attitudes

The one distinguishable trait that all predators have in common is that they harbor deviant sexual attitudes and/or behaviors. However, not all predators who sexually abuse children are sexually aroused by children. There is a distinct difference between pedophiles and molesters. *DSM-IV, Diagnostic and Statistical Manual of Mental Disorders*, which is published by the American Psychological Association, offers the definition of *pedophilia* as "recurrent, intense, sexual urges and sexual arousing fantasies of at least six months in duration involving sexual activity with a pre-pubescent child." Thus the target of a pedophile's sexual fantasy will be a child.

A child molester who is not a pedophile is referred to as a *situational molester*. According to Kenneth Lanning, an FBI supervisory agent, situational molesters aren't necessarily sexually inclined toward children but turn to them to gratify their needs because they are available. They may, for example, use sex with children as a way to alleviate boredom, stress, or anxiety. However, their choice to sexually abuse children is often dictated by the fact that children are "easy victims." Their innocence, their subordination to adults, and their naïveté make them accessible victims to predators. Situational molesters are often angry men who have a pattern of acting out their hostility on others in violent and harmful ways. Sexual abuse for these men is often just another way of releasing their aggression on others.

Many people ask the question, "Is it true that most sexual predators have been abused as children?" While the answer to this is yes, it needs a qualifier. Studies have shown that most child sex offenders do have a childhood history of abuse, whether it was emotional, physical, or sexual. Yet this does not mean that all sexually abused individuals grow up to be predators. As mentioned before, there are more abused children who will live their lives without harming another person than there are abused children who become perpetrators.

When sexual predators are asked to look into their past, a majority of them confirm some sort of exposure to sexual abuse. Sexual abuse creates its own brand of psychological damage. Because sexual contact with an adult can be stimulating and exciting for a child as well as shameful and degrading, it is confusing, overwhelming, and extremely harmful to the child's developing ego.

One of the most harmful and pervasive scars that it leaves is a skewed view of sexuality. Sexually abused children learn that sex is often paired with aggression and that sex is a shameful, painful, but often stimulating experience. When children are exposed to adult sexual stimuli at too early an age, they become overwhelmed. It is as if their sexual thermostats have been turned on to high, and they are left defenseless to battle such over-powering feelings. Left to their own devices, eventually abused children will act out their sexual stimulation by excessive masturbation, inappropriate sexual play with other children, a preoccupation with sex, and the development of deviant sexual attitudes and behaviors that continue into adulthood.

There are clear warning signs that will inform you when a man has deviant sexual attitudes or behaviors. An important red flag that indicates a predator's propensity to view women or children as sexual objects is the consistent use of pornography. Pornography depicting children or young teens in a sexual manner is a clear indication of deviant sexual attitudes. The excessive use of pornography of any kind is a sign that the user is substituting the gratification he receives from viewing sexual objects for the intimacy and satisfaction of a healthy adult relationship.

It is not uncommon for sexual predators to use pornography as a means to lure and captivate victims. Children are naturally curious and stimulated by sexual images. A predator may begin his or her seduction by leaving *Playboy* or *Penthouse* magazines on display for children to explore. This will arouse the children and prime them for sexual exploration. The predator is likely to increase the explicitness of accessible pornography in order to intensify the potential victim's arousal. Pornography depicting children may also be used to "normalize" the sexual abuse by presenting it as an "ordinary activity" that adults and children engage in.

The accessibility, ease, and relative anonymity of pornography on the Internet have made the use of pornography more widespread than ever, and, for predators, cyberspace pornography is dangerous territory to enter. A majority of pedophiles collect child pornography and view it on the Internet without ever physically harming a child. However, for those se-lected few who do choose to act out their deviance on children, the use of Internet pornography only serves to stimulate their fantasies and sexually arouse them to higher and more dangerous levels.

Ted Bundy, during a taped interview shortly before his execution, talked about the effects that pornography had had on his deviant sexual behaviors. He alleged that he had been exposed early in his childhood to pornography and become obsessed with the sexual images he'd discovered. According to Bundy, it was his early fixation on pornography of a violent sexual nature that eventually led to his sexually criminal behaviors.

Many predators talk about the impact that pornography had on them as children. They discuss their obsession with it and how it motivated their behaviors and organized their lives. Unlike the other children who were busily engrossed in Little League games, monster movies, and comic books, predators recall becoming singularly focused on pornography. They structured their time so that they could be alone with their stimulating collection of erotica. However, eventually, the pictures, movies, and other pornographic materials did not suffice. As they grew, they began to need more and more stimulation, which led to their decision to act out their fantasies.

Marc, a highly intelligent man in his late thirties, discussed the role that pornography had had on his sexually abusive behaviors.

"When I was a kid, I found pornography in my uncle's house. I was so turned on to it that I began looking forward to coming home from school so that I could lock myself in my room and look at these pictures. I would wake up in the middle of the night, stay at home during weekends, and pretend that I was doing homework at night just so I could be alone on my bed staring at those stimulating and erotic sights. As I got older, I began to purchase pornographic movies and magazines and hide them throughout my home. I knew something was wrong with me, especially since, as I got older, I continued to gravitate toward pornography that depicted adolescent girls.

"I got married, had children, and was employed in a high-level executive position in my company, but my fascination with pornography never ceased. I kept it secret from everyone, including my wife. Eventually, with the advent of the Internet, my preoccupation with pornography was heightened. I could now spend countless hours in the privacy of my home, or even at my office, surfing the Net for those sites that displayed teens in compromising and sexually arousing ways. I fantasized about those young girls and what it would be like to really have sex with them.

"And then one day my fantasies became a reality. I met a young girl at a track meet for my oldest daughter. She was my daughter's classmate, and she was also on the team. She was very friendly, and over the course of time, we got to know one another. I took her swimming with me in the early mornings, and eventually I began visiting her late at night outside of her home.

"She would leave her house in the middle of the night and meet me around the corner. We would spend hours talking and petting in my car. I thought I was in love with her. What I realize now was that she was the incarnation of all my sexual fantasies. She represented all the young girls who had ever exposed themselves in the magazines, movies, and on the Internet sites with one difference, she was here with me, a breathing, warm, and beautiful young female who professed to be in love with me. I know that what I did was terribly wrong; but from the time I was young, I was so obsessed with pornography that it seemed inevitable that the day would come when I would cross the line to become a sexual predator."

John, Rick, Dr. Season, and Mr. Rook have the potential for deviant sexual behavior. John is a selfish, immature man who would use children to fulfill his needs because he feels intimidated and controlled by women and is therefore unable to have long-term, satisfying sexual relationships with adults. His need for control and power is expressed through his sexual domination of young people.

Rick has a great sense of inadequacy that comes from years of being ostracized by his peers. He feels unacceptable and terribly lonely, and these feelings have settled deep within him to create a seething anger. Unfortunately, the anger and his need for acceptance find their expression in sexually inappropriate ways. Rick's adolescent sexuality has no healthy outlet; therefore he seeks gratification from the younger children who look up to him.

Middle-aged Dr. Season, although not a pedophile, derives satisfaction from sexual activity with young women because it makes him feel desirable and youthful. His objectification of women as sexual objects is in character with his tendency to see the world as "his for the taking."

And finally, Mr. Rook, the embodiment of the "dirty old man," has been a pedophile all of his adult life. He had successfully hidden his child pornography from his wife; and if their sexual relationship was wanting, neither partner discussed it. Mrs. Rook, born in a time when sex was rarely discussed, would have been too embarrassed to confront her husband about his lack of sexual desire for her, and therefore Mr. Rook's perversions went unchecked. Left to his own devices, Mr. Rook developed sophisticated and devious ways to lure young boys into acts that served to satisfy his perverse sexual desires.

Drug and/or Alcohol Abuse

There is no direct causality between predatory behaviors and substance abuse. The misuse of alcohol and drugs does not *cause* child molestation, and not every predator is a substance abuser. However, substance abuse and child molestation are connected by the fact that a majority of predators have a history of substance abuse. Studies from the Department of Justice indicate that at least 40 percent of predators admitted to drinking or using drugs during the period of time that they were abusing children.

Many individuals who abuse alcohol or drugs are using these substances to "medicate" themselves. Because they have not developed the internal mechanisms needed to successfully navigate their lives, they have learned to rely on outside sources to help them stay afloat. The characteristics of a predator already mentioned, such as low self-esteem, a lack of empathy, troubled childhood, and failed past relationships, define an individual who has significant problems coping with life, and alcohol and drugs are often used as crutches for these emotionally handicapped individuals.

For the insecure predator, alcohol may mask the sense of inadequacy and the fear of failure that continuously plague him or her. Inebriated, and thus temporarily free from an inadequate sense of self, the predator can move about with confidence. It is often during these times that a predator's true personality characteristics will be revealed. Under the influence of alcohol or drugs, the inhibitions that serve to restrict someone who is prone to sexually acting out are significantly lessened.

Other predators may find that alcohol and drugs fill the emptiness inside of them. This inner void has been created by years of disillusionment, early abandonment, and disappointments in work and relationships. With a dried-up reservoir thirsting at the emotional needs of an already depleted individual, alcohol and drugs can feel like a temporary oasis. Many predators feel an inner sense of loneliness, helplessness, and frustration; and when these emotions surface, they cannot tolerate them. For these individuals alcohol and drugs are a way to numb the painful emotions that they have been avoiding for years.

There is a high correlation between antisocial individuals who repeatedly engage in illegal actions and the abuse of substances. Antisocial individuals are often characterized as "thrill seekers" who strive for the incredible "highs" they experience in unlawful activities, illicit sexual behaviors, and the use of illegal substances. Under the influence the thrill seeker may engage in deviant sexual behavior to intensify the high.

The use of alcohol and drugs clouds perceptions, impairs judgments, and significantly influences decision making. Therefore an individual who has the characteristics of an abuser is more likely to act on these traits when under the influence. Thus, one of the fundamental prescriptions for an offender in treatment is that he or she abstain from the use of all harmful substances.

Now that you have learned the ten warning signs of a predator, you can better identify a potential sexual offender and prevent that person from harming your children. If Sylvia, Sally, Beth and George, and Cindy and Justin Morgan had had the list of the ten most common characteristics of a predator, it might have been easier for them to answer those questions they were left with after meeting John, Dr. Season, Rick, and Mr. Rook. The answer to all of their questions should have been an undeniably, "No," to Sylvia's continuing her relationship with John, to Sally taking Kim to Dr. Season, to Beth and George leaving their son at the camp, and to the Morgans allowing their twin sons to continue visiting Mr. Rook. For in saying, "No," they would also be saying, "Yes," to the continued safety and protection of their children.

Being aware of the ten most common characteristics is the first step in identifying a predator. Yet remember that an individual can have a number of these characteristics and still not be a sexual predator. In the next chapter you will be given another vital tool in assessing whether you or your children have come in contact with a predator. By becoming familiar with the five stages of abuse that predators use to identify, stalk, groom, and maim their prey, you will have the advantage of being able to recognize their patterns of behavior and plan your defense accordingly.

The Five Stages of Abuse

Every relationship develops in stages. A romantic sojourn begins the moment you meet someone. You move through the awkwardness of those first few dates until you embark on the exhilarating highs of a new infatuation. As you travel further down the road of intimacy, you learn more about your partner. You witness their habits and moods, and you share ordinary days filled with work and chores as you decide whether or not to continue heading toward commitment. At any juncture you may depart as friends or go your separate ways.

An abusive relationship also follows a pattern that progresses through stages. Yet when a victim embarks on a journey with a predator, the final destination is not a happy union or an agreeable parting. From first glance, the stages in an abusive encounter may appear much like those in a "normal" relationship. Therefore it is critical that you understand what these stages are and how they differ from the development of a healthy relationship.

Like any other close relationship, developing a connection with a child takes time. A child needs to become familiar and comfortable with another person and establish an alliance that considers his or her developmental needs. Because children are dependent on adults for their survival, their relationships are often based on the implicit trust that adults will know what is best for them.

When a sexual predator stalks a child, he or she will use the stages most commonly found in a romantic relationship in order to seduce and overpower a young victim. Treating the child like a special person who has been bestowed with a unique ability to meet an adult's needs, the predator will entice the child into a relationship. Therefore it is the parents' responsibility to protect their children from someone who has the power to manipulate and abuse the innocence of youth.

STAGE ONE: DETECTION

An abusive relationship begins with detection. In this stage the predator searches for his or her next victim. The initial meeting is a critical maneuver because the sexual predator will notice details that will help him or her evaluate the strengths and weaknesses of a potential victim. And this information is essential for planning a strategic seduction.

Children are often easy targets for sexual predators because of their natural state of vulnerability. So how does a predator detect those children who would be the most defenseless against sexual abuse? To find out more about this, let's visit the playground of an ordinary preschool and observe the initial interactions between a sexual predator and the five-year-old children he has recently met.

On an unseasonably warm fall day, Savannah, Jensen, and Hannah are playing together. They have been inseparable best friends since they met at the preschool and always have a wonderful time sculpting clay figures, setting up puppet plays, and cascading down the red slide on the playground. Savannah, the smallest of the three, is the leader of the group. Quick minded and verbal, she commands the other two through a potpourri of creative games. She concocts fabulous stories of magical princesses and daring knights, and single-handedly directs, casts, and stars in these imaginative productions. Jensen's practicality and his eagerness to please complement Savannah's fanciful nature. He has a strong and sturdy frame, and he is an expert at building the castles and digging the moats that are needed to protect Princess Savannah and her royal family. He is as resourceful as Savannah is fanciful. Hannah, on the other hand, is a soft-spoken child with an angelic face. With her blonde bangs framing aquamarine eyes, she appears feminine and sweet. She is always selected to be the "baby" or the "pet" in their make-believe family. Most of the time she doesn't mind, except just once she would like to be the princess.

A new person has just come to work at the preschool. The children call him "Mr. Bob." He has come to help their teacher, and the children have already accepted him as an adult in authority who can tell them when they should come in for naps and what to eat for snacks.

Mr. Bob seems nice, and the children are just getting to know him. Savannah, however, doesn't like him. She thinks he is "weird" and gets annoyed when he wants to join them in their play. She doesn't have the patience for an adult who wants to talk when kids are busy playing.

Hannah is quiet around new people, and she doesn't like it when strangers touch her hair. It took her a long time to feel comfortable around Savannah and Jensen, but Mr. Bob makes her feel shy. He does seem nice, and he even brought them candy once when they were playing outside. That almost never happened, except on special holidays like Halloween. Hannah thinks that maybe she could like him if she knew him better.

Jensen has already made up his mind that Mr. Bob is nice, and he could be an asset to their group. Jensen tells them this while building a castle for their new play. "I like Mr. Bob; he's cool. None of the other teachers ever play with us. I bet he'll help me dig the moat."

Savannah stops her search for a magical wand long enough to confront Jensen. "He won't do that."

"Yes, he will. He's nice. I'll go ask him." Jensen jumps up and runs toward Mr. Bob, who has just emerged from the building.

Hannah, who has been quiet up to this point, approaches Savannah. "I want to be princess this time. Maybe Mr. Bob will let me."

"He's not the boss of us," Savannah retorts.

At that moment, Jensen returns with Mr. Bob in tow. He asks them what they are playing.

"We're playing castles," declares Savannah, "and I'm the princess."

"She always gets to be the princess," Jensen explains.

"Well, is that so? And what about you, Hannah, who do you play?" Mr. Bob kneels down to face her.

"I play the baby," Hannah says softly.

"You don't like that very much, do you, Hannah?" Mr. Bob continues.

"No."

"Well then, how about this? Why don't the two of you girls be the princesses, and Jensen and I will be your knights?"

Savannah voices discontent, but Mr. Bob intervenes. "I'll tell you what, Savannah. You can be the magic princess, and with your powers, you can make me a knight and Hannah your princess sister."

The children agree and the play begins.

As you may have already assumed, Mr. Bob is the sexual predator. He is in the first stage of detection, and he must carefully assess each child as he decides who will be his next victim.

Jensen is a pleasing boy, and he has already accepted Mr. Bob as his friend. But is he the most vulnerable child in the group? Mr. Bob has already observed that Jensen readily follows the orders of the spunky and outspoken Savannah. Does this mean that he would be easy to manipulate? Savannah, on the other hand, might be tough to lure into his web for she is a determined child and already suspicious of Mr. Bob. From first glance, sweet and shy little Hannah seems the most obvious choice, but she is slow to warm up to him. Mr. Bob will need to spend more time with the children to see how they react to his manipulative ploys.

Factors That Determine
a Child's Vulnerability to a Sexual Predator

There are a number of factors that make children susceptible to a sexual predator. One is age. *The younger the child, the more vulnerable he or she is to sexual abuse.* The children that Mr. Bob has met are all preschoolers and therefore are receptive to the manipulations of an adult. Adults naturally have authority over young children, and Mr. Bob's role as teacher's aide at the preschool places him in an automatic position of power over the children.

Another important factor is availability. In fact, as you will learn, availability is often considered the most important condition for sexual abuse to occur. You will see in future chapters how teachers, counselors, baby-sitters, siblings, stepparents, and medical professionals had unlimited and unsupervised access to the young children they sexually abused. And, un-fortunately, all three of the preschool students you have just met are easily accessible to Mr. Bob.

Research has attempted to identify certain personality characteristics that make children more vulnerable to a sexual predator, such as compli-ance, friendliness, and sympathy. However, consistent results have not been found. For every acquiescent and docile child who has been sexually abused, there is a fiery-spirited one who has also fallen prey to a sexual predator. We do know that girls are more likely to become victims, but is that a result of certain personality traits inherent in females or is it because, throughout history, they have been labeled and treated as the more vul-nerable sex?

However, certain traits *can* be directly correlated to the degree of vul-nerability in children. And Mr. Bob has an excellent opportunity to detect these traits in the children he has met by assessing their social and aca-demic performances at the preschool. Intellect is an important factor. Chil-dren who are intellectually impaired are at a higher risk for sexual abuse. These children are often at a distinct disadvantage because they have def-icits in their memory, perception, judgment, and in their level of self-care. They tend to be easily led, and their ability to discern dangerous situations is often limited.

Another prominent factor that directly relates to children's vulnerabil-ity to abuse is their self-esteem. We know that children who don't feel good about themselves are more prone to abuse. Those who are ostracized from peers and ridiculed by others are often more susceptible to the manipu-lations of a sexual predator, who is all too willing to give them the praise, recognition, and attention they so desperately crave.

Children who are depressed or have recently suffered a loss, such as a death or divorce, are also at risk. These children may be experiencing sadness, confusion, and a sense of abandonment that may be temporarily lessened by the deceiving attentions of a predator.

For a multitude of reasons, children who have been sexually abused are, unfortunately, more likely to reexperience abuse than children who have never been victimized. Sexually abused children are often precocious in their sexual development because, as noted in chapter 1, their early exposure to adult sexuality turned up their "sexual thermostats." They have also learned to be a "victim," and therefore assume this role with others. For these reasons they are often more vulnerable to continued victimization.

A child's knowledge about sexual abuse and the level of preventative education that the child receives at home also make a difference. Parents must educate their children about sexual abuse. Identifying body parts and knowing which ones to keep private, saying, "No," to inappropriate touch, and identifying those situations that signal danger are critical defenses for a child.

Yet these preventative measures are not enough. A child must be taught not to keep secrets from family members and that open and honest communication is always expected. A child should also know that private relationships with other adults are never acceptable. Children who are taught these lessons are less vulnerable to sexual abuse.

Finally, parents must take charge of monitoring their child's environment. The parent who visits the preschool, communicates frequently with the personnel, and drops by unannounced to check on the status of the child is minimizing the chance that sexual abuse will occur. Parents who inform baby-sitters, day-care providers, or preschool staff that their family is aware of the issues involved in sexual abuse are warning potential sexual predators that their child is "off-limits."

With this in mind, let's return to the three children Mr. Bob has met and see if they display any of the above determinants that would make them more vulnerable to him.

All three children are bright and respond well to their teachers. They get along with their peers, and the bond they have established with one another reflects their ability to form and maintain friendships. They come from middle-class families and haven't had previous experience with abuse. Their parents are involved with the preschool and volunteer to bring treats for the children's snacks, but this is where the similarities end.

Savannah lives with her parents and a younger sister. Two blocks away, Hannah lives with her parents and two older brothers. Jensen's house is on the outskirts of town in a wealthy subdivision that was built for the executives of a company that had been recently relocated to their town.

Six months ago, Jensen and his mother had moved into his stepfather's home. Jensen likes his new stepfather, Roy, but he can't get used to the idea that his mother spends all of her time with Roy. Jensen liked it when he and his mother lived all alone in that yellow house at the end of Spruce

Street because she played with him all the time. Jensen learned to ride his three-wheeler on that street, and that is where he found the stray dog that would later become his pet. Roy was allergic to animals and the dog was the first to go, along with Jensen's neighborhood friends and his bedroom with the yellow wallpaper decorated with his favorite baseball players.

Just last Saturday, Jensen wandered into the living room to ask his mother for a peanut butter sandwich, and he found his mother kissing Roy. "Yuk, that's disgusting." Jensen remarked, as he watched his mother quickly disengage herself from Roy's arms.

"Don't say that, Jensen. Kissing can be nice. It's something people do when they're in love. You'll understand someday," Roy explained.

"I miss my dad," Jensen said, as he walked upstairs and slammed the door to his room.

Jensen had not seen his father for almost a year. When his father heard the news that Jensen's mother was getting married, he moved to Alaska. Jensen wanted to go with him, but his father said that Alaska wasn't a place for young boys. And besides, he needed to stay with his mother. Jensen argued that his mother didn't need him anymore now that she had Roy, but his father wouldn't listen.

So now you know a little more about the three children who are being appraised by Mr. Bob. He has spent weeks with the children; and along with school records and teacher's conversations, he has obtained enough information to assess the susceptibility of each child. *Jensen, feeling abandoned by his father, rejected by his mother, and out of balance in his new family, is the most vulnerable child.*

STAGE TWO: THE APPROACH

After the predator detects a potential victim, he or she moves into the Approach Stage. During this stage the predator will attempt to get closer to the intended victim. There are many ways that a predator can get near his or her victim, but an initial ploy will always involve some sort of seduction. A predator is masterful at attracting children because the predator can don a disguise as anyone he or she thinks the child wants. The predator will tailor his or her behaviors to appear as "the perfect friend."

Mr. Bob quickly understood the need for Savannah to be the leader, Hannah to play a princess, and Jensen to have male support. In one fell swoop, he landed in the center of their circle and changed the entire dynamics of their friendship. And slowly he began to isolate Jensen by forming a special alliance with him that excluded the other two children.

A sexual predator in the Approach Stage will be on his or her best behavior. The predator will continue to beguile the children with a nefarious charm while keeping an eye on the hold he or she is gaining over the potential victim. Mr. Bob masterminded this stage with cold and calculated moves.

He assessed that Jensen was a sensitive and needy child who looked for approval in almost everyone he met. He preferred playing with girls because he had spent so much time alone with his mother. He knew that girls appreciated his kindness and warmth, and he enjoyed the feeling of being needed. Ever since his father left, Jensen had made sure he told his mother how much he loved her so that she wouldn't be lonely or miss his dad too much. When he told her how pretty she looked one day, her gleaming smile told him that he had said the right thing. Jensen had liked the special relationship he had with his mother, and he was sorely disappointed when it came to an end shortly after she met Roy.

But Jensen also needed a father, and this was the weakness that Mr. Bob so cunningly assessed in the Detection Stage. During the Approach Stage, Mr. Bob had used this need to get closer to Jensen. Mr. Bob spent a great deal of time talking to Jensen. While making sand moats, wooden boats, and shields made of fallen bark, Mr. Bob and Jensen talked. Jensen told Mr. Bob how much he missed his father and how much he wanted to live with him.

Mr. Bob learned that Jensen's father was a mechanical engineer and had taught his son how to build wooden airplanes. Together, Jensen and his father would take their model planes to the wide-open spaces outside of town and launch them into the wind. He knew that Jensen missed this; and right before Christmas, Mr. Bob surprised Jensen with a model airplane kit. Mr. Bob suggested that they assemble it together; and for the next few weeks, instead of joining his friends on the playground, Jensen would go with Mr. Bob to the art room and work on their special project.

An important tactic that predators use during the Approach Stage is to meet the parents of the intended victim. If the predator is successful in establishing a relationship with the parents, he or she will have more opportunity for unsupervised time with their child. With this in mind, Mr. Bob decided to visit Jensen's mother and stepfather. On the pretense of letting them know how their son was doing in school, he dropped by Jensen's home and was invited for dinner.

Jensen's mother appreciated Mr. Bob's relationship with her son. She had been concerned about the sudden change in Jensen since her remarriage. On occasion Jensen was argumentative and sullen, and she knew that he resented Roy and missed his father. Although Roy was a caring man, he was far too preoccupied with his real estate business to spend much time with Jensen. Mr. Bob appeared at just the right time in their lives. Jensen brightened when he was in Mr. Bob's company, and his entire attitude had changed since Mr. Bob had taken an interest in him. And because of this, his mother was only too glad to allow her son to spend time with his teacher.

STAGE THREE: SUBJUGATION

If the Approach Stage was well planned and successfully executed, the predator will now move to the Subjugation Stage. During this phase he or she will devote energy into gaining control over the victim. At first, the control may appear subtle, as the predator offers friendly advice, suggestions, reminders, and occasional criticisms. However, over time, the predator's control will increase. Remember that the predator must render the victim helpless, isolated, and defenseless for the abuse to occur.

A predator gains control by slowly alienating the child from outside influences. By forming an exclusive and unique relationship, the predator begins to separate the child from his or her parents, friends, and teachers. In the following conversation, Mr. Bob is subtly luring Jensen away from his parents and friends by offering him a special type of friendship.

Mr. Bob and Jensen are sitting at a table during recess gluing the decals on the wings of the model airplane they have just completed.

"Jensen, you're really great at making these models. I bet your dad was a really good teacher. You must really miss him."

"I don't see him anymore."

"Do you talk to him on the phone?"

"On my birthday he called. He said he was sending me a present."

"Does your stepdad play with you?"

"Nah, he's too busy."

"What about Mom? Does she spend time with you?"

"She's with my stepdad all the time."

"You must really feel left out."

"It's okay, I guess."

"Well, your parents don't know what they're missing. You're a great kid. I love playing with you. I just wish your dad could see you now; he'd be so proud."

"My dad and I made an airplane like this, but I don't have it anymore. It broke when we moved. Mom can't fix it. I threw it away."

"Hey, I just had a great idea! Why don't we take a picture of our plane and send it to your dad. I bet he'd love it!"

"Right now?"

"Well, how about we take the picture when we bring it to the airfield on Saturday?"

"And Mom and Roy can come, too."

"Sure, if they're not too busy. I already talked to your mom about Saturday, and she said that Roy had to work and she is playing tennis with her friend. And I don't think they'd get up that early on the weekend. We're going to get up at the crack of dawn to fly our plane into the sunrise so we can get a really good picture to send your dad. Besides, do they really like model airplanes?"

"I don't think so."

"Well, your dad will really like this one. I promise you that."

Jensen nods his head enthusiastically as he pastes down the last decal.

In the above conversation, Mr. Bob seems to be sensitive, caring, and completely empathic with Jensen's grief over his absent father. However, his words reflect the skillful manipulations of a predator who is attempting to maneuver a child into an exclusive relationship. He has already isolated Jensen from his schoolyard friends by taking on a special project that involves only the two of them. He has also capitalized on Jensen's jealousy and resentment toward his mother and stepfather to further alienate Jensen from his family.

STAGE FOUR: GROOMING

Now that the predator has complete control, he will tend to the business of grooming the victim. In the Grooming Stage the predator will prepare his victim for the abuse. He will use subtle and devious methods to further isolate the victim from others. Buying expensive gifts and planning special activities will intensify as the predator lures the victim further into his web.

At this stage the predator will test the boundaries of the relationship by experimenting with overt displays of affection. The predator will look for opportunities to get physically close to the victim, such as kissing, hugging, or wrestling. Rewards of special gifts that are given to the child following physical displays of affection ensure continued cooperation.

An important aspect of this stage is securing secrecy in the relationship. Unless the predator is able to solicit the child's cooperation in *keeping a secret*, the sexual abuse can't occur. In the beginning the predator will prepare the child for secrecy by setting up several situations that require the child to maintain silence. Important decisions, special promises, and any clandestine activities that the predator engages in with the child are preliminary trappings that set the stage for secrecy.

Jensen has already promised Mr. Bob that he won't "tell a soul" about the important phone call they are planning to make to Jensen's father in Alaska. Mr. Bob told him that this summer he was planning to visit Alaska; and if Jensen's father agreed, Mr. Bob would take him up there to see him. But he makes sure that the trip is contingent on Jensen keeping it a secret from his mom, Roy, and his friends.

And Jensen must also keep secret those brand-new binoculars that Mr. Bob bought him so that they could watch their plane fly up close. Mr. Bob thought that Jensen's mom would make him give them back if she knew how expensive they were. Instead, Mr. Bob told him that they could keep them safe in his car so that they could use them when they went out to the airfield.

Engaging the child in a special relationship is an important tactic that maximizes the chance that the child will ultimately submit to the sexual abuse. A predator will manipulate the child into thinking that he or she has power over an adult. By elevating a child to an adult status, a predator can then ask that child to fulfill adult sexual needs. Mr. Bob "confided" in Jensen in order to make him feel special. The "secrets" that he divulged to Jensen were important, and he "trusts that Jensen will not tell anyone else about them." In this manner, Jensen feels special and privileged and is primed to believe that he can fulfill adult needs.

In the following conversation you will discern how Mr. Bob grooms Jensen by telling the boy that he, too, has experienced losses and that his relationship with Jensen has been instrumental in healing his wounds.

It is a brilliant day, with the clouds drifting swiftly across the morning sky. The airplane that Jensen and Mr. Bob have just launched is gliding many feet above their heads. They have already taken a number of Polaroid shots of the plane, and the binoculars will help them spot the craft as it lands. For the next few moments, they stand in silence enjoying the sense of accomplishment that soars each time the plane arches a graceful turn in the air.

Mr. Bob breaks the silence. "Hey, Jensen, look at that plane fly. That's really something. We did it!"

"It's cool. Can we take it out again next week? I want to show it to Mom and Roy."

"Of course we can; they'll love it. But remember, don't say anything about visiting your dad in Alaska or the binoculars. They're our special secrets."

"I know, I won't. I haven't told Savannah and Hannah, but they don't play with me a lot anymore. They think I don't like them."

"Of course you like them, Jensen; it's just that us guys need to be together and do special things. And we have to keep our secrets, right?"

"Right."

"You're such an incredible kid. I haven't told you this before, but I want to explain something to you."

"What?"

"I want you to know how important you are to me, Jensen. You see, two years ago, my little boy lived with me." Mr. Bob assumes a sad look as he reaches out to stroke Jensen's hair.

"Where is he?"

"He's not here anymore. You see, his mother took him far away from me. Just like your mom, his mom got married to someone else and they moved to another state."

"Alaska?"

"No, but somewhere very far away."

"Do you get to see him?"

"No, almost never, because his mother and his new stepfather don't like him to come out to see me."

"Why not?"

"Because they don't think he is big enough to fly on a plane all alone. What do you think?"

"I never went on a plane by myself."

"But you could if you wanted to. You're a big guy now."

"I know, I'm almost six, and I'm not afraid to go on a plane by myself."

"That-a-boy, Jensen. You're great. Just wait till your father finds out that you are flying all that way just to see him. I know how your dad misses you because I miss my kid so much. But you know what? I feel so much better because you are here. When I'm with you, I don't feel so lonely. You're just like my big boy."

Jensen looks up at Mr. Bob, and, in a rush of emotion, he throws his little arms around the big man's waist and buries his face in the soft down of his sweater. Mr. Bob reaches down to cradle Jensen's head and together they stand in this embrace until the plane gently cascades down to earth.

STAGE FIVE: THE ABUSE

The sexual predator will ensure that all of the previous stages of abuse are reinforced and firmly established before he enacts the sexual abuse. Equally important is the level of control, secrecy, and cooperation of the victim in order for the abuse to continue. Therefore it is not uncommon for the predator to revert back to the previous four stages as he or she further strengthens those bonds that will keep the victim trapped. It is only when one of these factors becomes weakened that the victim has a chance to escape.

Mr. Bob's sexual abuse of Jensen occurred on one of their "special Saturdays" as they got ready to launch their plane. It was a cold spring morning, and Jensen and Mr. Bob were sitting in the car with the heater still blowing. Mr. Bob shivered and asked Jensen to come closer so they could help each other get warm. With Jensen on his lap, he explained that touching one another in special places was one way they could express their real friendship. He told Jensen that he was so lonely for his own little boy that he needed the special attention Jensen gave to him. Explaining to Jensen that fathers normally do this with their boys so that they can learn about sex, he molested Jensen.

To ensure that the abuse would continue, the predator needs to fortify the child's compliance and secrecy. To do this he uses a combination of pleadings, promises, and threats. Promises of exciting vacations and the acquisition of long-sought-after toys are made by the predator to ensure the child's cooperation and secrecy. And although some of these promises are fulfilled, others are held out to further entice a victim.

In most cases the predator will also voice a number of threats that will frighten the child into secrecy. Threats may take on the form of a warning that harm will come to the victim's parents, friends, pets, or to the predator, if the silence is broken. Children are gullible, particularly when it comes to adults. They have been taught to believe that adults tell the truth, and that they mean what they say. At a young age children are naive about the world, and their dependence upon adults leads them to assume that adults are capable of carrying through with their threats. Therefore statements such as: *If you tell, your parents will be very angry with you and probably send you away to live in a foster home,* and, *If you say anything to your parents about this, they will send me to jail forever,* are highly effective in frightening a child into secrecy.

Predators will capitalize on a child's sense of guilt and shame, which inevitably result from sexual abuse. Because young children naturally engage in magical thinking that presumes that they are the center of the world and everything that happens is a result of them, they will blame themselves for the predator's behaviors. This sense of shame is exacerbated when the predator makes the following threat: *What we are doing is special to us, and no one else will understand. So if you tell your parents, your friends, or any other adult, they will think that you are bad and you will be in big trouble.*

Following the initial act of sexual abuse, Mr. Bob told Jensen that if he told, they would not be able to do any of their special activities anymore. Further, their model plane and binoculars would be taken away, and their special plans to visit his father would never happen. He also threatened that if Jensen told anyone, Mr. Bob would be sent away forever, just like Jensen's dad, and that they would never see one another again. Mr. Bob told Jensen that no one would understand their friendship, and that everyone would be very mad at both of them for what they had done. In fact, he warned that once Jensen's mother and stepfather found out, they would have to send Jensen away to a foster home until he grew up.

In this manner Mr. Bob was able to continue the sexual abuse for over three months. And although Jensen kept his promise not to tell anyone, the changes in his behavior spoke loudly of emotional damage. He either clung to his mother in desperation, or spent an inordinate amount of time alone in his room or staring at the television. He began to urinate in his bed at night; and, on a number of occasions, he wet his pants at school. Jensen's mother noticed that he had regressed to baby talk and sucking his thumb, habits that he hadn't done for at least two years. Initially she assumed that these changes were a result of his problems adjusting to his new home. When she tried to talk to Jensen, he refused to respond. Distraught and confused, she decided to bring him to his pediatrician.

Jensen's doctor also noticed a worrisome listlessness in the once happy and outgoing child. Jensen appeared anxious and very uncomfortable with the examination, particularly when the doctor attempted to examine his genitals. He asked Jensen if anyone had ever hurt him or touched him; but once again, Jensen remained mute.

After consulting with Jensen's mother about his concerns, the doctor advised her that she continue her attempts to talk to her son. He also suggested family counseling to further ascertain whether Jensen's behavior problems stemmed from his difficulty adjusting to his new family. When she took her son home that afternoon, they sat at the kitchen table over a chocolate sundae.

"Jensen, what is the matter? You can tell me, I'll understand. Is it Roy?"

Jensen continued to spoon the whipped cream into his mouth as he shook his head.

"Well then, has anyone made you mad at school? Like Savannah or Hannah?"

Without looking at his mother, he replied, "They don't play with me anymore."

"Why not?"

"Mr. Bob said that they are girls and that I should play with him."

A hot flash of fear spread throughout her body as Jensen's mother leaned toward him.

"What else did Mr. Bob tell you?"

"Nothing."

"Jensen, do you like being with Mr. Bob?"

"Sometimes."

"Does he ever do anything to hurt you?"

"No, not all the time."

"Did he ever touch you anywhere that he shouldn't?"

Jensen remained quiet as he stirred the spoon in the soupy chocolate mixture.

"Jensen, look at me. It's important that if anyone has touched you, you tell me."

Jensen finally looked up at his mother and what she saw in his eyes frightened her. "He'd be mad, Mom. And then I couldn't see my dad. It's a secret."

"Jensen, you shouldn't have any secrets from me. Some secrets are not good to keep, especially if they are about someone touching your body."

Jensen immediately started to cry. "You'll send me away."

"Jensen, I would never send you away. Did Mr. Bob tell you that?"

"He said that you would send me to live in a foster home. I don't want to go to a foster home, and I don't want Mr. Bob to go to jail forever."

It didn't take long for Jensen's mother to reassure her son and release him from the stronghold of his fears. And when the final bastion of resistance was torn down, Jensen told his mother about Mr. Bob, and at last, his torturous ordeal of sexual abuse came to an end.

Jensen would eventually recover from the shame, humiliation, and the sense of betrayal created by the sexual abuse. But it would take some time. Jensen's teacher and his parents also felt a great deal of guilt since they had not been able to detect any of the warning signs of sexual abuse.

Jensen's mother was a loving and caring parent, and her devotion to her son had never faltered even through her new marriage. However, she had been distracted by the demands of a new household, and she'd mistakenly interpreted her son's sullen misbehavior as an "adjustment period." She'd made an egregious error when she believed that Mr. Bob had the best interest of her son in mind and therefore allowed him to have unsupervised access to Jensen.

Mistakes are most often made when we have insufficient information to guide us to the right decisions. Now that you have the information on how a predator can lead his victim through the five stages of abuse, you can recognize the warning signs ahead of time.

Being able to identify the ten most common characteristics of a sexual predator and the five stages of abuse is a formidable armament against the sexual offender. However, these seemingly indomitable adversaries often intimidate us because they appear to us as incomprehensible individuals who commit unexplainable acts. Therefore, in the next chapter, you will have an opportunity to become familiar with four predators in order to understand more about how and why they commit such heinous acts of abuse. In learning about these predators' early histories, the formation of their deviant fantasies, and in what manner they seduced their young victims, you will come to a better understanding of how they present themselves to the world, and most important, why they are so successful in obtaining child victims.

Chapter 3

Four Types of Male Predators

Predators do not fall into distinct categories. They are an extremely diverse population represented in all occupations, religions, races, and cultures. You don't have to go to a therapist's office, psychiatric hospital, jail, or the back alley of a pornographic movie theater to meet a child abuser. Many of us have met them in our children's schoolyards, the pews of our churches, executive office suites, and at the playgrounds and parks of our neighborhoods. They are as likely to lurk in the crime-infested trenches of our inner cities as to occupy next-door residences in our quiet, affluent suburbs.

Despite the popular notion proliferated on television and film, predators are not always those unspeakable monsters who inhabit the dark shadows of our fears or the incorrigibly violent inmate who sits in a jail cell seeping in ignorance and hatred. They're often likable and highly engaging individuals who have achieved top positions in their chosen professions. They may appear as harmless as the boy next door or as meek as the quiet librarian who finds comfort among the archives of the books that surround her. They may be as friendly as the most popular guy you once knew in your high school class or as charming as the handsome young intern who administers gentle cures to your child's aches and pains. It is virtually impossible to detect predators by certain physical, occupational, or racial characteristics. What then makes a predator so different from the well-intentioned and harmless people who make up the vast majority of our world? The answer lies in their decision to act out sexually harmful behaviors on children.

In interviewing predators I was surprised to discover that, excluding the more violent or antisocial sexual offenders, I actually liked these people. They were engaging, intelligent, and often had an appealing personality. As I interviewed predators who had inflicted immeasurable damage on defenseless children, I found myself smiling in response to their humor and nodding my head sympathetically as they related the horrors of their own childhoods.

Some of them appeared to have insight, and quite a few had a good sense of humor. Many of them willingly admitted to the pain and suffering they had caused others, and the guilt they bore at times seemed genuine.

Because so many of these predators were successful in presenting themselves in a sympathetic light, I would often leave an interview feeling sorry for the unfortunate circumstances that had led them to prey on children. Yet as soon as I got into my car, turned on the ignition, and waited for the engine to warm up, I realized that my emotions had misled me. The individuals I had been interviewing were not harmless victims of their circumstances; they were dangerous predators who had seduced and violated children. As I drove out of the parking lot, I realized that if someone like myself, a trained clinician with years of experience in the field of victimization, could respond to them in such a sympathetic manner, then what protection did the average person have against such potentially dangerous individuals?

In order to become more familiar with the personalities of these individuals so that you will be less susceptible to their manipulative ploys, you will meet four different types of sexual predators. As you discover the pain, loss, and abuse that they experienced in their childhoods and trace the formation of the obsessions and compulsive behaviors that eventually led them to sexually abusing children, you will have a better understanding of how each of these individuals operates.

As your familiarity with these predators increases, you will experience the wide range of emotions that they engender in all of us. You will feel distaste, anger, and revulsion as you witness their abusive acts toward children. Yet you will also experience compassion and empathy for their early childhood experiences that are familiar to so many of us, whether it be poverty, parent alienation, abuse, or unpopularity with peers. This is what makes the task of characterizing predators so difficult. Like you and me, these individuals withstood many trials and tribulations throughout the difficult journey of childhood and adolescence; and yet unlike the vast majority of us, they broke one of society's most fundamental taboos by sexually exploiting children.

It is important to emphasize that the unfortunate circumstances that existed in the predators' pasts are not presented as excuses for their acts of abuse. These men are responsible for their choice to engage in despicable acts against children. No mitigating circumstances can obscure this fact. For we know that for every child who has suffered tragedy in his or her life and later decides to inflict this pain on innocent people, there are many more who survive disastrous home lives and do not grow up to prey on others.

Each of the many predators I interviewed was a unique person with his own set of thoughts, emotions, and personal history. However, similarities in childhood history, patterns of thought, grooming behavior, and sexually deviant acts did emerge that could be organized into distinct categories. Thus, I chose to group these male predators into four different classifications: the narcissist, the inadequate, the antisocial, and the pedophile.

Not all predators fall into one of these four categories, for as already noted, predators represent a diverse group of people who in many ways defy categorization. Nevertheless, by choosing four male predators who embody the characteristics of each category, it will be easier for the reader to grasp the quality, style, and personality of each type of offender.

THE NARCISSISTIC PREDATOR

The first predator you will meet is the narcissist. When I entered graduate school, I believed that the narcissist was like the handsome Greek youth who gazed a bit too long in the river at his magnificent reflection and, in doing so, lost his footing, fell in, and drowned. I soon discovered that this ancient myth was, in fact, the origin of the psychiatric name for a personality disorder that involves a dangerous fascination with one's self-worth. A narcissistic person is one who long ago in childhood received unrealistic messages about his self-importance. As he was glorified, sanctified, and idolized by his parents, he learned that his accomplishments and attributes made him lovable and beyond reproach. He learned to hide unacceptable feelings, desires, fantasies, and behaviors from the rest of the world, and at times even from himself, and therefore his "true" self was never fully recognized.

Yet unlike the Greek god Narcissus, who perished as a result of his self-love, the narcissistic individual is more likely to cause pain and suffering to others. To narcissists, the world is theirs for the taking, and they are exempt from the everyday rules and regulations that govern the rest of society. The narcissist, who has never really experienced unconditional love and acceptance, exists only for the continued pursuit of attention, recognition, and praise from others. The narcissist will hurt and destroy others because he has an endless need for recognition that does not allow room for the give-and-take that is found in healthy relationships.

Let us now meet Harvey, a man whose handsome face is accentuated by his intense blue eyes. Before his arrest and conviction for sexually molesting a teenage girl, Harvey was employed as an English teacher at a prestigious private high school in the charmingly affluent countryside of Vermont. From outside appearances, Harvey had a bright future. He lived in a remarkably quaint, remodeled carriage house with his attractive wife and a new baby daughter.

> Harvey came from an upper-class family with a long lineage of well-bred, sophisticated, and highly accomplished patriarchs. As the firstborn male of a wealthy attorney and a homemaker, Harvey was expected to carry on the family tradition of excellence. His father, a dominant and autocratic ruler of the household, held a tight rein on his wife and children. His punishments were swift and severe, and his strict sense of right and wrong wore heavily upon the members of the family. Everyone moved around in a quiet manner to please Harvey's father. Although the living room furniture was carefully designed and color coordinated, the meals exquisitely planned, and the gardens tended with precision and grace, the atmosphere in the home was cold and heavy.
>
> Harvey's older sister, relegated to second-class status as a female, deeply resented the birth of her younger brother. She was uncontrollably jealous of the adoration and attention he received, and, in private, she acted out her rage on baby Harvey well before he ever had a chance of defending himself. Helpless and trapped by this indomitable foe, Harvey increasingly retreated within him-

self and found his only solace in food. His parents, unaware of the negative impact that his sister's jealousy was having on him, berated him for not living up to their expectations. While Harvey was getting fatter, his sister was blooming, basking in her victory over the domination of her younger brother.

Thus Harvey entered kindergarten as an overweight, sullen, and withdrawn child. He was fearful and timid with his classmates, and it did not take them long to figure out that Harvey was an excellent target for mockery. Poor little Harvey struggled in school as his internal pain made it impossible for him to concentrate on his lessons. He had a tough time learning; and combined with his awkwardness out on the playground, Harvey was not a popular child.

Harvey's parents were terribly disappointed and embarrassed of their only son. They hid him away from prying relatives and made him stay at home when they left, resplendent in their attire, to take part in the social scene at their country club. As time went by, Harvey, alone, abandoned, and afraid, became angrier, sadder, and heavier.

To make matters worse, just as Harvey was entering third grade, twin boys were born into the family and Harvey's status became even more compromised. Left alone once again, as his mother and the nanny were remodeling the new nursery and putting beautiful matching clothes on screaming infants, Harvey began to display his pain and anger in different ways. He stole from his parents, classmates, and teachers, and often lied about his life to get the attention he so desperately desired. He got into many scuffles on the playground that left him bruised and battered and often resulted in detention and harsher consequences from his father.

Let us now flash forward to the summer of Harvey's twelfth year when he was initiated into the "forbidden" world of sex. His sister, now a headstrong teenager of fifteen, was displaying her own brand of rebellion against years of parental neglect by becoming wildly promiscuous. She had what appeared to Harvey as a never-ending string of long-haired, drug-using boyfriends who would slink into the house when their parents were away. Harvey would hide from view and secretly observe the sexual fumblings of his sister and her latest paramour. And as the petting increased to more advanced forms of sexual behavior, Harvey watched his sister lose her virginity.

Harvey's sister was not daunted by the loss of her innocence, and she plummeted into a series of casual, drug-induced sexual encounters. During one fateful night when Harvey was hiding in his sister's closet waiting for the next "show to begin," he was discovered. His sister and her boyfriend reacted with vengeance as they beat Harvey about the head and back with their fists. Harvey cried profusely and begged to be released from the torrent of blows. Eventually, they let him go with a warning that if he told, dire consequences would follow. Harvey slunk out of his sister's bedroom, shamed, angry, and bruised.

Once in the safe confines of his room, Harvey found himself battling with the most confusing feelings he had ever known. Aside from the deep humiliation that he suffered, he was filled with rage. However, accompanying these emotions, there arose an overwhelming sense of sexual stimulation that Harvey could barely contain. Harvey was having his first experience with the powerfully destructive mixture of aggression and sexuality that was to become the hallmark of his later abusive behaviors. For young Harvey, the pattern had been set; sexual gratification obtained through any means available would help relieve his pent-up anger and resentment.

As fate would have it, like the ugly duckling that turned into a swan, pudgy Harvey matured into a splendid adolescent. His childhood fat filtered down to expose a lean and well-proportioned young man. As he entered high school, he shed the skin of his former self and exposed to the outside a shiny new exterior that was seemingly free of the scars that had deformed him in his childhood.

It was in this manner that Harvey became popular. He gained notoriety as the captain of his high school football team and was recognized as a bright student who excelled in his studies. The girls flocked to him, and he had the pick of the finest, most nubile young females his school had to offer. He regularly seduced them into sex with his winning looks and the sense of control he had learned so adeptly from years of watching his father brandishing power over others.

Harvey's parents were beside themselves with joy. Their long-lost son, the hope for their future, the designated bearer of the family's pride and achievement had finally materialized. They lavished him with praise and rewards until nothing was beyond reach of Harvey's desires. He drove a sporty car, and his attire reflected the newest trends in fashion. He was the epitome of an accomplished, happy, and self-assured youth. Nothing to the naked eye could mar this picture of perfection. Yet underneath Harvey's winsome exterior lurked the pudgy, angry, and sexually aroused child who had been so shamefully banished from his sister's room years ago. And at certain times, during stressful periods, when alcohol had gotten the best of him or when the memories of his lonely and miserable childhood began to compromise his perfect world, his "damaged child" would surface.

The "angry little boy" within Harvey continued to seek revenge on innocent others for all of the injustices he had suffered. A bewildered and vulnerable high school girlfriend of Harvey's would confide in her best friend that, at times, Harvey would become physically aggressive with her and demand sex. He would threaten her with abandonment and tell her that he would tarnish her reputation by spreading stories of their sexual exploits throughout the school. Ashamed and scared, Harvey's girlfriend would succumb to Harvey's manipulations and inevitably give him what he wanted. Harvey gloried in the ease of his conquest and began to treat other girls in a cavalier manner. He "dumped" them as soon as he got them into bed, and he never looked back as he rounded the corner in search of a new victim. Harvey's career as a sexual predator had begun.

Harvey graduated from high school with honors and was accepted into an Ivy League school. His sexual exploits tempered somewhat in college, as he was often seen in the company of one particular pretty sorority girl who complemented his own good looks. With years of experience marveling his audiences with stories of adventure and intrigue, it was inevitable that Harvey excelled in writing. Despite his father's enticing arguments to take over the successful law firm that had been in the family for generations, Harvey chose teaching as a career.

Harvey married his college sweetheart, and they moved into a small, affluent neighborhood not far from his childhood home.

He procured an especially sought-after position as an English teacher at an exclusive prep school and almost immediately immersed himself in campus life. He became coach of the girls' tennis team and an academic sponsor for the school's yearbook and weekly newspaper. All of this allowed him ample opportunity to spend time alone with young girls. Life was good for Harvey as he once again found himself at the apex of high school life. He was a popular teacher, a favorite among the multitude of girls who harbored secret crushes on their handsome and attentive English instructor.

After Harvey's first year of teaching, his wife became pregnant. Unfortunately, she had a difficult pregnancy that forced her to be bedridden for most of the nine months. She was often unavailable to Harvey emotionally and sexually, and Harvey began to seethe with resentment. He felt banished from his marital bed, much as he had felt long ago when he had been beaten and thrown out of his sister's room. Unable to utilize the same authoritarian manner as his father had employed to dictate the behaviors of the other family members, Harvey felt powerless and out of control. A sense of impotence and self-deprecation began to reawaken the childhood feelings that had sentenced him to years of humiliation from his peers and his sister.

But things were different for Harvey at school. His sense of entitlement and his need for recognition were finding full expression in the admiration from his students and the power and control he increasingly exerted over their lives. Harvey believed he was king, and he needed only to look around at the adoring faces of his young subjects to know that he reigned supreme.

On a number of occasions, when Harvey found himself alone with a particularly attractive female student, he fantasized about engaging in a sexual encounter with her. He rationalized these flights of fancy as natural reactions to the constant unavailability of a sick and pregnant wife. Occasionally, he would find himself embracing a tearful tennis player after a bad match; and if the hug lasted long after the crying had stopped, Harvey felt no responsibility, for he believed that the young girl was the one who sought solace in his arms.

The second year that Harvey taught, a bright and precocious

student professed her love for Harvey. She believed that Harvey returned her affection and had written him enticing messages suggesting that they consummate their attraction to one another. Harvey told his student that nothing could happen between them, but he continued to read her sexually explicit letters. Harvey kept these letters, never informing the administration of their existence, for in secret he derived a great deal of sexual satisfaction from them. At graduation, this persistent girl, regal in her cap and gown, proposed that Harvey meet her after the ceremony to celebrate this rite of passage. Harvey agreed to meet her at the back of the high school stadium after everyone had left. Believing that she was now free from the restraints of student life, Harvey passionately kissed the graduate and fondled her firm, young breasts. They promised to meet during the summer, but Harvey ignored his student's attempts to contact him. Although he had been very aroused by the encounter, he dismissed the incident as just another student's obsession and thought little of it for the rest of the summer.

In the spring Harvey's wife had given birth to what Harvey saw as a screaming and demanding little imp who never slept. Harvey resented the baby in much the same way as his sister had once been offended by his birth. Harvey elected to sleep on the couch rather than be wakened by the hungry wails of his newborn. It was during this time of banishment, resentment, and frustration that young Michelle came into Harvey's life.

Michelle with her bright smile, cascading blonde hair, and lithe athletic body had just enrolled in Harvey's freshman English class. Barely fourteen years old, Michelle had not yet discovered the full power of her sexual attractiveness, and she was unaware of the effect that her pubescent appearance was having on her attentive English teacher. Harvey quickly sized up Michelle's athletic potential and placed her on the tennis team, even if it meant he had to give up a few extra hours after school or an occasional Saturday morning to coach the fledgling player. The seduction had begun.

Harvey soon became aware that Michelle had family problems. At times she came to class tired and distracted, and on occasion he noticed a puffy redness around her eyes. When he offered to help her after class with a particularly difficult writing assignment, he asked her about her personal life. It did not take long for Harvey to become a confidant to this troubled youth. She told him things she had never shared with anyone, including her best friend. Michelle had a volatile relationship with her father, who was a prominent and wealthy banker. Michelle confided in Harvey that her father often drank and that when he did he would become quarrelsome and verbally abusive to his wife and children. Harvey commiserated with Michelle as he himself had struggled with a successful and domineering father. The boundaries between student and teacher were getting smaller each day as Harvey began to believe that he had "fallen in love" with Michelle.

It was not surprising that right before the Christmas season, Michelle experienced the first pangs of "love." She began to blush in Harvey's presence and even planned the clothes she would wear to appear more seductive on those days that they had their special tennis lessons. Harvey was well aware of his student's developing infatuation and did nothing to prevent it. In fact, he played into her adolescent crush by teasing her, winking at her during class when he thought no one else would see, and placing affectionate kisses on her cheek after tennis practice.

The situation in Harvey's home deteriorated. Harvey and his wife had become more and more distant from each other. They rarely made love since Harvey found it difficult to become aroused by his wife, who was always disheveled, tired, and had a baby glued to her hip. Instead of talking about their situation, Harvey retreated into his den and planned the seduction of Michelle.

At school, Michelle and Harvey's relationship escalated. They exchanged furtive glances throughout class and spent more and more time alone after tennis practice, reveling in the anticipation of their as yet unconsummated passion. Harvey began to share more and more with Michelle about his dissatisfaction at home and how he longed to be important to someone again. He told her that she made him feel special, young, and vital, and that he regained his lost youth when he was with her.

Michelle fell prey to the seduction; and in the spring of her freshman year, and five months before her fifteenth birthday, she lost her virginity to her high school English teacher. Although she believed she was "in love," she was not physically or emotionally ready to handle the sexual demands of a twenty-nine-year-old man. Although the loss of her virginity was a difficult experience for her, it paled in comparison to what would follow. For Harvey, sexual intercourse with Michelle was only the beginning of his reign of terror, which would eventually plunge Michelle into a nightmare of shame, manipulation, and control.

The subjugation of Michelle was evident in Harvey's increasing possessiveness over his teenage victim. He strove to control her every move. He wanted to know where she was at all times and admonished her for the time she spent with her friends. He would seethe with jealousy if he saw her talking to a male classmate and made her promise that she would exclude all social activities from her life that made her unavailable to him. He began to call her home and request that she meet with him, making up excuses about a below-average term paper or the difficulty she was having with her tennis game.

As the reins tightened, Michelle began to feel the dangerous control that her English teacher was exerting on her life. She was caught in a terrible struggle. Her ever-increasing sense of guilt and her fear of being exposed immobilized her and caused her to withdraw from her friends and family. Her difficult relationship with her father only intensified her feelings of shame, isolation, and fear of retribution. She became wan, lost weight, and often appeared anxious, tired, and distracted. Her grades plummeted as Michelle found it impossible to concentrate on her studies.

A few months after their sexual relationship began, Michelle suspected she was pregnant. She was paralyzed by fear. After discussing the matter with Harvey, they decided that she would have an abortion that would be arranged and paid for by Harvey. In the days leading up to the procedure, Michelle became so anxious and distraught that she fainted one afternoon during her gym class. Lying on the white cot behind the drawn curtains of the nurse's office, Michelle began to cry uncontrollably. She turned her face to the wall; and as the tears cascaded down her face, the school nurse quietly entered the room. Michelle had been a vivacious and healthy adolescent when she'd first entered the school; but what the nurse now saw, lying cuddled around a white sheet, was a thin, pale, and frightened little girl. It didn't take long for her to get Michelle to talk; and when she did, the nurse was horrified at what she heard. The sordid details of this young student's affair with her English teacher were revealed. The nurse was obligated to call the authorities, and the veil of secrecy was finally torn down.

The ending to this story is not a pretty one—as it never is with sexual abuse. Fortunately for Michelle, she was not pregnant. Her physical symptoms were a manifestation of the trauma she was experiencing, and they had served to alert the adults around her that she was in danger. Subsequently, Harvey was arrested at his home, handcuffed, and whisked off to jail. With the local reporters flashing their cameras and writing down the details of this illicit affair, Harvey was charged with child sexual assault from a person in a position of trust. During Harvey's well-publicized trial, a number of his former students came forth with allegations of sexual molestation. In front of the well-bred community, the angry parents, the crying teenagers, and his shocked wife and parents, Harvey was sentenced to seven years in prison.

Harvey will never be able to teach again. It will be a very long time until he can have unsupervised access to children or adolescents, and he will be listed as a sex offender in the registry in whatever community he chooses to live. Yet Harvey, the enduring narcissist, will survive. He may have been knocked down a few notches from the top rung of the ladder, but Harvey will attempt to climb up again. He may choose to move to another state and reside for a while in obscurity from his infamous past. And unfortunately, the likelihood that Harvey will reoffend is very high.

Now that you have met a narcissistic predator, it will be easier for you to detect this type of person. Remember Harvey when your daughter's swimming coach asks to take her to the pool in the early mornings before school or when your son's journalism teacher begins to spend too many evenings alone with him arranging the layout for the school newspaper. Even though the narcissistic predator may have a winning smile and an alluring appeal, you are better prepared to question his intentions than your naive and impressionable adolescent. Always be concerned when a teacher or any adult in a position of authority spends an inordinate amount of time alone with your child. Do not assume that this person is safe merely because of his or her status. Get to know the professional involved with your child.

No aspect of an adult's relationship with your child should be secret. Parents should be allowed to join in on the activities at anytime. Unfortunately for Michelle, her parents did not suspect that Harvey was a predator, and they falsely assumed that his interest in their daughter was purely professional. Therefore they did not accompany Michelle to her "private" tennis lessons with Harvey or ask to be included in their "early morning meetings" about Michelle's schoolwork. For if they had, they would have discovered that Harvey was a sexual predator who was grooming their daughter for abuse.

THE INADEQUATE PREDATOR

The next man that you will meet, the inadequate predator, appears very different from the narcissist. Unlike the narcissist, who is usually accomplished and adept socially, the inadequate individual has not achieved much in life. These individuals cannot find fulfillment in adult relationships and therefore turn to children as a source of companionship and sexual fulfillment. Narcissistic predators will also turn to children for companionship and sexual gratification; however, their motives are entirely different. Harvey was able to have relationships with people his own age, but he chose young Michelle because she was an easy target for his sexual manipulation. For Harvey, the world was his for the taking, and his exploitation of Michelle was a manifestation of his belief in his own self-importance. For inadequate predators, who have little belief in their self-worth, perceive children as their only recourse for fulfillment.

Let's now meet Andy, a perennial adolescent who, despite his forty years on this earth, has never accomplished anything significant. Currently, he lives in a remote town in northern California. He wears his long hair tied carelessly at the nape of his neck, and he carries around a backpack filled with cigarettes, unemployment checks, video games, and other paraphernalia that serve to distract him from the responsibilities of life.

How did Andy become such a vagabond misfit who only felt comfortable hanging around smoke-filled bars with the younger generation or playing Nintendo games with his girlfriends' kids? And more important, what generated his sexual abuse of children? By examining Andy's early childhood and understanding more about the circumstances that had led him to his present situation, we can trace the evolution of this inadequate predator: He victimized children because he himself perceived that he was still a child.

There is a suburb of Detroit that is, for the most part, a blue-collar neighborhood. It has about as much aesthetic appeal as the discarded and rusted cars that often litter the driveways and backyards of its inhabitants' homes. It was in this neighborhood that Andy was born. Andy's mother gave birth to him, and then four more children followed in rapid succession. Both of Andy's parents worked full time just to keep gas in the truck and food on the table. They had little time for their children, and they made that known from the start. Andy's father often used threats of violence to keep the children quiet and out of the way.

Both parents did their share of drinking, and the tension eased considerably when they were inebriated. It was during these evenings that Mom and Dad would join the kids to watch the endless streams of vapid sitcoms that flickered on the television screen.

As Andy grew, he was expected to earn money. Andy mowed lawns and bagged groceries for less than minimum wage, and, without much fuss, he gave most of his meager earnings to his parents. They didn't seem to notice his efforts. In fact, they rarely noticed Andy unless they were drunk.

While the parents dictated the family activities and how much beer could be bought with their savings, the streets belonged to the kids. The juvenile pecking order was established early on at the broken park benches and among the weed-infested backyards of their homes. Because of Andy's small stature, he was assigned a low position on the social totem pole. Andy was the gang's errand boy, the kid who was easily ignored but could always be counted on. He was just another kid who hung around with the group, his hair falling down over his face as he stared relentlessly at the ground beneath his feet.

Andy labored through school under the weight of an undiagnosed learning disability. His reading was poor, and his writing was almost illegible. Andy didn't mind that he failed many of his classes because he never thought about the consequences. With his worn sneakers shuffling reluctantly through the halls of his school, and his eyes forever fixed on the ground, Andy didn't need to look ahead because emotionally Andy never grew up.

Andy was exposed to the normal rites of sexual passage for preteen children. The neighborhood boys would gather together frequently to gawk at the naked breasts in the *Playboy* magazines they stole from their parents. Because the adults in their lives were largely unavailable to these pubescent boys, they were left on their own to grapple with their burgeoning sexuality.

Aroused by the sexual stimuli to which he was being exposed, Andy began to act out sexual fantasies with his younger siblings. Playing "doctor" was quite frequent during those afternoons after school when Andy and his siblings were lounging on the couch in front of the television or in the evenings when his parents were out drinking.

Somewhere between the graphic stimulation provided by his friends and the frequent sex play with his siblings, habits of a more deviant nature were beginning to form in Andy. At night, after everyone had gone to bed, he would creep into his sisters' room. He would become sexually stimulated at the sight of his sisters' half-naked bodies, so vulnerable and defenseless in their sleep, and he would begin to masturbate. At times, he would lower his pants and rub his genitals against his sister's bodies. As Andy obtained sexual gratification from the defenseless posture of his sleeping sisters, the sense of inadequacy and helplessness he experienced in every aspect of his life diminished. It was in this fashion that the young Andy, aroused as he stood in the darkened doorway, began his tragic career as a sexual predator.

Out on the streets, the gang was careening toward adolescence. As they traded their bikes in for used cars and their pockets of candy for cigarettes and beer, they also strove for more intense forms of sexual stimulation. One of the guys had a rather extensive collection of pornography that he had stolen over the years from his uncles. Every afternoon the boys would race down to his

house and hide in the basement looking at porn flicks and graphically explicit pictures in magazines. Andy never felt quite comfortable with all of this for he harbored his own brand of sexual
fantasies that could never be shared with the guys.

One by one the boys and girls lost their virginity and began to
pair up until only Andy was left. With a cigarette dangling from
his mouth and the trademark cascade of hair falling down over
his eyes, Andy sat on the park bench, alone, passing time. Andy's
younger brothers and sisters remained his closest companions;
and when he grew tired of sitting at the park, he would shuffle
home to join them in front of the television.

Somehow Andy graduated from high school; and, diploma in
hand, he walked right back into the cluttered living room of his
childhood home to resume his place on the couch next to his
siblings. No one ever expected much from Andy, and therefore
nothing much ever took place in his life except for the sexual
gratification he obtained from his routine nightly vigils over his
sisters' slumbering bodies.

Because his father demanded higher rent from Andy after he
turned eighteen, Andy eventually went to work at a local gas station. He pumped gas, cleaned the grease off tires, repaired broken
mufflers and flat tires, and swept the floor clean each evening. It
was there, among the smell of gasoline and oil, that he met Dawn.

Andy watched as Dawn drove into the station in a dilapidated
car with two little kids in the back and a flat tire. As she emerged
from the car, he saw that although she was still in her mid-
twenties, she already had lines of wear and tear etched on her
heavily made-up face. She had a great body, though, and all the
guys at the station turned to admire her as she strolled up to the
counter asking for help. Andy volunteered to fix her tire and thus
began their courtship.

Within a few weeks the relationship had progressed to Andy
spending a great deal of time at Dawn's house. Although Dawn
wanted sex from the start, Andy was uncomfortable with this type
of intimacy. In fact, Andy was uncomfortable with any type of
closeness that required more of him than sharing a beer and a
space on the couch. Yet because Andy felt that he needed a refuge
other than the crowded confines of his own home, he acquiesced

and began a sexual relationship with Dawn. Andy tried to accommodate Dawn, but he never felt truly comfortable in her bed. He was awkward and unsure of himself sexually, and Dawn's voluptuous body and adult desires were too much for him to handle. He began using alcohol to mollify his anxiety; and instead of making him more competent in bed, it created more problems. He was often unable to maintain an erection and would fall asleep before Dawn ever had the chance to demand more of him.

Andy continued his work at the gas station; but because he was drinking heavily, he often came in late and was unable to perform even the most menial of tasks. Eventually Andy was fired; and instead of looking for another job, he marched down to the unemployment office to fill out the necessary forms.

With Andy out of work, Dawn offered him a place to stay. He moved his scant belongings into her home, and he quickly found his place among the living room couch and the lounge chairs in the backyard. While Andy collected his unemployment checks, Dawn continued her full-time job as a bookkeeper in a large manufacturing plant. She had worked there for six years, ever since her ex-husband had left her and the children to fend for themselves. Dawn was a reliable employee, and the benefits she received were well worth the drudgery of her nine-to-five position. She was a good mother, but she was often so tired and worn out from her work that she had little energy left in the evenings to cater to her children's needs. She did, however, manage to cook dinners, clean the house on a regular basis, and supervise the kids as they brushed their teeth and dressed for school each morning. Andy offered little help in the financial and physical maintenance of the home except for the occasional hamburger he would throw on the grill; but as Dawn frequently remarked, "He is great with the kids." Dawn appreciated the attention he gave to her children, and that was the reason she allowed Andy to hang around for so long.

Dawn's children were friendly and sweet. They adored their mother but tended to gravitate toward Andy, since he always seemed to be around, lounging in the sunlight, watching television, or fixing his car. At eight, Dawn's daughter, Lisa, was in desperate need of a father. She clung to Andy and basked in the attention he gave to her. Lee, the little six-year-old boy, was also hungry for male companionship; and he begged Andy to teach him how to ride his two-wheeler and play baseball. Andy was only too happy to oblige since he had always enjoyed being with kids. In fact, since Andy had never grown up, Dawn's children became his friends, his confidants, and his escape from the responsibilities of adulthood.

Instead of spending hard-earned money on after-school day care, Dawn allowed the children to come home from school to be with Andy. It served everyone just fine, except, of course, the children. For as they became closer and closer to Andy, they were inching nearer and nearer to the destruction of their innocence.

With the sexual tension mounting as a result of Andy's impaired performance in bed, Andy allowed himself to project his sexual desire onto the children. He knew that this was wrong, just as he knew that every time he had masturbated at the doorway of his sisters' bedroom he was doing something wrong. But Andy had few resources to deal with his increasing sense of frustration. He felt inadequate as a provider and as a lover; but just like he'd done when he was young, Andy decided to stay put. He neither ventured out the door in pursuit of other means of gratification, nor did he stop himself when he chose to stare at Lisa's frilly underwear as she swung on a park swing or at Lee's crotch when he raised his legs over the monkey bars. He had began to view the children as objects to relieve his sexual frustration.

Eventually, Andy began to groom the children, and they formed their own special clique that had a code of secrecy that purposely excluded Dawn. Andy would cuddle with them on the couch, wrestle them to the floor in fits of uncontrollable laughter, and help them with their evening baths before their mother came home. They began to do things in secret, such as going to the movies in the afternoon when they were supposed to be doing their homework and eating candy and drinking pop before dinner. In much the same manner as his inebriated father once had done with him, Andy began to tease and mock the children into feeling weak, defenseless, and under his control.

Summer finally came, and the kids, released from the restraints of school, rushed excitedly home in anticipation of the long, hot days alone with Andy at the swimming pool or in the park. And this is just what happened, except that the kids now had to pay a price for Andy's undivided attention. He had begun to molest them, and his sexual exploits became more sinister as the summer wore on. With the veil of secrecy protecting them from outside scrutiny, Andy had free reign over his victims in a way that he had never experienced before. He felt powerful for the first time in his life; and despite the occasional twinges of guilt and self-recrimination, he was free to explore the endless possibilities of being in control.

By now Dawn was aware of a change in Andy and her children. Andy had almost completely withdrawn from her as he numbed himself with nightly drinking and insisted on remaining frozen in front of the television. More often than not, he slept on the couch, passing out in a drunken stupor before he ever made it to their bedroom. She also noticed that the children were fussier; they seemed to be fighting with each other all the time, and Lisa was complaining of stomachaches. Lee had wet himself a number of times, and he had begun to talk in a babyish manner.

When Dawn tried to talk to Andy about the children's changed behavior, he dismissed it as just a phase they were going through. He promised that he would talk to them and keep a closer eye on their activities. Dawn was not reassured. She was tired of Andy's lack of drive and immature behaviors, and she worried about his singular focus on her children. Yet she didn't have the strength to kick Andy out of her home. Her children seemed so attached to him, and she just couldn't bear to have them lose another male in their lives.

When school started in the fall, the teachers also noticed a change in the two children. No longer were they the well-behaved, attentive, and friendly students who had skipped down the halls of the school eager to join their classmates. They were now shy and withdrawn, reluctant to engage in playground activities.

Mrs. Jones, Lisa's perceptive and caring teacher, was the first to notice Lisa masturbating beneath her desk. Without making it public, Mrs. Jones quietly walked past Lisa's desk and gently tapped her on the shoulder. Lisa was jolted from her hypnotic state as she put both of her hands up on her desk. During recess that day, Mrs. Jones asked Lisa to stay inside and help her decorate the bulletin board for Halloween. It was then that Mrs. Jones, in her gentle yet persistent manner, obtained the information from Lisa that unlocked the mystery to her dramatic change of behavior: Lisa was being sexually abused.

Following Lisa's disclosure, a series of interviews ensued. Police detectives, social workers, and therapists all intervened on behalf of the children, and Andy was ordered out of the home. Because of the trauma that had been inflicted on the children, it would take months before the entire sordid story was revealed but not before Andy had a chance to escape. Free on bond, Andy took his truck, packed his meager belongings, and without looking back, drove cross-country to hide in obscurity in a small mountain community in northern California.

Andy, now a forty-year-old unmarried man, continues to avoid responsibility and uses adult relationships as a way to gain access to children. But his story is not meant to frighten you for you can now identify Andy and other inadequate predators like him. You will be able to spot him several feet away as he sputters down the street in his road-worn truck with empty bottles of beer littering the floor of his cab. And if he ever stops to say a kind word to your children or offers them his friendship with candy, pop, and special attention, you will know better and whisk your children away as fast as you can. Further, now that you have been introduced to Andy and his kind, you will never believe that this man-child is innocent and harmless. You are aware that he will never be able to have a responsible adult relationship, and therefore you will protect your children from becoming his only resource for companionship, solace, and sexual gratification.

Tragically for her children, Dawn was too busy to spend quality time with them. For the sake of convenience and out of the necessity to provide the basics for her family, Dawn worked long hours and allowed Andy to assume a great deal of the parenting responsibilities. Without knowing the characteristics of inadequate sexual predators, she did not detect many of the warning signs that Andy gave indicating he was immature and used children to meet his needs. When Dawn noticed the changes in her children's behaviors, it was already too late. She erroneously assumed that Andy was taking care of her children and allowed her own internal warning signs of danger to go unheeded. Therefore the sexual abuse continued until Lisa's disclosure put an end to it.

THE ANTISOCIAL PREDATOR

The men you have met so far have had some sort of conscience. Whether it was not fully developed or it was marred by a toxic environment, their conscience allowed them to believe they had developed feelings for their victims. They may not have set out to intentionally harm another, although this is exactly what they did. Often their faulty and irrational thinking led them to justify their actions as an expression of their caring for their victims. Harvey believed he was in love with Michelle, pursued her with intensity, and suffered feelings of guilt and remorse when their affair came to an end.

But what about the individual who feels no remorse, who has no respect for the value of others' feelings, does not attach to his victims, and views all others as objects that can be used only to gratify his own needs? This predator is the antisocial, the individual with no conscience.

From ancient times the great minds in philosophy, religion, and science have grappled with the concept of conscience. Sigmund Freud theorized that the superego housed the conscience. The conscience was considered to be an essential part of the personality that develops early in life as a way to keep in check the unacceptable impulses with which we are born. It was also postulated that the father has a central role in handing down the scepter of the conscience, and it is through the child's identification with the father that he or she learns to internalize right from wrong.

Research in the decades following Freud's publications supported the theory that the father is essential in developing a conscience in a child. When they examined the early childhood of criminals, they found that a large proportion of them had been raised in a single-parent home without a father. Therefore it was often assumed that a boy raised alone by a mother was at higher risk for antisocial behavior.

Recent studies, however, have disputed this notion. A significant amount of dangerous juveniles have come from intact homes; and on the other side of the equation, many children from single-parent homes where the father is absent do not display antisocial behavior. Further, it has been demonstrated that morals are developed from a variety of sources, such as siblings, extended family members, the neighborhood environment, peer influence, and the media. And undisputably a mother is also a vital contributor in the child's developing conscience.

It is also disputed whether environment is solely responsible for the antisocial tendencies in certain individuals. Genetic research has sought to locate a defect in the DNA programming of antisocial individuals in order to predict and therefore prevent antisocial behavior. There are brain researchers who point to the fact that antisocial individuals have trouble with certain areas of cognitive functioning and the regulation of emotion, which suggests a physiological basis for antisocial behavior. Yet these studies, like environmental research, have been inconclusive. However the most widely accepted theory today is that antisocial behavior is a result of the interaction between the genetic predisposition of an individual and a toxic environment.

Antisocial individuals display warning signs of their lack of conscience early on in their development. As children they engage in aggressive and destructive behavior, such as setting fires, cruelty to animals, bullying their peers, and even attacking their own siblings and parents. They are frequently suspended from school and often have difficulty learning. Their parents report them to be difficult to control; and despite the consequences, nothing seems to deter these children's errant behavior.

Because the antisocial individual lacks the internal mechanism to inhibit him from acting out against others, his only deterrent is his fear of getting caught. Therefore the antisocial predator, to avoid detection, is cunning and deceptive. Like a chameleon, he can change his appearance with lightning speed so that he appears to be a perfect match for his environment. Place him at a socialite's ball, and he will be bedecked in splendid attire as he glides around the dance floor waltzing with the pretty debutantes. Ask him to attend a business lunch at a pricey restaurant downtown, and he will don his most stylish suit and skillfully negotiate international deals while causally sipping Perrier. Admire him as he effortlessly glides down the most challenging ski run, or listen to him as he shoots the breeze with the guys at the local bar while drinking shots of tequila.

This is why the antisocial individual is so difficult to detect because once you think you have him pegged in that square hole, he changes shape. He is the charmer, the quintessential seducer, the man who can make you sympathize with him for his unfortunate circumstances and believe in him for his outward display of courage and triumph. However, this is only an illusion, for he is the sorcerer of trickery. He is skilled at making others believe in him, and that is how he snares his victims.

In this next section you are going to meet an antisocial individual and have an opportunity to examine the chameleonlike behaviors, cavalier attitude, and lack of empathy that were evident in his early childhood.

> Thomas is a large, dark-haired man who has always maintained a good physique. He works out regularly in the gym and chooses the foods he eats very carefully. He is an excellent cook and has been known to entertain people with his wonderfully exotic meals and his endless tales of adventure, travel, and intrigue. Thomas has done just about everything. He has a fascinating history that began in a foreign land as the child of an American diplomat. He has traveled the world over as an enlisted soldier in Vietnam, a photographer, a journalist, a poet, and an entrepreneur. He has made millions and lost even more. He has been married once, and that marriage ended in a bitter divorce. But before we go on about Thomas's life, let's reel back to his childhood and examine the early budding of his antisocial behaviors.
>
> Thomas's father was working for the U.S. government when he met and married Thomas's mother. The couple then moved to London, where Thomas and his three older sisters were born. The family lived in an expensive apartment and led a privileged life. The children were educated in private English schools. They had little contact with their father, who was always ensconced in private political meetings that seemed to last all day and well into the evening. The children grew up in the care of a succession of nannies, who changed their diapers, fed them bottles, and, as they grew, accompanied them to an array of horseback-riding lessons, sailing instructions, and dance classes.
>
> Thomas never liked these activities very much; and more often than not, he would skillfully escape from his nanny's scrutinizing eye and wander off to enjoy some other form of entertainment. Thomas always found London fascinating and was drawn to the street life. It was there, amid the cabarets, gambling halls, and pubs, that he began to meet many of the people who would shape his life. He befriended a vagabond poet from India, a successful Oriental rug dealer from Syria, and a notorious race-car driver

from France. They all marveled at Thomas's maturity, which went far beyond his eleven years. Although Thomas was not very big for his age, he carried himself with the assurance of an adult. While his looks may have been unassuming, his posture spoke of a confidence that others found quite alluring.

A prostitute inducted Thomas into the world of sex at the age of eleven. This act propelled Thomas into a series of sexual encounters with older women who were only too happy to oblige the eager and willing young novice. By the time Thomas was fourteen, he had amassed a great deal of sexual experience.

While Thomas's life was blossoming on the streets of London, his family quietly continued their political and social obligations. His sisters grew to be perfect little ladies, stifled in their school uniforms and quieted by the requirements of socially acceptable behavior. Thomas abided by none of these. With a cigarette dangling from his mouth, Thomas would intrigue the other students with fabulous stories of life on the streets with his infamous friends. Eventually, Thomas's unsavory attitude caused too great a stir among the faculty and students, and he was expelled from school.

Like an unruly racehorse being sent back to the stables for more training, Thomas was banished from the London penthouse and sent to the States to live with relatives. His aunt and uncle had reluctantly agreed to let him stay with them, and they resented his presence even before his plane landed on the tarmac. But this did not seem to concern Thomas at all; for at the age of fourteen, he was in no mood for a guardian, and he let that be known from the start.

It was in this setting that Thomas's adolescence continued its acceleration. Thomas did poorly in school, and he was frequently suspended from his classes for one infraction or another. He had a series of girlfriends, and each one represented a different turn that his life had taken at that particular moment. Using the characters he had befriended on the streets of London, Thomas took on many roles. For a few months, he became a philosopher carrying around a backpack filled with tattered poetry books. And when he tired of that, he would dump his artsy girlfriend and turn to the miniskirted blonde who flirted with him in math class as he donned the attire of an entrepreneur. The next bend in the road might find Thomas fancying himself as a race-car driver, sitting beside a sultry, tattooed brunette, as he flashed into the high school parking lot in his turbo-charged car ready for the race to begin.

Thomas had not given much thought to what he would do after high school. Graduation night left Thomas exceptionally drunk, and he didn't sober up until he left the army recruiting office the next morning with his papers to go to Vietnam. The fact that there was a war going on had little meaning for Thomas. His whole life had been an adventure, and now it was time for more excitement and fun.

In Vietnam, the air was hot and sticky, and most of the men were restless and scared. But Thomas found himself quite at home in this foreign land amid the unfamiliar young men who shared his bunker. He listened sympathetically to their stories and even helped them write poignant love letters to their girlfriends back home.

Face-to-face combat had little meaning for Thomas since he felt little remorse at the act of killing. The soldiers found him courageous, and the officers described him as exceptionally skilled and obedient. He was decorated, and he became a hero. Thomas's inability to truly feel for others was an asset in this jungle of pain, misery, and death.

Beside the carnage of battle, the nightclubs teemed with life. The prostitutes flourished amid the fear and chaos of war as the soldiers sought respite in the arms of these desperate girls. For Thomas, his exposure to this type of sexual encounter was not unique. However, in Vietnam it was more extreme. Thomas found that his appetite had no limits as he chose the youngest of Vietnamese girls to fulfill his increasingly depraved sexual acts. No one thought anything about Thomas's activities. In fact, most of the men had suspended whatever restraints and pangs of guilt they may have ordinarily felt to enjoy their reckless pursuit of pleasure amid the horrors of war. But for Thomas, the behaviors that were being enacted in this war-torn country were carving deep grooves in a psyche that was already marred with antisocial tendencies.

Thomas returned to the States, and he settled back into American society with relative ease. He quickly obtained a position as an insurance salesman in a prestigious firm. Thomas was in his element as he negotiated side deals that would not only benefit certain customers but would put extra cash in his pocket as well. He was also not above lying to potential customers in order to close an advantageous sale. It was only a matter of time for Thomas's activities to become known. When customers began to complain about Thomas, the branch manager was forced to let him go.

With the ink barely dry on his pink slip, Thomas walked across the street and obtained another sales job in a competing insurance company. Later he would laugh and tell his buddies at the bar that when the manager of the competing company found out that he had been let go because of allegations that he had lied to customers, he all but jumped at the chance to hire Thomas.

Thomas eventually was let go from three insurance companies on charges of unethical practice. He then decided to join the migration to Silicone Valley and learn the computer business. Thomas was adept at making the right connections; and in a short time, he secured a good job in this lucrative field. With all of this in place at the age of twenty-seven, Thomas decided it was time to settle down.

Thomas had done his share of dating since he'd returned to the States, and he continued to prefer young girls who would adore and worship him and expect little in return. He was never faithful to the girls he dated, and he justified this to himself by claiming that he had given five years to Uncle Sam and now he needed to take some time for himself. He continued to visit prostitutes even though he was never lacking for the opportunity to bed the many young women he escorted around town.

Thomas picked his wife the way others chose their cars or their penthouse suites. He looked for the most striking, sleek, and fully equipped woman he could find and then set out to woo her right up to the altar. Everything went as planned, and Thomas and his new bride made a striking couple as they bowed their heads in prayer, promising to love and cherish one another for a lifetime. Right before Thomas slipped the ring on his newlywed's finger, he caught the eye of a beautiful bridesmaid and they exchanged seductive glances.

With the wedding out of the way, Thomas was now free to

conduct his business in any manner he chose. He began to have outside dalliances within six months of his marriage. Once again Thomas justified his actions by claiming that he had made a mistake, and that he was too young to be married. He felt righteous in his decision to stay with Jennifer and make good on his promise to support her. After all, she should be grateful that he was going to buy them a brand-new house in a posh suburb only three miles from the ocean.

At the office Thomas and another top employee were secretly planning to take over the business. By altering files and redirecting proceeds to their own accounts, Thomas and his cohort managed to swindle almost a million dollars from the company. By writing illegal contracts and promising unrealistic financial gains to customers, they managed to undermine the credibility of the top executives, and piece by piece, the conglomerate toppled. Thomas and his buddy were there to pick up the pieces.

As a part owner in a new and promising enterprise, Thomas was riding high on the crest of success. He bought a sporty new convertible, donned a Rolex, and had all of his suits handmade at an expensive Italian clothier. He and Jennifer took frequent trips to exotic places, and as his tan deepened so did his ambition.

Thomas eventually ousted his partner and began to invest in other business ventures. Overextended financially, Thomas ran his companies like he raced his cars—reckless and out of control. When the loans came due and Thomas could borrow no more, he immediately filed for bankruptcy and skillfully hid most of his assets. By that time, Thomas and Jennifer had two small girls who were conditioned to the good life. They were used to swimming in their heated outdoor pool, attending private schools, and being chauffeured around by nannies. Something had to be done to ensure a continued life of privilege.

Being adept at computers had its advantages, and Thomas soon discovered that a great deal of money could be made in Internet pornography. Since smut was a field in which Thomas was comfortable, he obtained loans from friends in order to start his own on-line pornography site. This business venture became extremely successful. Once again Thomas could afford to cruise the highways in his sports car in search of new challenges.

Thomas's entrepreneurial endeavors were not limited to adult pornography. Thomas anticipated higher profits using children as sex objects, and thus he purchased a number of child pornography sites. As Thomas became more involved with child pornography, he resparked his sexual interest in very young girls.

In a situation where an individual is incapable of bonding with another, a marriage of convenience will soon become stale. Jennifer, tired of Thomas's philandering, moved out with the girls one day in the late fall, leaving Thomas with the large house and a browning lawn covered with deadened leaves. Thomas and Jennifer engaged in lengthy court battles that involved a never-ending array of arguments about alimony, child support, and custody; and he rarely saw his children.

Thomas continued to thrive on a variety of business ventures. He became the owner of a trendy restaurant, purchased a cable company, and continued his Internet businesses. He had a string of girlfriends who occupied the spaces that Thomas's family had left. They swam naked in the pool, careened drunkenly around the billiards table, and slept late on the silk sheets in the king-size waterbed.

One particular girlfriend lasted longer than the others. Nina had the right combination of savvy, sophistication, and looks to maintain Thomas's interest for a while. The fact that she was a single mother with an eleven-year-old daughter did not deter Thomas.

Nina was a successful real estate agent who was often too busy to take much notice of her daughter, Cassie. With Thomas around, however, it seemed easy to pretend that they were all one happy family. Cassie was drawn to Thomas's charm and wit. He treated her like an adult, and she was often allowed to take part in the social activities that took place at his house. Weekends at Thomas's place would often involve an entourage of characters that sat poolside with drinks and other stimulants that kept them amused and tirelessly giddy. During this time Thomas discovered the power of cocaine to accelerate the pace of his pleasure seeking. Nina also enjoyed the exhilarating highs of the drug, and they often partied with reckless abandon well into the night. During these times Cassie would eventually retreat alone to her bedroom, stimulated and overwhelmed by the adult cavorting she had witnessed all night long.

One particularly hot summer day, Nina and Thomas were out

at the pool lying in the sun trying to melt away their hangovers. Nina finally gave up and decided to take some aspirin and retire to the air-conditioned bedroom. The effects of the cocaine from the previous night had left Thomas irritable and anxious, and he soon decided to join Nina for a nap.

Walking into the house, he saw Cassie, still in her T-shirt and underwear, watching television in the family room. Thomas sat next to her and pretended to watch the show, but found himself distracted by her scantily clad body. All of a sudden he no longer felt tired and edgy; he was ready for a new adventure. He asked Cassie if she wanted to take a swim with him. She agreed and before she could run upstairs to get her bathing suit, Thomas suggested that she should swim in the nude. Cassie replied that she could never do that, but Thomas began to coax her with teasing remarks. Cassie agreed to swim without her shirt if she could get into the water without Thomas looking. While Thomas poured himself a Scotch, he watched from the kitchen window as Cassie ran out to the pool, took off her T-shirt, and hastily dove into the cool water.

When Thomas finally entered the pool, he began to play with Cassie. They splashed around and dove to the bottom to retrieve shiny pennies. Cassie was having so much fun that she forgot that she didn't have on her T-shirt. When they emerged from the pool, Thomas suggested that they relax in the hot tub. Among the frothing white bubbles, Thomas began to groom Cassie. He complimented her on how beautiful she had become, "just like her mother." He told her that he enjoyed being with such an intelligent and mature young woman, and that he felt that they had become very close.

Thomas asked her about her interest in boys, and when Cassie replied that she had a crush on a classmate, Thomas agreed to help her out. He told her that boys liked "sexy" girls, and she needed to learn how to become more appealing to them. He asked her if she would like him to teach her how to be sexy, and Cassie innocently agreed. Thomas reached for Cassie and began to kiss her. As they kissed, he praised her for how wonderfully she was doing. Continuing his soothing and seductive approach, he then fondled her body. When he put his hands down her pants and inserted his finger into her vagina, Cassie protested in pain and pleaded to leave the hot tub. But before she did, Thomas asked her to keep the incident "their special secret." Thomas watched as Cassie, still half-clad, climbed out of the hot tub and ran into the house.

Cassie never again allowed herself to be alone with Thomas, and by September she had confessed the entire incident to her mother. Nina, shocked and furious, called the authorities. The allegations were investigated, and Thomas was charged with child abuse. The FBI had already been looking into his child pornography Internet sites, and he was under suspicion for having sex with minors, money laundering, illegal gambling, and fraud. Unfortunately for the many victims that Thomas would eventually harm, he was released from prison after serving only two years. His mandatory attendance at the offender treatment program was merely an act of superficial compliance; and as he had done with most other people in his life, Thomas succeeded in charming the treatment providers into believing he was genuine. He never believed for one moment that he was a sexual predator; and once released from the confines of treatment, Thomas left the whole messy incident behind him. Today you can find him among the glitzy dinner parties of the rich; or if he is not there, look for him at the pornographic theaters or behind the smoke-filled bars of a topless nightclub. But be aware that whatever costume he is wearing, beneath the façade lurks a very dangerous man.

THE PEDOPHILE PREDATOR

Most people assume that all child molesters are pedophiles. But as noted previously in chapter 2, not every predator has a sexual preference for children. Take, for instance, Harvey and Andy. Neither of these men had a sexual obsession for children. Rather, they used children as available targets to discharge their frustration and anger and ameliorate their sense of isolation, loneliness, and sexual tension. Harvey and Andy are considered to be *situational* molesters and not true pedophiles, and as an antisocial, Thomas's interest in young girls reflects his tendency to use any object available to gratify his needs rather than a true sexual desire for children. On the other hand, the pedophile does have a *sexual* inclination toward children, and therefore his act of molestation will be a pervasive fulfillment of his deviant sexual desires.

No one is certain what causes an individual to develop a sexual interest in children. Although pedophilia has existed as far back as recorded time and can be found in almost every culture, some critics of modern society claim that it is more prevalent today because of the emphasis placed on youth. We live in a society where our young are worshiped and increasingly exploited. Pubescent adolescents are often portrayed as sexual ideals. In almost every top fashion magazine, models barely out of junior high grace the pages with moistened lips that speak of a sexuality far beyond their years.

From the scandalizing pages of *Lolita* to the near-nakedness of a twelve-year-old Brooke Shields, in *Pretty Baby*, the images of sexualized kids have seeped into our consciousness. The androgynous ads so blatantly exposing Calvin Klein models, with their seemingly prepubescent shapes, send a message that a childlike body is sexual and can be exploited. Therefore, argue certain social theorists, this type of exposure conditions society to view children as viable sex partners.

A predator may desire a sexual relationship with an adolescent in order to regain the vitality of the past. Fantasies of sexual exploits in high school when he was young and admired may create a longing in a man to have an adolescent girl fall in love with him. These men are not necessarily pedophiles since the young girls they are pursuing represent youth and an ideal of female sexuality. However, true sexual arousal by children is considerably more deviant.

Researchers have looked into the childhood histories of pedophiles in an attempt to better understand the origin of their obsessions, and, as yet, no definitive answer has been found to explain sexual interest in children. A history of sexual abuse in childhood, as stated previously, does not automatically sentence a person to pedophilia. It is true, however, that sexual abuse of a chronic and profound nature, such as ritualistic abuse, will damage children and cause severe disruptions in almost every area of their lives. But it does not, in itself, brand a child as a future pedophile.

Interviews with pedophiles reveal unusual interests and sexual behaviors that began early in their lives. Because they were so ashamed and guilt-ridden over these unexplainable fantasies, they did not share them with anyone. Their compulsion to act out their sexual fantasies usually began early in adolescence when experimentation with sexuality is common. They may have had a few relationships in high school, but they were not satisfied with these relationships. They felt empty and hollow with girls their own age, and these relationships rarely led to sexual fulfillment. They may have found solace and satisfaction in being with young children. As youth counselors, baby-sitters, and neighborhood "big buddies," these adolescents began to gravitate toward children, and little by little their relationships with people their own age diminished. They may have found themselves looking at children at the swimming pool or at clothing stores. Their fascination and sexual attraction to little bodies could often be discovered in their collection of child photos cut out from magazines that they kept safely tucked away in their bottom drawer.

You are now going to meet Mitchell. He is a pedophile. You will see in his story that he was not sexually molested as a child, and that the only sign that anything was amiss was his early sexual arousal to children. Eventually Mitchell was convicted of sexually assaulting over forty children. And he will tell you that this number is not accurate; for since he was a teenager, he must have molested over a hundred children. Tragically, this number is lower than the amount of child victims who fall prey to a typical pedophile.

If you could turn back the hands of time and see little Mitchell, with his shock of blond hair and a sprinkle of freckles that ran fetchingly across the bridge of his turned-up nose, you would never imagine that he would have grown up to be such a person. But Mitchell will tell you, in soft-spoken tones that carry a hint of the Midwest farmlands in which he was raised, that unless he attends his treatment program on a regular basis, he is likely to reoffend. His sexual desire for children runs strong and has existed within him for as long as he can remember.

Mitchell doesn't remember much of his childhood except that he was always a loner. He loved to wander the vast countryside and found himself content to sit for hours on the bank of a river. In fact, Mitchell had long periods of time that were lost in daydreams.

Mitchell's family was uncommunicative. After the evening grace, they would devour their food without talking. Mitchell's father worked long hours as an accountant, and he also served on the town council. He was well-known in the town and liked by everyone. Mitchell never became close to his father, maybe because they had so little in common. Mitchell's dad would obligingly take his son on seasonal hunting, fishing, and camping trips, but it never seemed to bring them any closer. Mitchell's father never did understand his "strange son," who would rather spend hours alone in his room than throw a football with the other guys.

To the rest of the community, however, Mitchell appeared to be an ordinary boy who obtained average grades in school, rode his bike to the store, and could often be seen mowing the lawn or washing his dad's car on Saturdays. But a dark and frightening presence was growing inside of Mitchell, one that he could not share with anyone and one that was slowly gaining more control over his life.

The first time Mitchell realized that he was sexually attracted to children was when he, himself, was only a child. In the summer of his eleventh year, Mitchell's cousins came for a visit. At seven and four years of age, the little girls were welcome playmates for Mitchell. The three of them swam in the river and played among the banks of the creek, collecting bullfrogs and tiny green turtles. As evening drew near, Mitchell and the girls would come home, undress, and jump into the outdoor shower to wash away the day. No one ever paid much attention to the giggles and shouts that emanated from the backyard for they were only children having fun. But for Mitchell, the "fun" was tinged with sexual arousal. At night he would masturbate to the images he had collected during the day, and on occasion he would steal his cousins' underwear and use it to enhance his self-stimulation.

By the time Mitchell reached adolescence, he was adept at hiding his preference for children. He participated in many high school sports, drove a pickup truck that had belonged to his father, and even took up fishing and hunting as a means to prove his manhood. He dated girls on and off throughout his junior and senior years of high school and did his share of kissing and fondling in the cab of his truck. However, he never truly found pleasure with the awkward groping; and when he would return home, he would satisfy himself while gazing at the collection of child photos that he had collected from mail-order catalogues over the years. These advertisements showed young children in their underwear in various poses that were meant to encourage mothers to buy the merchandise for their youngsters. For Mitchell, however, his collection of child advertisements carefully hidden behind the balled-up socks was his only source of true sexual gratification.

The summer of his junior year, Mitchell procured a job as a

counselor at a local day camp. Although his father scoffed at the idea of Mitchell playing with kids all day, Mitchell was delighted at the prospect of spending time with children. As the summer wore on, Mitchell and his campers formed a special bond. They swam away the heat in the local pool playing water games that allowed Mitchell the opportunity to hold a child's silky leg underwater or to encircle his arms around the waist of a young novice swimmer. The contact with their young bodies gave flight to Mitchell's hidden desires, and his sexual appetite for children grew with rapid intensity. Instead of being satisfied with the photographs of child models in the magazines and newspaper ads, he began to collect child pornography.

A few of the campers thought that Mitchell was "strange." These particular children stayed away from Mitchell in the pool, on the playground, and during excursions to the zoo. If someone would have asked these children why they did not want to hold Mitchell's hand at the park or let him push them on a swing, they would have shrugged their shoulders and replied, "I don't know; I just don't want to." Their lack of comfort with Mitchell found no words. As for the other children, they were too distracted by the time Mitchell spent teaching them how to swim, swing a bat, and dive off the high board to notice the danger that lurked beneath his touch.

Mitchell had also been a volunteer at the local Boy Scout troop for over a year; and the summer of his senior year, he was asked to accompany twelve ten year olds on their first overnight camping trip. The scouts were excited as they stuffed their backpacks with hunting knives, fishing gear, and rain ponchos. The climb up the mountain to the lake was fatiguing, but they arrived just before sunset. Mitchell helped the boys set up their tents and open their sleeping bags, preparing for the cold night to come. After a meal of fire-roasted hot dogs and canned beans, they sat around a roaring blaze, toasting their marshmallows and singing camp songs. The campers became tired and, despite their best efforts to keep awake, began to drift off to sleep beside the warm and crackling fire. Mitchell and the scoutmaster helped the boys into their tents, tucking them into their sleeping bags.

During the climb that afternoon, Mitchell had paid particularly close attention to the little red-haired boy who seemed to have a more difficult time than the others negotiating the rocks and crossing the streams. Little Jacob was not as athletic as the rest of the boys, and, in fact, his parents had considered not allowing him to go on this excursion. Jacob had developed a severe case of pneumonia when he was only two years old, and the medication he had taken for the following year and a half had compromised his growth. Jacob had always struggled with being the smallest kid in his class.

Jacob's plight did not go unnoticed by Mitchell, who began to encourage the young hiker up the mountain. He relieved some of the weight in Jacob's backpack and gave him extra water and nourishment as they journeyed together toward the peak. Jacob was beaming as he climbed the crest and stood proudly with Mitchell, his new best friend, at his side.

Because there were not enough tents for all of the campers, Mitchell had offered to share his with Jacob. With the fire crackling its last embers, the campers settled in for the night, and Mitchell planned his approach. After climbing into the tent, Mitchell asked Jacob if he wanted a massage. Jacob sleepily agreed, but when Mitchell's hands began to caress his genitals, the little boy resisted. Mitchell beseeched Jacob to cooperate because they were friends and Mitchell had done Jacob a favor by helping him up the mountain. Now he was asking Jacob to return the favor. Believing himself to be puny, powerless, and insignificant, Jacob closed his eyes and, frozen with fear, succumbed to the abuse.

Jacob never told anyone about the incident. Mitchell had shamed and frightened Jacob into secrecy by whispering into Jacob's ear the terrible consequences that would occur if he ever told anyone. The next morning, as the sun glared resplendent in the blue sky, the campers fished, swam, and hiked some more until it was time to descend. Climbing down the mountain was easier for everyone except for little Jacob, who was now burdened with a weight that was heavier than any backpack he would ever carry. Lumbering down the mountain with his shoulders sagging from shame and humiliation, Jacob was hobbled by the crushing blow of sexual abuse.

Undaunted by his victimization of Jacob, Mitchell spent the rest of that summer molesting other small children. He found young girls and boys at the park, at the swimming pool, or in the homes where he baby-sat the neighbors' children; and, tragically, he was never caught. No one seemed to notice how little time Mitchell spent with his peers as his relationships with his friends dwindled and his encounters with girls his own age became non-existent.

When he began college in the fall, Mitchell safely secured an apartment off campus and began his studies. Alone, without the prying eyes of his small-town friends and relatives, Mitchell continued his pursuit of children. He majored in sports rehabilitation, and he began doing his field placements at elementary schools, recreation centers, and other youth facilities. He was a good student but made sure that he received little attention from his professors and his peers. He eschewed the bustling activities of the fraternity halls, student centers, and college parties; and he kept himself immersed in his studies and in his pursuit of children. He befriended lonely children from the poorest parts of town, the ones he found clinging to the walls of the recreation center, unsure of themselves and shunned by their peers. They believed he was their savior as he rescued them from isolation and their impoverished existences; and even when he made that first sexual advance, they often allowed it because of the good things Mitchell had brought into their lives.

Mitchell, too, convinced himself that he was helping the children he pursued. After all, he loved and befriended them, and they shared something so powerful that it transcended the ordinary rules that govern other people. Mitchell initiated them into sex; and because he told himself that he loved and cared for them, he deluded himself into believing that sexual education was as normal as helping them learn long division or how to shoot a basketball effortlessly through the net.

Mitchell entered the professional world as a rehabilitation specialist, a career that would offer him many opportunities to satisfy his sinister longings. His first job was in a hospital that specialized in childhood injuries. He may have been a novice in physical rehabilitation, but he was already, at the age of twenty-two, an expert pedophile, skilled in seducing and sexually molesting young children. While employed at the hospital, Mitchell damaged countless children under his care.

At the age of thirty, Mitchell met Shirley, a quiet woman with unassuming looks and a gentle manner who ran a day-care center in her home. Mitchell saw an opportunity in this relationship since Shirley's day care could provide him with an easy access to children. Shirley was pleasantly surprised when Mitchell proposed; and a year after they met, they married.

Mitchell fulfilled his conjugal duties on their short honeymoon and then settled into Shirley's home more like a boarder than a husband. In fact, he requested a separate bedroom because he complained of sleeping problems. While Shirley cooked and cleaned, Mitchell continued to prey on children. The marriage suited Mitchell because now, as a respectable married man, he was freer than ever to conduct his clandestine abuse away from the scrutiny of suspicious eyes.

Shirley's day-care center became a repository for Mitchell's sexual fantasies and a resource for his deviant behaviors. Shirley thought it was wonderful that her husband would offer to come home at the lunch hour to watch the children while she ran errands. And while the diligent Shirley was out buying groceries for the children's lunch, Mitchell was playing tag football with them out in the backyard. Grabbing buttocks and genitals as he wrestled the children to the ground, Mitchell was consummating his persistent passion for sexual contact with children.

Mitchell continued to molest children for the following twelve years before he was caught. He wreaked havoc on the lives of many innocents, who left Shirley's day-care center each day with new scars emblazoned on their psyches. These children held themselves together with the threads of hope and a blanket of denial that was unraveled each time they came into Shirley's home. Some of the children who had been molested did not want to return to the day-care center; and without uttering a recriminating word, their cries of refusal were interpreted as separation anxieties. Mitchell was actually questioned a few times by parents of children who claimed he had touched them. Each time, Mitchell would explain his behaviors as an "accidental touch that may have occurred while they were playing games." Shirley, na-ively unaware of her husband's abuse, consistently defended her husband against these allegations, and the two of them erected a seemingly impenetrable barrier to the truth.

In the year before his arrest, Mitchell became more careless in his pursuit of children. In fact, he later admitted that his reck-lessness was a plea to be caught in order to free him from the grip his sexual obsession had on his life.

The year before his arrest, two young sisters had been enrolled in Shirley's day-care center. At seven and four, these girls were rambunctious and eager to engage in physical contact. They loved to wrestle and play tag football with Mitchell, and they would jump on his lap every time they settled down in front of the television. Nap time was especially difficult for those two; and on occasion, when Mitchell would put the rest of the children down for a nap, he would allow the two sisters to stay awake and play. It was during these afternoon interludes that Mitchell began to sexually abuse the girls.

It was the seven-year-old Janelle who finally put an end to the reign of terror that Mitchell had begun long ago in his childhood. One evening, at home, while the girls were bathing in the tub, Janelle reached for her younger sister. She then climbed on top of her and began moving her hips in a sexually suggestive manner. When their mother came into the bathroom to wash the girls' hair, she was shocked by what she saw. She quickly grabbed Ja-nelle off of her sister and began to question the girls. As they toweled the soapy suds from their bodies, they told their mother of the activities that had occurred at Shirley's day care. Their mother immediately notified the authorities; and after a lengthy investigation, Mitchell was arrested on charges of child sexual assault.

When law enforcement decided to question other children who had been at the day-care center, they found a pattern of sexual abuse that spanned over a decade. But Mitchell main-tained his innocence until a seasoned defense attorney advised him to plea-bargain to a lesser offense. Mitchell was found guilty and sentenced to fifteen years in jail.

Mitchell spent the next seven years in prison and the following eight years attending an outpatient treatment program for sexual offenders. He currently has a parole officer whom he meets with regularly; and with all of this in place, Mitchell still feels the sexual urge that, without these outer restraints, would propel him into sexual activity with children.

Even though Shirley lost her day-care center, her dignity, and her trust in her husband, she remained by Mitchell's side, and to this day, he cannot understand why this sweet, compassionate woman is still with him. But now at sixty, Mitchell feels grateful. He will tell you that getting caught was the best thing that ever happened to him because it finally released him from the shackles of his hell of shame and horror. He can never take back all of the harmful actions that he inflicted upon countless children; and to this day he cannot explain his sexual cravings for children. And because there will always be that sexual attraction to children, Mitchell avoids all contact with them.

Pedophiles like Mitchell are *among* us. They may take the form of a kindly minister, an overinvolved gymnastics coach, or a friendly baby-sitter. They may believe that they genuinely love children, and their sexual attraction to them propels them ever forward into intense and intimate relationships with them. Yet their love is destructive and painful, and their interest in children is never healthy.

Now that you have had the chance to meet Mitchell, remember him when you are examining the relationship your child has with the swimming coach, the youth counselor, or that friendly teenager down the street. A relationship with a child must be balanced with other interests. A person who spends an inordinate amount of time with children and avoids relationships with adults can be dangerous. Relationships with children that are secretive, prolonged, exclusive, and intense should be closely scrutinized for they may indicate a potential for sexual abuse.

Activities that offer an adult the opportunity to have physical contact with children should not be encouraged. Wrestling, tickling, and massaging should not become routine; and adults who consistently engage children in these activities are sending a warning sign about their need for physical contact with children. Although Mitchell's football games and roughhousing with the children appeared benign, they demonstrated an inappropriate pattern of behavior that reflected deeper and more serious concerns.

•   •   •

The men you have just met represent four major types of predators. Yet as noted previously, predators do not always fall into these four categories. Most of them, in fact, have one or more traits of each type. For example, the narcissist and the antisocial may appear indistinguishable since they share certain characteristics. They are both self-involved, have a tendency to objectify others, and have a difficult time with adult relationships.

However, upon closer inspection, the narcissist is able to form some type of relationship with others, and he may even believe that he is "in love" with his victim. For although the narcissist has the tendency to use other people for his own gratification, it is not uncommon for him to become attached. On the other hand, the antisocial predator does not have the capacity to really connect with another person. This individual, like the narcissist, will use others to gratify his needs, but these needs are often fleeting and could just as easily be met by anyone. Therefore the person who is serving to meet the needs of the antisocial is only a fleeting object who will soon be discarded as he aimlessly pursues greater heights of pleasure, satisfaction, and excitement. Relationships with a narcissist will deplete others and make them feel betrayed, hurt, and confused, while encounters with an antisocial will leave people feeling empty.

The antisocial and the pedophile also share certain traits. The pedophile is an individual whose abuse of children demonstrates an antisocial tendency to blatantly ignore the needs of others in order to satisfy libidinal urges. And the inadequate predator may also have characteristics of a narcissist or an antisocial. For example, inadequate individuals suffer from a damaged self-esteem that may not manifest itself in exactly the same way as narcissists' tendencies toward self-involvement. But nevertheless, the inadequate predator is consumed by an injured sense of self that results in abusive acts toward others. An inadequate predator's inability to take any responsibility for the care of others, and the fact that he will experience little regret for his immaturity, clearly reflect antisocial tendencies.

Now that you have become familiar with these four types of predators, you will be better able to identify them. Yet remember that they come in all shapes and sizes and can be found in all walks of life and in every location where there are children. They may appear normal at first, and this is what makes the task of identifying them so difficult. It takes a long time to familiarize yourself with another person. To really understand people you need to know their history, understand their attitudes, and observe their patterns of behavior. And this type of knowledge is often inaccessible to parents who will need time to evaluate the appropriateness of an adult's interactions with their children. So even though you may not be able to fully analyze these people when you meet them, look for the initial ten warning signs that indicate danger and then observe their relationship with your children. Do they seem to be taking you and your children through the stages of abuse? Do you sense seduction, control, and intimidation in his or her relationship with you or with others? Be aware that it takes time to develop a healthy relationship, yet often a predator will trap a victim in a union that appears to be traveling at a whirlwind pace.

Finally, don't be afraid to investigate someone's past. Make sure that you gather information from what someone says and through the messages you receive from his or her behavior. Look at how he or she interacts with your children and remember the rules that you need to have in place to ensure the safety of your children. Don't allow secrecy and exclusion of others to be a factor in someone's relationship with your child, and make sure that the lines of communication are open between you and your child at all times.

While most of the male population would never harm children, these four types of male predators can cause immeasurable damage. Therefore it is crucial that you take the necessary steps to prevent any of these predators from ever gaining access to your children.

Almost all of the sexual predators you have met so far have been men. Yet females also sexually offend against children. In the next chapter, we will examine women offenders in an effort to understand their similarities and their differences in relation to male predators. Like the male offenders you have met, you will be able to examine female predators' patterns of behavior and learn more about the development of their deviant sexual behaviors in order to understand their unique patterns of abuse against children.

C h a p t e r   4

Female Predators

Tina and her two children have just arrived at an all-inclusive resort located on a lovely Caribbean coast in Mexico. As a single mother, Tina has worked hard to afford a luxury hotel, but it was worth the sacrifice. After they unpacked their bags, thirteen-year-old Daniel and ten-year-old Jill ran out to the sea to swim and snorkel. Tina carried a romance novel and suntan lotion as she followed her children to the beach. She sat under the cool shadow of an umbrella and began to read.

In less than an hour, the sun was positioned directly overhead, and the beach sizzled with heat. As Tina got up to prepare for a swim, she gazed down the sunny stretch of white sand and looked for her children. She spotted Jill, alone by the water's edge, sculpting a sand castle. Tina cupped her eyes to take in a wider expanse of the beach as she searched for Daniel. Farther down the shoreline, Tina detected two figures. As they moved closer into Tina's view, she recognized Daniel walking with an older woman. Tina watched as Daniel and his companion slowly made their way out into the ocean. Daniel appeared to be captivated by this woman, as he smiled and laughed in response to whatever she was saying. Tina sat back on her lounge chair and opened her book, but she could not concentrate. She found herself looking up more than once to watch Daniel and wonder why he was spending so much time with a woman who seemed to be Tina's age.

Daniel was an exceptionally good-looking boy, and he had always been mature for his age. He genuinely cared about others, and his pleasing, warm manner had often attracted compliments from Tina's friends. Tina felt proud to have raised such a remarkable son.

Lunchtime was approaching; and as Daniel remained by his companion's side, Tina's uneasiness increased. She decided to leave the shady outline of her beach umbrella and join Daniel and the woman in the water. As Tina approached them, her wariness increased as she saw them sitting in the shallow water, laughing as the waves washed over their bodies.

"Hey, Mom." Daniel waved enthusiastically to Tina. "I want you to meet my friend Anne." Tina introduced herself to Anne, who she learned was thirty-five and had come alone to the resort to nurse her grief over a recent divorce. Tina found Anne to be quite pleasant and exceptionally attractive. She told Tina that she thoroughly enjoyed Daniel's company and marveled at how sensitive and mature he was. Tina thanked Anne and then asked Daniel to get his sister and come up to the hotel for lunch.

"Can Anne eat lunch with us?" Daniel pleaded.

Tina looked at her son's handsome and eager face and replied, "Sure, why not. Anne can join us for lunch."

Jill also found herself attracted to the pretty, older woman, who smiled encouragingly at her. Tina had to admit that Anne exuded a certain charm that made others want to be with her. Tina asked Anne if she had any children of her own. Anne looked sad as she replied, "No, I was never able to have children. That was one of the reasons my marriage didn't last. It became too difficult for us to deal with, and I think that my husband wanted children so much he decided to have them with someone else."

"Well, then, pretend we're your kids for the vacation," Daniel offered with an eager smile.

Anne looked affectionately at Daniel and placed her hand on his. "That is awfully sweet, Daniel. You are so wonderful. But you already have a mom, so you and Tina can be my special friends."

After lunch the children invited Anne to join them at the pool. When Anne was not teaching Jill how to dive, she was lounging next to Daniel, talking to him about his interests in music, movies, and sports. Tina could not relax. Hours ago she had thrown her book aside as she spent much of her time mulling over the situation. Maybe she was just jealous of Anne's beautiful smile, perfect body, and the seemingly effortless way she'd captivated her children.

The afternoon segued into dinner with Anne as they participated in the hotel's fiesta on the beach. Anne taught the children how to dance to the salsa beats of the Latin band. As the piñata broke into a thousand pieces, and candy and fireworks fell from the starlit sky, Tina wondered at what point she should politely remove her children from Anne's influence.

Tina found the opportunity the next morning. At breakfast Daniel excitedly told his mother that Anne had asked him to accompany her on a sailboat that afternoon. They were planning to sail to a small cove a few miles from the hotel and have a picnic.

Jill looked up from her bowl of cereal. "Can I go, too?"

"No, you can't go. There's only room for two on the sailboat," Daniel retorted.

Tina's response was swift and firm. "You can't go, Daniel."

"Why not?" he protested.

"Because, I don't think that it's appropriate for a thirty-five-year-old woman to be spending so much time alone with a thirteen-year-old boy," Tina explained.

"Mom, you're being ridiculous," Daniel protested. "Anne is nice. She's here all alone, and she likes to talk to me. I like her. What's the big deal? I want to go!"

"No, Daniel, I don't feel comfortable with the situation, and you will have to trust me on this one. Let's plan to do something special this afternoon. How about renting jet skis?"

"I want to!" Jill shouted enthusiastically, but Daniel remained silent.

Tina sipped her coffee and stared at her son, who was obviously struggling with his disappointment. Tina thought to herself, *I hope I am not overreacting.*

Was Tina overreacting? Can harm befall a thirteen-year-old boy who has caught the attention of an older woman? When Tina returned from her vacation and told a number of her coworkers and friends about Daniel's interactions with Anne, she received mixed responses. Some of the men thought that it was more than all right for an older woman to take an interest in Daniel. Her office mate chuckled when he heard about Daniel and Anne. "Hey, Tina, maybe if your Danny-boy had played his cards right, he would have become a man down there in Mexico."

While none of Tina's female friends reiterated the common male response that "Daniel had missed the sexual experience of his young life," they did minimize Tina's concerns. After hearing about Daniel and Anne, one of Tina's closest friends replied, "Well, Tina, what were you so worried about? It's not as if this woman could have done anything to him. Daniel is a big boy; he can take care of himself."

Tina was shocked by these responses and more confused than ever. Why had she reacted in such a protective way toward her son when so many others felt that it had not been a dangerous situation?

GENDER STEREOTYPES

The answer to Tina's question can be found in society's beliefs about the gender differences that exist in regard to sex and aggression. If Tina peeled away the layers of opinions she received from friends and coworkers about her thirteen-year-old son's interactions with a thirty-five-year-old woman, she would uncover a traditional conviction that men are sexually aggressive and their victims are women.

I must admit that I also fell prey to this stereotypical gender view of sexual abuse. When I first prepared my outline for this book, I chose to completely omit the discussion of female predators. Yet as I reviewed a multitude of case histories in preparation for writing about predators, I was faced with the fact that a female had been the perpetrator in approximately one in ten cases involving child sexual abuse. I recalled the number of children who had come into my clinic as victims of child abuse by females. They suffered the scars of abuse from female baby-sitters, nannies, day-care providers, preschool teachers, aunts, older sisters, and, on rarer occasions, their own mothers. And yet despite the proliferation of evidence I had that females are capable of sexually abusing children, I did not propose to write a chapter on female predators. For I, like Tina, her coworkers, friends, and the vast majority of people in our society, found it difficult to acknowledge a behavior that deviates as much from the social norm as the sexual abuse of a child by a female.

The three common misperceptions pertaining to female predators are that: women are not capable of committing sexual abuse on their own, women must be mentally ill in order to sexually abuse a child, and women are not naturally sexually aggressive. Evidence of these beliefs was abundant as I interviewed colleagues and discussed women predators in preparation for writing this chapter.

> Isn't it true that in most cases, women don't act alone; and when they do perpetrate abuse, it is most often because they are being forced into it by a man?
>
> I thought that women perpetrators were an exception; and when they do sexually abuse children, it must be because they are mentally ill.
>
> Female perpetrators are very different from male perpetrators because women are not naturally sexually aggressive, and they are often in love with their victims.

In some instances, the above statements are true. However, research has demonstrated that women *are* capable of perpetrating sexual abuse in the absence of a man's influence. Further, not all woman claim to "be in love with their victims," and women do not have to be mentally ill to sexually molest a child.

Traditional beliefs that designate women as victims and ascribe men to the role of sexual aggressors have some validity. In the July 2000 report from the Bureau of Justice Statistics, 86 percent of all reported sexual assault cases in the United States were perpetrated by men. (This figure includes adult sexual assault victims.)

Although the percentage of female predators may be far lower than men, women are still responsible for victimizing a significant number of children. In 1991, Craig Allen published his study, *Women and Men Who Sexually Abuse Children: A Comparative Analysis.* He cited that, in 1989, it was estimated that over 3 million children had been sexually abused by women. In *The Social Organization of Sexuality,* by Laumann, Gagnon Michael and Michaels, it was reported that in 1994, 7 percent of males surveyed had had childhood sexual contact with an older female. And the most recent data collected by the National Center for Juvenile Justice cited that in 1998 women were responsible for over 8 percent of the total number of sexual offenses committed against children.

I experienced a curious phenomenon when I conducted the interviews of female predators in preparation for writing this chapter. I was startled by the degree of psychopathology I saw in these women. In contrast to the men I had talked with, I found that these women had suffered more severe abuse in their childhoods and had serious impairments in their ability to function. They had chronic histories of failed relationships, and a higher degree of financial problems than the men. And most notably, a majority of the women I came in contact with had committed some of the most severe acts of child sexual abuse.

As I became aware of society's overall denial that females are capable of sexual offenses, I understood that the women I had interviewed had come to the attention of the authorities because they had committed the worst forms of child sexual abuse. And because only the most egregious acts of sexual abuse perpetrated by women are prosecuted, the statistics on female predators are significantly underestimated. Boston psychologist Laurie Goldman, in her article "Female Sex Offenders: Societal Avoidance of Comprehending the Phenomenon of Women Who Sexually Abuse Children," analyzes the ways society minimizes the scope of child sexual abuse by females. In her article, Goldman maintains that even the systems that are designed to protect children, such as our courts, deny that women could perpetrate sexual abuse. As an example, she cites a case in the state of Washington where a judge dismissed a case against a woman who was accused of child sexual abuse by declaring, "Women don't do things like this."

Craig Allen also supports the fact that society has a difficult time seeing females as sexual offenders. He notes that only severely disturbed women who have committed the most deviant sexual offenses come to the attention of therapists or the judicial system since courts weed out many female sexual predators by prematurely dismissing their cases. This, Allen argues, is a reflection of society's denial of women as sexual aggressors.

Ruth Matthews, a Saint Paul psychologist, provides another reason that child sexual abuse perpetrated by women is underreported. In the case of child abuse where the mother is the offender, child victims are often unwilling to turn against their abusers. Maternal dependency is so primal and powerful that a child's attachment to a mother can endure years of profound abuse and neglect. Matthews explains that when a single mother is the offender, disclosure most likely results in the child being removed from the home and placed in foster care. Therefore to avoid this, many abused children do not make outcries, and thus many maternal incest cases go unreported ("Female Perpetration of Child Sexual Abuse: An Overview of the Problem," by Lisa Lipshires, published in *Moving Forward News Journal*, Volume 2, No. 6, July/August 1994).

Another important factor that leads to the paucity of data on female predators is that women are given more latitude than men for intimate acts with children. Although fathers do take part in the care of children, *sleeping next to a fretful toddler, bathing, applying medicines to genitalia, and the caressing of the infant while at the breast have been traditionally assigned to the mother.* Therefore it is often difficult to determine just when a mother crosses the physical boundaries of nurturing and enters the realm of sexual abuse.

If society tends to deny the existence of female sex offenders, and child victims are fearful to sacrifice what little sense of security they have to make an outcry against their own mothers, how can we determine the actual incidence of female predation? We can do so by talking to adults who had been sexually abused as children by females. Yet collecting data from these retrospective studies can be a problem since a significant percentage of boys who had sexual contact with older women do not report these incidents as abuse.

When an adolescent female and an older man engage in sexual intimacy, the girl automatically becomes the "victim" and the man is identified as the "predator." Yet when the situation is reversed, the same labels are not often applied. Debbie Crapeau, who facilitates treatment programs for female sexual offenders at the Resource Center for High Risk Youth in Denver, Colorado, discussed the phenomenon of the sexual differences that exist in victimization. "When a young girl is engaged in a sexual relationship with an older man, she is a *victim*; but when a young adolescent boy has a sexual relationship with an older woman, he is not considered a victim, he is considered *lucky*."

Even the victim himself, a teenage male who was lured into a sexual relationship with an older woman, will discredit the notion that he was violated and is more apt to classify the "abuse" as *a mutually satisfying experience*. The reluctance of an adolescent victim to acknowledge that a relationship with an older woman could be considered abuse was demonstrated in a twenty-eight-year-old man who sought therapy as a result of his inability to have a satisfying relationship with a woman. When reviewing his background, he noted that he first became sexual with his high school English teacher at the age of fifteen. When he was told that sexual intimacy between an adult and a child is considered "abuse," he reacted with marked indignation. He was adamant that he had not been a victim, and that his relationship with his teacher was totally consensual.

> It was my first sexual experience, and it was incredible. I wanted it as much as she did, and I was so lucky to have an older woman teach me about sex. I couldn't believe she had picked me. I mean, I was not that great looking in high school, but she thought that I was special. She really took care of me, and I learned so much from being with her.

As therapy continued, he explored these memories and began to see that he had been overwhelmed by the "relationship" with his teacher.

> My teacher began to get possessive with me, and I found myself in an awkward situation. I wanted to be a high school student just like everyone else, but I had to pretend that I was a lot older than my friends because I was her boyfriend. After a while I wanted to break it off, but I couldn't. How could I have ignored her; she was my teacher and she had power over me? I wanted to get into a good college, and I needed her recommendation. The relationship ended when my dad got a job in another state and we moved. I was secretly happy that the whole thing was over.

My client at that time was a vulnerable adolescent, and his teacher was not his "first love" or "the embodiment of his fantasy," she was a *predator* who led him through the stages of abuse. This female offender identified the vulnerability in her insecure fifteen-year-old student. She then went on to use her power and position over him to groom him for the abuse. She rewarded his compliance with special attention and recognition. She swore him to secrecy and established power and control over him, isolating him from friends and family. Once the sexual abuse occurred, she strove to maintain it by increasing her influence, power, and control over this young boy's life.

Further exploration of this man's contact with his high school teacher years ago revealed that it did have a profound impact on his developing sense of sexuality and future relationships. The experience had overwhelmed, confused, and shamed him. He admitted that he knew what he and his teacher were doing was wrong, but he was sworn to secrecy and he eventually felt trapped in a situation that he was not ready to handle. He had no outlet to process the experience, and left to his own, he could not sort out the kaleidoscope of emotions that whirled through his mind. He had trouble concentrating at school, became progressively isolated from his peers, and found it impossible to sleep at night. For many years following this incident, my client found it difficult to connect with girls his own age, and he muddled through a series of failed relationships with feelings of guilt and shame until he finally sought treatment.

Now that you are aware of the issues involved with female predators, let's return to that Mexican coast with Tina and her children. Was Tina overreacting to the situation with Daniel and thirty-five-year-old Anne? Was she responding with jealousy when she did not allow Daniel to go sailing with Anne? Absolutely not! Tina demonstrated appropriate parental concerns, and her actions protected her son from possible abuse. Maybe nothing would have happened on that deserted beach cove. Yet if Anne had attempted to seduce young Daniel, he would not be "lucky," as many of Tina's friends had told her; Daniel would have become another child victim of sexual abuse.

CHARACTERISTICS OF FEMALE PREDATORS

Since the majority of identified perpetrators of child abuse are men, the characteristics of female predators are often compared to male predators. And in many respects, they do share common traits. However, in Craig Allen's comparative study of male and female predators, he notes that demographics of female offenders differ from their male counterparts in the following ways:

> - Female offenders generally have lower income levels and lower occupational status.
> - Female offenders are less residentially stable.
> - Female offenders are on the average younger than male offenders.
> - Female offenders are less likely to exhibit other aggressive forms of antisocial behavior.

➤ Female offenders have more traumatic childhood histories, including a higher degree of sexual abuse within their immediate family.

➤ Female offenders are less likely to admit that their sexual acts were abusive.

In summary, the above differences tell us that female predators may be more financially, educationally, and mentally unstable than their male counterparts. However, these generalizations about female predators may not be accurate in representing the entire female offender population because of the limited number of female offenders who come to the attention of the authorities.

Debbie Crapeau also acknowledges some fundamental differences that exist between male and female predators that relate to the characteristics of the sexual offense:

➤ Women use a victim stance more often than men and tend to blame their offensive behaviors on men.

➤ Women are more likely than men to be involved with co-offenders even if they started the abuse on their own.

➤ Women tend to romanticize the abusive relationship more than men.

As well as determining the differences in male and female predators, Ms. Crapeau highlights the similarities in their behaviors:

➤ Women are just as likely as men to deny their abusive actions.

➤ Many female sex offenders also have a history of deviant sexual behavior.

➤ Female offenders are just as likely as men to engage in more than one form of sexual abuse.

➤ Women offenders also use distorted thinking and rationalizations to justify their behaviors.

➤ Women predators have the same likelihood of reoffending.

One of the most distinguishable differences between male and female predators is the way in which female predators view their offense. Females are traditionally relationship driven, and they tend to see their actions as a result of their attachment to a significant other. Therefore, when the victim is an adolescent boy, it is common for a female predator to couch the abuse in terms of a relationship. They may rationalize the abuse by viewing themselves as "providing education" or as a "loving partner to a lost and lonely young person."

Melanie's Story

An example of how a female predator can couch the abuse in terms of a relationship can be found in Melanie's story of her sexual contact with a young boy. Melanie, a psychiatric nurse working in a private mental hospital on an adolescent unit, rationalized her abusive behaviors by telling herself that her fourteen-year-old victim desired and needed her. Yet in reality, Melanie dominated her victim; and every step of the way, from the grooming to the actual act of abuse, Melanie skillfully led this young boy into a helpless state of submission.

> Tyler, a troubled adolescent, ran away from home, did not attend school, and was physically aggressive with his parents and siblings. Every intervention had been tried from medication to outpatient therapy. He had even been placed in adolescent group homes, but nothing seemed to work. Tyler appeared incorrigible, and as a last resort, he was referred to a private mental institution in a secluded northwestern state.
>
> Tyler was immediately put into isolation on the locked unit. His parents were told that he could not have any phone calls from them or visitors until he was "fully under control." With no privileges and no contact with the outside world, Tyler was completely dependent on the staff to meet even his basic needs. And Melanie was his primary care nurse.
>
> Melanie, an overweight and plain woman in her forties, had been struggling for years with a series of unsatisfying relationships with men. She had married in her teens and had a grown son. Her son had been a difficult child to raise, and he and Melanie had never been close. At the time of Tyler's hospitalization, Melanie was living alone in an apartment close to the hospital. Her

life had become focused on the care she gave to the adolescents on her unit. The staff described Melanie as a "dedicated and competent professional."

Melanie was immediately drawn to the challenge of "reaching" Tyler. Because of his involuntary hospitalization, he had become withdrawn and sullen. One evening, while Melanie was on the night shift, she heard sobbing from the isolation room. Peering into the glass window, she saw Tyler huddled on his bed crying into his pillow. Melanie unlocked the door, entered the room, and comforted the frightened and lonely adolescent. Thus began the seduction.

Melanie did a thorough job of grooming Tyler. She paid special attention to him, making him believe that she was the only one who really cared about him. She encouraged his anger at his parents for placing him in the hospital and confirmed his belief that they did not understand him. She rewarded his compliance to her orders and the attention he paid her by giving him special treats, such as scented shaving cream, a new toothbrush, candy bars, and cigarettes. Tyler's "counseling sessions" with Melanie became an opportunity for Melanie to snare her victim further into her web of seduction. During these times, they shared confidences and explored their secret fantasies and desires. Melanie made Tyler believe that she was his lifeline and his only hope for escaping his psychiatric "imprisonment."

Melanie also wrote Tyler letters telling him that she cared about him and that he was special. She acknowledged the pain and suffering he experienced as a result of his "traumatic childhood" and promised him a better life with her. She confessed her love for him and detailed the ways in which she wanted him to physically love her. Tyler responded with written pleas to Melanie to free him from the hospital so that they could "be together." He confessed his devotion to her and told Melanie what she wanted to hear, that she was "beautiful and desirable." Melanie swore Tyler to secrecy by warning him that she would be fired and that his chances of leaving the hospital would be considerably lessened if he ever told anyone about the letters or their "special" relationship.

Tyler kept the secret and Melanie responded by giving Tyler

special privileges. She allowed him to leave his isolation room and took him with her to run errands. She awarded him responsibilities outside of the unit and justified this to the staff as Tyler's reinforcement for progressing in his therapy. During these forays, Melanie would take the opportunity to get physically close to Tyler. They began kissing and fondling one another in deserted offices and among the secluded greenery of the hospital grounds. One day, approximately two months into Tyler's hospitalization, the final act of abuse occurred.

Melanie told Tyler that he was going to clean the administrative offices that day and that she would help him. Riding up in the elevator to the third floor of the hospital, Melanie told Tyler to hold her in his arms. She embraced Tyler passionately; and when she sensed reluctance in him, she demanded that he comply with her requests or else she would take him back to his isolation room.

When they entered an unoccupied office, Melanie ordered Tyler to undress and lie down on the floor. He did as he was told, and it was there on the carpet of a darkened, abandoned office, in the third floor of a psychiatric hospital, that Nurse Melanie raped her fourteen-year-old patient.

Tyler was terribly ashamed about having sex with Melanie, and following that incident, he began to withdraw from her. Melanie became anxious about Tyler's reactions and her threats increased.

Eventually, Tyler was released from isolation and placed on an open unit. Once removed from Melanie's influence, Tyler confessed the incident to his roommate, and the secret was finally set free. When the roommate told the staff, shortly after Tyler's confession, they were shocked and outraged. That evening the police were called into the unit to question Tyler. When Melanie returned to work the following day, she was escorted from the grounds by armed police and charged with child sexual assault. She received a sentence of incarceration for one year; and because this was her first offense, it was lessened to in-home detention. Her nursing license was revoked, and Melanie was prohibited from ever working with young people again. As a condition of her probation, Melanie was ordered into offender treatment for six years.

To speak to Melanie today, you would find it hard to believe that this mousy, unassuming woman was capable of committing such aggressively destructive acts on a naïve young boy. A year into her treatment, she still maintained that she and Tyler had been "in love." She believed that she understood him and that her connection with him transcended the conventional boundaries of nurse and patient. She felt committed in her attempts to "cure" Tyler and had fantasies about their life together when he was released from the hospital. She persistently denied the damage she had inflicted on such a troubled young boy, for she clung to her belief that he wanted her as much as she wanted him. She continued to refer to her victim as "the most beautiful person I have ever met. He was courageous and smart but terribly misunderstood." She rationalized her abuse of this defenseless child by stating, "I was the only one who really knew Tyler, and I had the keys to unlock him from his isolation and pain. No one will ever understand our relationship. They judge it only because of our age difference."

Now that you have met Melanie and Tyler, and witnessed Melanie's insistence that she and Tyler were "in love," do you believe that Melanie sexually abused Tyler? If you do, then the following exercise will only strengthen your conviction. Picture in your mind the dowdy middle-aged Melanie having sex with her fourteen-year-old male patient. Then close your eyes and change Melanie into a forty-five-year-old man named Mark. Then transform Tyler into an adolescent psychiatric patient named Teresa. Last, envision Teresa following Mark's orders and lying naked on the carpet of the empty office on the third floor of the hospital. Is Mark a predator, and do you see Teresa as his victim? Most likely you do because, as discussed previously, societal norms make it easy for us to view Mark as the sexual aggressor and Teresa as the defenseless and exploited victim. However, despite the gender reversals in Melanie and Tyler's case, the same labels apply. Melanie was the sexual predator, and Tyler was her victim.

TYPES OF FEMALE PREDATORS

In their book, *Female Sexual Offenders*, published in 1989, Ruth Mathews, Jane Kinder Matthews, and Kathleen Speltz identify three types of female predators based on the predator's choice of victims and whether the female offenders acted alone or with a partner. The three types are as follows:

- ➤ Teacher/Lover
- ➤ The Predisposed Predator
- ➤ The Male-Coerced Predator

Although the traditional belief has been that female offenders most often commit abuse with a partner, the female predators are evenly distributed across these three categories. Because of the severity of the abuse perpetrated on child victims by females in conjunction with partners, it is likely that these types of female offenders are prosecuted more than the other types, particularly the teacher/lover. This may be one explanation for the preponderance of these cases in our legal system.

Teacher/Lover Predator

You have already met Anne, the high school English teacher, and Melanie. They are all teacher/lover predators. And as you have become aware, these types of women justify their abusive behaviors by telling themselves that they had a special bond with their victims. They have a very difficult time coming to terms with the consequences of their abuse, and they are tenacious in their beliefs that sexual intimacy between an adult and a child is justified if those involved are in love.

The teacher/lover female predator usually chooses prepubescent or adolescent males as her victims. Her motives for the sexual offense are teaching her young victims about sexuality or obtaining love from them. She is likely to see her contact with her victims as positive. This type of predator is searching for power and control. Like Melanie, these women are insecure, angry, and have many unresolved issues about dependency and abandonment. They usually have a number of failed relationships in their past and come from homes where they were sexually, physically, or emotionally abused.

Details of Melanie's childhood revealed that she was one of four children who were born to an unstable and neglectful mother. Her father had abandoned the family when Melanie was just an infant, and as a result, they lived in poverty. Melanie's mother was more interested in her never-ending succession of boyfriends than in caring for her children. Eventually, after Melanie's mother left her children alone at a motel for three days while she cavorted with her latest boyfriend, social services took charge. They forced Melanie's mother to relinquish custody, and the children were sent to different foster homes. Melanie never had a consistent and loving environment, and as a result, she grew up to be a needy and terribly insecure woman.

A teacher/lover predator takes her young victim through the same stages of abuse that you read about in chapter 2. Even though they may rationalize their behaviors by couching it in terms of developing a relationship, they are in actuality detecting, approaching, subjugating, grooming, and eventually sexually abusing their victims.

Women predators often choose adolescents because they have identified them as vulnerable to sexual abuse. Adolescents are easy prey for female predators because of their natural tendency for sexual experimentation and the confusion and susceptibility that arise from their search for identity. Further, many adolescents are in the process of pulling away from parental control, and the alienation that results from their quest for a separate identity can leave them vulnerable to the cunning seduction of an adult predator.

Melanie and the high school English teacher were in positions of power and trust over their victims. They misused this power to gain control and total dominion over their victims. The next teacher/lover predator you will meet was not a professional in a position of power; she was the seemingly devoted mom-next-door. However, the power and control she had over her adolescent victim came with her status as an adult and a mother.

As you read the story of Janice and her adolescent victim Sean, watch how Janice takes Sean through the five stages of abuse, from detection to the actual act of abuse. Also look for the warning signs that indicate Janice is a predator. Does she have one or more of the ten characteristics that most commonly define a predator, such as depression, low self-esteem, poor impulse control, substance abuse, or a lack of empathy? Although we have already defined Janice as the teacher/lover predator, which one of the four types of male predators does she most resemble—the narcissist, the inadequate, the pedophile, or the antisocial? And finally, can we consider Janice's actions toward Sean to be abuse?

After twenty years of marriage and a full-time career, Janice felt incomplete. She was bored with her husband and believed that her two teenage sons did not need her anymore. She worked as a sales representative and her hours were flexible, leaving Janice with a lot of free time on her hands. It was in this setting that Janice met fifteen-year-old Sean. He was the best friend of her younger son, Riley.

Sean often told Riley that he thought Janice was a "cool" mom. His own mother, a single, working woman with two other children, had little time to spend with her family. Sean often complained about the messy condition of his house, how his mother smoked all the time, and how she was always passed out on the couch in front of the television, "too tired to cook dinner." He rarely saw his father, who lived in another state and never paid child support. He was a lonely and neglected boy, and Janice immediately detected his need for adult contact. She began to make herself available to the boys after school, baking them treats and talking to them about school, their friends, and their interest in girls.

Janice became aware that Sean was awkward with girls and that his self-esteem was poor. Sean learned from his absent father and his mother, who paraded different men in and out of Sean's life, that relationships are fleeting and insincere. Although he longed to have a girlfriend, Sean avoided the opposite sex as much as possible.

Janice began to invite Sean to stay for dinner, and he eventually became a regular at their household. Janice lent a sympathetic ear to Sean during those times when he was fighting with his mother and complained that "no one understood him." She comforted him when he felt alienated from his peers at school or ignored by the girl he secretly admired. Sometimes, even when Riley was at home, Sean would seek out the company of Janice. Sitting opposite Janice at the kitchen table in the late afternoons, he felt the comfort of adult companionship and a sense of security that he had never experienced before. Janice sympathized with Sean's plight and agreed with him that his mother did not understand him and did not have the time to give him what he needed.

Sometimes when Riley was not around during these discussions, Janice would offer Sean a glass of wine. As they slowly sipped their drinks, she told Sean that he was very special and that she thought of him as intelligent and mature. She criticized Sean's mother for not taking the time to appreciate who he was, and she reassured Sean that she noticed how unique he was.

One weekend when Riley was away at a baseball training camp, Janice suggested that Sean stay over for the weekend. Janice's offer seemed like a welcome respite to Sean, who was growing weary from the constant fighting that took place in his own home. Unbeknownst to Sean, Janice's husband had planned a hunting trip that weekend, and their older son was spending a few days spring skiing with friends. So it would be just Janice and Sean in the home alone all weekend.

With the proper grooming in place, it was not difficult for Janice to move the seduction along to physical intimacy. The first evening they were alone, Janice and Sean sat close on the couch watching one of her favorite foreign films. She marveled at how insightful Sean was as they discussed the meaning of the movie. The movie was erotic, and its sensual scenes aroused Sean. After a few glasses of wine, he felt afloat on a sea of warmth and acceptance, and he was becoming sexually aroused. Janice took the cue; and moving closer to Sean, she enticed him into kissing her. After a lingering kiss, Janice pulled away in "mock horror" at what they had just done. She told Sean that he was much too young for her and that physical intimacy between them was impossible. Sean then played right into her pretense of restraint and told Janice that age should not be a factor if two people really loved one another.

There followed another night of kissing and fondling that was immediately followed by a rash of recriminations from Janice. Finally, on Sunday, Janice "gave in" to what she told herself was "Sean's desires" and led him to her bed.

After that night Janice plunged Sean headfirst into a sexually abusive relationship. She became his "sexual educator" and "mentor" in all areas of his life. She changed the way he cut his hair, the clothes he wore, and even the type of music he played. Sean was fully under Janice's control; and although their relationship was clandestine, Sean believed that everyone could see that he was "in love." Because their relationship was a "secret," Janice became more distant from her own sons, particularly Riley, who had become confused and hurt with Sean's sudden withdrawal. Since Sean felt uncomfortable being with the son of his lover, he no longer came over to the house when Riley was at home. Sean shunned his former best friend until their relationship drifted apart. A number of times Riley tried to confront Sean, but it was to no avail. No one could reach Sean except for Janice.

Six months into the affair, Janice began suffering from severe headaches. She went to the doctor, who diagnosed stress and gave her prescription medications and advice to see a therapist. Her marriage was falling apart, and she was in chronic fear that her relationship with Sean would be discovered. Her connection to her sons had deteriorated to hasty pecks on their cheeks as they ran out the door. She could no longer sleep, and her lack of concentration reduced her work performance to a precarious level. She decided to end the "affair" with Sean.

Over a candlelit dinner at a remote restaurant, where Janice had more than once treated her young lover to an expensive meal, she told Sean that their relationship must end. Sean was hurt and confused. He felt betrayed and abandoned, and he reacted with threats of self-harm. Janice did not take Sean's threats seriously, and she dismissed his outcries as adolescent "hysteria." She told Sean that he would get over her and that now that he knew the "secrets of adult love," he could have any girl in the school. Humiliated, Sean ran out of the restaurant, leaving Janice to offer apologetic glances to the rest of the patrons as she paid the bill.

A few weeks passed before Janice heard from Sean again. Late one night he called Janice at home and told her that his pain was too great and that he wanted to say good-bye to her. He still cared for her, and she would always be the "one and only love of his life." After he hung up the phone, Janice lay awake in bed unsure about her next move. But unbeknownst to Janice, the next move would be made for her.

For that night, after hanging up the phone, Sean quietly entered the bathroom and took an overdose of his mother's pain medication. As he was becoming groggy, he wrote a good-bye letter to Janice detailing his last wishes and expressing his hurt and disappointment over their terminated romance. He told her that he would die with the memory of their true love and signed it, "Yours forever, Sean."

Early the next morning Sean's mother discovered her son as he lay unconscious on his bed with his note grasped in his hand. She called an ambulance, and Sean was rushed to the emergency room. Once he was stabilized, he was moved to the psychiatric unit for evaluation. It was during the clinical interviews with the therapist that Sean disclosed his affair with Janice. The authorities were notified, and Janice was arrested.

The next time Janice and Sean saw one another, it was in the courtroom during a highly publicized trial. She told the members of the courtroom that she had never truly been in love with Sean, and that she had tried to discourage his physical attraction to her because she knew it was wrong. She described how she had first tried to help him and nurture him the same way she did with her sons, but that Sean had been sexually aggressive with her. She claimed that he wanted her, and she gave in because she felt sorry for him. On the stand she testified that she did not believe that she had done anything to harm Sean because a physical relationship was what he really wanted. But as Janice explained, when Sean began to fall in love with her, she had to put an end to the relationship.

Despite her attorney's argument that this was Janice's first sexual offense and that she was suffering from a depression that clouded her judgment, the jury found Janice guilty. She was sentenced to eighteen months in jail and three years of probation. As for Sean, he was left with a much greater burden to bear. As a victim of sexual abuse, he felt shamed and alienated. He had lost his best friend, his belief that Janice had truly cared for him, his self-respect, and the innocence of his childhood.

Through the help of a gifted and caring therapist, Sean did finally make his way through the maze of confusion, anger, and betrayal he'd experienced following the abuse. He learned that Janice had not been an adult confidante or a sexual mentor, and never his lover. She had been a sexual predator who had identified, groomed, and abused him for her own gratification. He finally understood that the relationship with Janice had not been an exciting affair; rather it had been an abusive interaction between a victim and an offender.

Tragically, Sean was not the only adolescent victim in this story. Janice's two teenage sons were also deeply marred by their mother's sexual contact with Sean. Riley struggled with the sense of betrayal that had cost him, not only his best friend, but the trust and respect he had once had for his mother. Both boys felt extremely uncomfortable with Janice, and their anger intensified their alienation from her. When Janice's husband asked for a divorce, both boys moved out of the house to live with him. It would take years of family therapy to heal the wounds that had been created by Janice's actions.

To understand more about the characteristics of this female predator, let's examine the way in which Janice led Sean through the stages of sexual abuse. First, she detected his vulnerability in his alienation from his parents and in his low self-esteem. She then approached him using the guise of an understanding adult. She gained control over him by further alienating him from his parents and presenting herself as the only one who appreciated him. She then began to groom him by offering Sean food, a place to stay, and arranging a special time when they could be alone. Offering him wine was just another prop in the grooming stage; and when everything was finally in place, Janice committed the final act of abuse.

Janice displayed a number of traits that are shared by all sexual predators. The most obvious one was her low self-esteem. She based much of her self-worth on being an attractive and attentive mother and wife. But since she was aging, her children were growing, and her husband was neglecting her, she felt abandoned and insecure. She believed that a sexual tryst with an adolescent would make her once again feel young, attractive, and valued. Janice's desire for power and control was also demonstrated in her need to be the center of activity in her household. She had a difficult time when she could no longer control her sons' lives, and her ability to dominate Sean gave her the sense of importance she felt she had lost years ago. Further, Janice had an alcohol problem that exacerbated her depression and caused her to act impulsively.

Finally, Janice's lack of empathy was paramount. When she decided to abuse an adolescent boy, she acted irresponsibly toward her own family, deeply betraying her own sons; and she manipulated an impressionable and lonely young boy into believing that he was in love with her. It was only when Janice decided that Sean was no longer useful in her life that she decided to end the abuse. When Sean gave Janice warning that the pain he was suffering was too great for him to bear, her lack of empathy allowed her to ignore his pleas. And this lack of empathy nearly cost Sean his life.

I am certain that a majority of you have concluded that Janice sexually abused Sean. The manner in which she identified, stalked, and planned out her seduction of this vulnerable youth clearly identifies her as a predator. The fact that she used her relationship with this young man to justify her actions does not exclude her from being labeled a sexual predator. In fact, a majority of predators develop some type of relationship with their victims well before the abuse takes place.

Janice was not necessarily sexually attracted to children like the predisposed predator you will soon meet. She merely took advantage of Sean's youth to control him. However, the predisposed female predator is often aroused by children and has a long history of using children to satisfy her sexual needs. This type of predator often has the most number of victims and is most similar to the male pedophile you read about in chapter 3.

The Predisposed Predator

This type of female predator is sexually aroused by children and has a chronic pattern of using children as sexual objects. She often has a childhood history of severe sexual abuse that was perpetrated on her at a very early age. Therefore she is likely to display more severe forms of mental illness than the other two types of female predators. The predisposed predator will function poorly in most areas of her life. These women often marry in their teens, but their relationships are unstable and they eventually live on their own. They also have trouble finding and keeping jobs, have chronic financial problems, and a lower level of education than the other two types of female predators.

In general, the predisposed predator has sexual contact with boys and girls equally; however, in the case of maternal incest, daughters are more likely than sons to be the victims. Predisposed predators often act alone, and their motives for the abuse may sound much like the teacher/lover predator's justifications. However, because the predisposed predators' prey are, on the average, younger than the teacher/lover's victims, it is harder to rationalize the abuse in the guise of a romantic relationship.

A predisposed predator's most accessible victims are her own children, and thus she is likely to turn to them for sexual pleasure and intimacy. However, if a female predator does not have children, she will find her victims through her extended family, neighbors, and friends. Statistics demonstrate that most child sexual abuse occurs within the child's home or in the home of the perpetrator and with someone the child knows. And in the case of the predisposed female predator this is especially true.

Next you will read about Belinda, a predisposed female predator who struggled with depression and anxiety throughout her life. She had a childhood history of sexual abuse. Belinda's stepfather had molested her at the age of ten; and although her mother had asked him to leave, Belinda had never received treatment for the sexual assault. Left on her own to cope with the terrible trauma, Belinda began to sexually prey on other children. She taught her brother about sex and sexually molested her younger nieces and nephews. By the time Belinda had graduated from high school, she had sexually assaulted over thirty children.

> As a single woman Belinda continued to live with her mother. Belinda also liked to spend the weekends with her siblings. All of Belinda's brothers and sisters were married, and Belinda had three nieces and two nephews. Tragically, some of these children became casualties of sexual abuse. Belinda chose her victims well. She relied on her predatory skills to select the most acquiescent and suggestible children, and she manipulated their developing sexuality to keep them aroused and involved. Because the children were sworn to secrecy, they did not tell anyone about the abuse. Belinda rewarded their subjugation with attention and presents.
>
> Belinda's life outside of her home was sparse. She worked as a receptionist in a small accounting firm. She was friendly to her coworkers, but they knew little about her life outside the office. Except for Robert, Belinda had no contact outside her family.
>
> Belinda and Robert had been dating for the past twelve years, and their relationship had never progressed beyond that. They'd met in high school, and since Robert lived in the same neighborhood as Belinda and he'd never moved out of his home, their relationship was easy and convenient. In fact, their relationship had never been sexual. Belinda had little interest in sleeping with Robert; and since he never pressed the issue, she was content to

keep him at arm's length as they sat beside one another at an occasional movie or at a concert.

Labor Day weekend marked the beginning of the end of Belinda's reign of domination and control over the children. Anthony, Belinda's favorite nephew and the latest inductee into her sexual lair, eventually broke the fortress of secrecy.

Anthony was five years old; and although he was small for his age, he had the spunkiness and intelligence of an older child. Belinda spent a great deal of time with Anthony grooming him for the abuse. In the guise of familial devotion, she taught little Anthony how to throw a ball, draw colorful pictures, read storybooks, and write his name. Anthony was deceived into trusting Aunt Belinda, and in her presence he believed he was loved and special.

Labor Day weekend was approaching, and the entire family decided to go camping. With all the necessary equipment packed in the cars, the family drove to the mountains. Anthony was excited because he had been chosen by Aunt Belinda to accompany her in her car. On the ride to their camping designation, Aunt Belinda told Anthony that this weekend was going to be very special for both of them. She explained to him that he was becoming a "big boy," and she had a secret for him. Anthony was bursting with anticipation.

Once the tents were set up, the family cooked hot dogs and hamburgers on the grill. As night approached, a campfire was started, and Belinda helped the children spear their marshmallows. The adults became restless and began to forage in the cooler for beers. Within an hour everyone was feeling fine. Belinda declined the beers because she did not like the "out of control" feelings she had when she drank.

Belinda offered to help the children prepare for sleep. She tucked each one of them into their sleeping bags and then turned to Anthony. "Because you were so good today, Anthony, you are going to sleep with Aunt Belinda tonight." Anthony, who was sleepy from the day's adventure, gratefully climbed into his aunt's arms as she carried him into her tent.

Outside Belinda's tent, the adults were loud and reckless in their merriment. Belinda held Anthony until he fell asleep and then put him into his sleeping bag and waited. Eventually the night air became quiet. Belinda woke Anthony and instructed him to join her in her bag. "It's cold, my little Tony, come and make your Aunt Belinda warm." Anthony did as he was told, and once in the confines of her bag, Belinda began to caress her nephew. Anthony appeared confused and when he tried to squirm out of her touch, Belinda told him that what she was doing to him was "their big secret." She went on to explain to him that he was her favorite, and that she only did this with the children she loved the most. Anthony, overwhelmed and confused, did the only thing he could to escape, he pretended to fall asleep.

The next morning Anthony acted as if nothing had happened. If anyone had paid close attention, they would, however, have noticed that Anthony was avoiding his favorite aunt. Instead of clamoring for her attention, he would swim in the creek with the rest of the children, fish with the men, or play hide-and-seek with his cousins. He even began to cling to his mother while she was talking with the other women or attempting to cook meals. "What is wrong with you, Anthony? Go play with the kids," she would say, as she pried her youngest son's hands from her waist.

Returning home was quite an ordeal. Anthony refused to drive with Belinda, claiming he was sick and wanted to ride in the backseat of his parents' van. Belinda reacted with hurt indignation and was sullen as she drove home with one of her sisters.

"What's wrong, Belinda? Are you upset about Anthony? Boy, you and that kid are really close. You should get married and have your own children. You really love kids," her sister suggested. Belinda remained silent.

After the camping trip, Anthony changed. He became more aggressive with his siblings and his parents. He wet his bed on a number of occasions and had a succession of nightmares. He had started kindergarten that fall, and his teacher remarked that he was withdrawn from the other children.

One day in late September, Anthony was found playing with a little girl in a secluded area on the side of the school building. Both children were unclothed and Anthony was ordering his class-mate to kiss his penis. The teacher asked the children to put on their clothes and come with her into the office. She called their parents; and when Anthony's mother came to the school, she questioned her son. "Where did you learn that from?" Anthony replied, "I can't tell you. It's a secret between me and Aunt Belinda." Promising that he would not get into trouble if he told, Anthony's mother extracted the "secret" from her son.

Needless to say, the events that followed created havoc in the family. Once Anthony broke the veil of silence, the other children escaped their captivity. Belinda's siblings were outraged, and the anger that ensued shred the family apart.

Belinda was charged with sexual assault on minors, and she was sentenced to eight years of probation. As a condition of her probation, she was ordered to attend an offender treatment program. Once in the program, Belinda talked about her own history of sexual abuse at the hands of her stepfather. Belinda learned that her own childhood molestation was a factor in her sexually abusive behaviors and that she needed to resolve this before she could ever be around children again.

Maternal Incest

A mother's sexual abuse of her own children is perhaps the most difficult for us to comprehend. A predisposed female predator who victimizes her own children, not only indelibly scars them for life, but also desecrates the sanctity of motherhood. The primal prescript for mothers to shelter and nourish their offspring is essential to our basic survival. Without this our species could not survive; therefore, incestuous mothers often appear as the most incomprehensible of all predators.

Because of the sanctions that govern motherhood, maternal incest is relatively rare as compared to the other types of sexual abuse. The number of predisposed female predators who sexually abuse their own children is considerably less than the number of men who sexually abuse *their* own children. According to the statistics provided by the U.S. Department of Health and Human Services in their 1998 report for "Child Maltreatment," approximately 3.8 percent of all child sexual assaults were perpetrated by a female parent as compared to 22 percent of sexual assaults committed by a father. (It is important to note that the term "female parent" refers to adoptive mothers and stepmothers as well as biological mothers.)

As noted previously, sexual abuse is perpetrated more on daughters than sons. Yet when mothers abuse their sons, these boys are left with profound psychological damage. When a boy is sexually abused by his mother, the devastation occurs not only because his basic trust in the world is shattered but the core are beliefs about his sexual identity is also threatened. Boys become aware at quite an early age that society expects them to be strong, assertive, and competent. When they are sexually exploited by their own mothers, the shame that ensues will create a deep chasm in their sexual development.

Mothers suffering from depression may be at higher risk for abusing their children than nondepressed mothers. Depression is an insidious disease because it drains the individual of the necessary resources needed to cope with life and deposits a trail of irritability and withdrawal. Therefore, a mother who is suffering from depression will be less able to handle the emotional and physical demands of child rearing. She may either retreat into a world of self-pity and sorrow or lash out at those around her in an attempt to discharge her pain. A depressed parent may also see her children as an outlet for her unmet needs or as available resources to fill her sense of emptiness.

Another critical factor in maternal abuse is the mother's own childhood history. Craig Allen discusses the incestuous female predator as a woman who, in many cases, had a childhood that was marred with chronic and early sexual abuse. Women who have emotional scars from their own history of sexual abuse may be at a higher risk for repeating these behaviors, particularly if they have not had the opportunity to resolve the abuse in treatment. As mentioned previously, a childhood history of abuse does not automatically condemn a survivor to repeat this pattern in adulthood. However, when this type of history is combined with other factors, such as depression, a lack of outside support, a low self-esteem, or substance abuse, the risk factor for a mother abusing her children becomes greater.

Even though research has taught us that victims of sexual abuse do not automatically grow up to be sexual predators, there is an interesting phenomenon that occurs when a female survivor of sexual abuse has her own children. There is a positive correlation between a mother's history of sexual abuse and her children's sexual victimization. In other words, a child is more likely to experience sexual abuse, whether it be within the family or by a third party, if his or her mother was sexually abused as a child. Why is this so since being a survivor does not automatically translate into being a predator?

The answer can be found in the scripts that were written for the survivor many years ago. Survivors of sexual abuse learned a number of lessons in their childhoods that were emblazoned in their memories. They were taught that love means physical and emotional pain and that the world is an untrusting place where very bad and uncontrollable things happen. Many survivors learned that they had to keep their shame a secret, and they believed that they were fundamentally "bad" people because they believed they were responsible for the abuse. They learned that sexual abuse may be accompanied by sexual pleasure but that "pleasure" has a lethal price. Parts of their souls were auctioned away for the price of secrecy and survival, and to get close to someone meant that you needed to use your body in exchange for a scrap of attention and caring.

Sexual abuse survivors, without proper intervention, may never have the opportunity to read a different screenplay and therefore are likely to re-create in their adult lives the pain and suffering they lived through as children. They will choose different actors, as husbands, boyfriends, or lovers, and the setting may change slightly. But the themes will be similar; and without therapeutic assistance, the climax and denouement will tragically follow suit in the sexual abuse of their own children.

For this reason sexual abuse rarely occurs in isolation, particularly familial sexual abuse. Sexual abuse is often intergenerational. When we ask parents of sexually abused children to trace their own family histories, more times than not we find that child sexual abuse has spanned many generations. The conscious and unconscious transmission of trauma seems to find its way into each new generation until a family decides to come to terms with its history and seeks to resolve the demons of the past.

Once again I will emphasize that a history of sexual abuse is not an excuse for the behaviors of female predators, just as it is not one for male offenders. It is offered as a factor in understanding some of the dynamics behind predators' behaviors. Ultimately, it is the choice of the person to act out sexually against children that defines him or her as a predator.

Male-Coerced Predators

There is a common belief that a man's will is the driving force behind a woman's sexually abusive behaviors. Certain feminist views espouse that, in many cases, aggression in women results from their defense against the violent potential in men. Women who kill husbands or physically attack their lovers are often viewed as defending themselves against hostile foes. And, in certain cases, this is true; however, as noted previously, women predators are capable of acting alone. Not all female predators have a co-offender, and we have already met a few of these women who acted alone. Melanie, the schoolteacher, Janice, and Belinda all perpetrated abuse without an accomplice. Yet approximately one-third of female predators do enact abuse as a result of their involvement with an abusive partner, and these are referred to as male-coerced predators or co-offenders.

Women who are co-offenders often claim that they were forced into perpetrating abuse as a result of threats made by their mates. A fear of abandonment or physical and mental abuse can be extremely intimidating for certain women, particularly those who bear the scars of their own childhood abuse. Women whose marriages are plagued with domestic violence are often so intimidated and controlled by their spouses that they feel they have no power to stop the abuse. Joining with their partner to abuse the children becomes another aspect of the violence, chaos, and loss of control that have characterized their relationship.

The male-coerced predator most commonly co-offends against her own children. The co-offender may be the biological father or more frequently a stepfather. As we have learned, it is not uncommon for a male predator to marry a woman in order to gain access to her children. Once this type of man is in the home, he can exert more influence and control over the family. In certain cases a woman may suspect that her husband is abusing the children; and when she finally catches him in the act, she may be reluctant to do anything about it because of the fears that threaten her own sense of safety.

The type of woman who co-offends with her partner has certain personality characteristics that make it more probable that she will attach to a deviant man and then become dependent on him to fill her emotional and physical needs. Craig Allen describes the "typical" co-offending female as someone who comes from a troubled and neglectful childhood, has borderline intelligence, and does not work outside the home. She has strong dependency needs and may therefore appear passive. She often has a low self-esteem and is involved with drug or alcohol abuse. Suicidal ideation, antisocial tendencies, unresolved anger, and deviant sexual behaviors are more common with this type of female predator.

•   •   •

In the following vignette, you will meet a male-coerced female predator, Charlene, a young mother with two small children. You will trace the development of her abusive actions and witness the decisions she had to make at every step of the abusive cycle. You will see how she allowed a predator to enter her home, groom her children, subjugate her and her children, and finally convince her to engage in the sexual abuse of her children.

> Charlene was only thirty-three years old when the father of her two infant children abandoned the family. Living in New York without child support, Charlene was forced to go on welfare. The family moved around frequently, and at times they even lived in motels. Alone and frightened, Charlene found herself attached to a series of unsavory men. She was desperately looking for some-one to take care of her and the children, but all she seemed to find were "losers" who were unemployed or drug dealers.
>
> Charlene had begun experimenting with drugs at an early age, and she was particularly drawn to cocaine. This drug gave her a remarkable high and allowed her to escape the barren monotony of her existence. However, after a bad experience with a dealer boyfriend who was arrested and sent to prison, Charlene had sworn off drugs.
>
> She had just moved into her first house, which had been sub-sidized through a government program. Charlene believed that she had turned a corner and was starting a new life. She and the children were busy painting rooms and putting up homemade curtains when Jerry appeared on her doorstep. He lived next door and invited the family for a barbecue that Sunday. Charlene ap-praised his long hair, tight jeans, and the tattoos he sported on his muscular arms. He looked like all the others who had sullied her doorstep, and she was tired of this look. But Jerry had a nice smile and straight, even teeth. "Maybe, just maybe," Charlene prayed, "this one will be different."
>
> Over hot dogs and beers, Charlene learned that Jerry had been married twice and he had a number of children scattered through-out the United States. He had a multitude of bad stories to share about his "witchy ex-wives who had their claws out for [his] money." He also had an unstable employment history, and as the

evening wore on, Charlene discovered that he, too, was a drug dealer. Charlene saw all the signs of disaster, but once again she chose to ignore them.

The kids seemed to like Jerry. He thrilled them with motorcycle rides and trips to the amusement park. It didn't take long for Jerry to miss a few rental payments and get evicted from his home. Moving in with Charlene and the kids was his best option.

Charlene was given a serious warning sign of the abuse to come when Jerry requested that the children join them in bed at night. He said that it made them close, "like one big family." He explained that when he was a child bad things would happen to him when he was alone in his bed, and that he wanted the kids to always feel safe and protected. Although Charlene felt uncomfortable with the situation, she acquiesced.

Soon after Jerry moved in, he and Charlene began using cocaine. And as drug use ransacked their lives, Charlene's children became more neglected. Charlene and Jerry were spending grocery and rent money purchasing crack, and they would remain high for days at a time. Ben, at seven years old, took care of his five-year-old sister, Jackie, as he scraped the bottom of the peanut butter jars to scrounge up a dinner for them.

Charlene and Jerry shared a history of childhood sexual abuse. When they were high and discussing their past, Jerry would become aroused by the memories and want to have sex. Gradually Jerry introduced the idea of including the children. At first Charlene was disgusted with the notion and flatly refused. However, as time wore on and the effects of the drug significantly altered her perceptions and decision making, Charlene became less and less resistant to the idea. One night when she and Jerry were high and having sex on the living room couch, Ben walked in. Years later, as Charlene describes the incident, it is obvious that she remains unaware of who coerced the little boy and how he was led into the sexual abuse. The last memory she has of that fateful night was of "having sex" on the couch with both Jerry and her son.

The next day Ben acted as if nothing had happened, but Charlene was consumed with guilt. She made Jerry promise that it would never happen again, and he agreed. But their agreement was short-lived; for the next time they were high, they went into the children's bedroom and sexually abused both Ben and Jackie.

The abuse occurred a number of times; and following each incident, Charlene was awash with grief and guilt. She often pleaded with Jerry to stop the abuse, yet she was unable to take a stand and end the terror they were inflicting on the children. Charlene lived in a nightmare, trapped in the memories of her unspeakable acts against her own children. She was terrified that if she reported Jerry to the authorities, she would be implicated and lose her children. She was also afraid to lose Jerry, her only connection to the outside world. Therefore she continued to be his partner in the abuse.

Three months later Jerry was arrested while driving under the influence of alcohol. While in custody, it was discovered that Jerry had violated the terms of his probation, and he was automatically sent to jail.

With Jerry safely behind bars, Charlene's own prison door of fear was unlocked. Within a few days Charlene approached the police station. Marching up the steps of the station, she told herself that this was the opportunity she had waited for. She could now free her children from the pain, humiliation, and suffering they had endured for the last three months. As she told the authorities about her children's abuse, she acknowledged that she had been a partner in the molestation. She claimed that she had done so only because she was afraid of Jerry. With tears streaming down her eyes, she admitted that she knew the abuse they were inflicting on her children was horrible and would do great damage to them and that was why she had to stop it, even if it meant losing them. In the end Charlene did lose Ben and Jackie. After two years in foster placement, social services advised her to relinquish custody so that the children could be adopted.

Today Charlene's life hangs in threads. She is disconnected from everyone she ever cared about, and her greatest fear has become a reality; she is totally alone. Her days are filled with treatment sessions, meetings with her probation officer, and a minute-by-minute accountability for every move she makes outside of the group home where she now resides.

Initially in offender treatment, Charlene blamed Jerry for the abuse of her children. She was convinced, and rightfully so, that he'd planned the abuse before he had ever moved into their home. And for many years following the abuse, she could not accept the fact that she was also a predator who had joined with another to sexually abuse her children.

Now that you have met Anne, the high school English teacher, Melanie, Janice, Belinda, and Charlene, you are in a better position to acknowledge the existence of female predators. You can see how their patterns of abuse parallel those of male offenders; and although some female offenders are more likely to disguise their abuse through a "caring or loving relationship," they, like their male counterparts, are merely rationalizing their offensive behaviors. And like male predators, female offenders will leave warning signs of their intentions before the abuse occurs. If you can identify these "red flags," you will be in a much better position to protect your children from female predators.

To understand the deleterious effects that female sexual abuse can have, keep in mind the female predators and their victims you have met in this chapter. Recall Tina's wise decision to curtail her son Daniel's activities with Anne well before anything harmful could take place. Learn through the pain and suffering of adolescent victims, such as Tyler and Sean, that women who engage in sexual relationships with minors are sexual predators, and use this knowledge to protect your adolescent from abuse.

It is acceptable for adults to take an interest in children; but if their attention to your child excludes other adults in your child's life and isolates your child from his or her parents and peers, then it is not a healthy interaction. Teach your children that women, as well as men, can harm them. Male predators are most often depicted in children's books and in the media as dangerous, and therefore a child may be more easily lured by a female predator because he or she was unaware that females are capable of harm. And remember that most sexual abuse occurs with someone the child already knows and not with a *stranger*. Therefore, it is important to teach a child to detect the same warning signs of inappropriate behaviors in both men and women, whether they are strangers or not.

Because society tends to view females as less threatening than men, women are likely to have greater access to your children. However, the same background checks and protective measures should be set in place when you leave your child with a female baby-sitter or allow your child to spend time with a female neighbor or relative. How much do you really know about the woman who is spending a great deal of time with your children? Does she single out one child from the rest? Does she favor that particular child with gifts and special attention?

More important, is your child able to talk openly about his or her relationship with an adult? If your child is keeping certain aspects of a relationship with an adult secret, this signals danger. Your child's relationships with adults should be completely accessible to you, including teachers, religious leaders, counselors, friends, and relatives. Never assume that a "secret" relationship with any adult is healthy for your child, and be assertive in your right to know about the details of your child's connections with others. If a female predator is aware that a parent will demand full access to her relationship with a child, that child will be less likely to become her next victim. Remember that predators choose their victims carefully, and a child who has no secrets from his or her parents will not be as vulnerable to abuse.

An adult female, whether it be a friend, neighbor, or relative, should never spend so much time with a child that it prevents that child from engaging with his or her family and with peers. Also, a female who is spending an inordinate amount of time with a child to the exclusion of her own friends and family is sending a warning sign. Even though women are taught to function as caretakers and nurturers, their interest in children should be balanced by their own interactions with adults.

A troubled adolescent may find a sympathetic ear through a kindly female neighbor or the mother of a best friend, yet his or her relationship with this adult should never encourage alienation from his or her own parents. Aligning with the adolescent against a parent can be a dangerous ploy by a predator to isolate the victim and establish a special relationship with him or her.

Melanie, the psychiatric nurse you met earlier in this chapter, seduced Sean by encouraging his anger and alienation from his parents and the rest of the staff. Although it may have been difficult for Sean's parents to monitor their son at the psychiatric facility, particularly since he was placed in isolation, it was up to the hospital staff to protect their patients. No one adult should assume total care for a child, particularly in the case where a child is utterly dependent on adults, as in the case of a psychiatric placement. In these situations it is critical that more than one adult assume responsibility. Therefore it is crucial that you carefully evaluate those situations in which your child will be alone with an adult. How well do you know the adult who will be alone with your child? And even if you feel that you are familiar with this person, will your child be totally dependent on him or her for a specified period of time? If so, realize that your child will be highly vulnerable to this person. Situations in which an adult and your child will be isolated from others, such as camping trips, hiking excursions, and other sporting activities such as sailing or cross-country skiing should be carefully examined.

Monitoring your adolescent's activities at school may be difficult, particularly if you feel uneasy about approaching school personnel. However, if healthy communication exists between parents and children, there is less likelihood that your child will be seduced into a secretive relationship with a teacher, counselor, or a coach. Listen as your children talk about their teachers. Crushes on teachers are common, especially with adolescents, but does your child's focus appear to be too fixed on one teacher? Do you know this teacher, and do the teacher and your child share their relationship with you? A warning sign of potential abuse is a professional who insists on privacy with a young person. Special activities that involve only a female teacher, counselor, or an adult friend and a child should be discouraged unless parents feel completely at ease with the situation. In the case of Anne and Daniel, a more comfortable scenario would have been one in which Anne invited Daniel's mother and sister to join them on the boat.

Now that you are fully acquainted with the characteristics, style, and behavioral patterns of both male and female adult predators, it is time to meet the adolescent who sexually abuses other children. These young offenders raise many difficult issues that need to be understood in order to avoid their abusive behaviors. In the next chapter, you will learn what problems are inherent in the classification, detection, rehabilitation, and prevention of adolescent sexual offenders.

Sexually Abusive Youth

hoosing a title for this chapter became a controversial issue. I discovered a vast difference in how professionals referred to youth who had sexually assaulted other children. Some of them likened these youth to "sexual predators," others labeled them as "young offenders," while some voiced an appeal that they be referred to as "sexually abusive youth." I realized that the discrepancy in the terms reflected the different attitudes and theories that professionals hold for children who commit sexual abuse.

Those who tend to view this population in the harshest light are often parole officers, prosecuting attorneys, and law-enforcement personnel. After years of watching young offenders parade repeatedly in and out of the legal system, they have come to believe that some of these children demonstrate similar behavioral patterns and personality characteristics as adult sexual predators.

On the other hand, a considerable number of the treatment providers, who tend to have a more "humanistic" perspective on juvenile crime, preferred to call their clients "juvenile sex offenders." This term recognizes the severity of the crime, but lightens the emphasis placed on the enduring personality characteristics that define adult sexual predators.

The least pejorative term, *sexually abusive youth*, was the one that I eventually chose as a title for this chapter. It is a description used by providers who have come to believe that not all young sex offenders demonstrate the fixed patterns found in their adult counterparts. This term also takes into consideration the proportion of young people who should not be classified as juvenile sex offenders. For in some cases, youth sexually offend against other children because of curiosity, experimentation, or peer influence. For these young people, a label of juvenile sexual offender may be too harsh.

The different terms that are used for young people who sexually abuse other children not only reflect professionals' attitudes toward this population, they have a great deal of bearing on the juvenile's prognosis. Gail Ryan, the director of the Perpetration Prevention Program at the Kempe Children's Center in Denver, Colorado, discusses the problems that can occur as a result of labeling a young person a "sexual offender." According to Ms. Ryan, the terms *juvenile sexual offender* and *juvenile sexual predator* may not be appropriate labels for sexually abusive youth. She notes that many of these youth have not established the patterns of sexual abuse found in adult sexual offenders.

An individual's sexual identity continues to take shape throughout the often turbulent years of adolescence. Most adolescents tend to be aroused by a wide variety of stimuli and have not yet internalized any one particular type of sexual behavior. Therefore adolescents are likely to explore and engage in sexual experimentation. For an adolescent who chooses to enact sexually abusive behaviors with another child, labeling him or her a "sexual offender" could have disastrous, self-fulfilling consequences and may define who that child will be years later.

Yet the controversy over what term should be used to identify youth who sexually abuse children doesn't mask the sobering fact that their abusive acts pose a real danger to children. Statistics from the U.S. Department of Justice published in July of 2000 reveal that 23 percent of all sexual offenders are under the age of eighteen, and that the largest number of sex offenders in *any age* group, are fourteen year olds.

Adolescents are not the only group of juveniles who sexually abuse children. An astonishing percent of sexually abusive youth are young children. Statistics from the Department of Justice classify children as young as *seven years old* as sexual offenders, and their most recent report noted that 16 percent of all juvenile sex offenders are *under the age of twelve*.

Not only do the statistics speak of the concern for young children committing sexually abusive acts, they also illustrate this population's vulnerability to sexually abusive youth. The most recent report from the Department of Justice states that 39 percent of the victims of sexually abusive youth are between the ages of seven to eleven and 40 percent of their victims are *under the age of six*.

While these numbers may appear startling, it is important to realize that only in the past few decades have we begun to collect statistics on juvenile sex offenders. It is likely that children have been sexually abusive for many years prior to the systematic collection of research data. However, since we now have the numbers that support the seriousness of this behavior, sexually abusive youth may appear to us as a relatively new national crisis.

Most professionals recognize that young children who have been exposed to sexual abuse are at high risk for victimizing other children. A vast majority of sexually abusive youth have experienced some form of trauma. For this reason, children under the age of twelve who were sexual abuse victims themselves and are acting in sexually aggressive ways toward other children are often labeled "sexually intrusive" or "sexually reactive." While these labels certainly take into account the precursors that lead to young children's sexual acting out, they send a clear warning that these behaviors are not acceptable. Once again, the point must be made that while a majority of sexually abusive children have themselves been victims, a majority of children who were abused *do not* reenact their victimization on others.

As alarming as these statistics may seem, they may, in actuality, be a low estimate of the true number of child offenders and child victims. Kim English, director of Research and Statistics for the Colorado Division of Criminal Justice, has conducted numerous studies of adult sexual offenders. Through disclosures from adult sexual offenders and adult victims about their experiences as children, she has come to believe that sexual crimes by children have been vastly underreported. In some cases, adults recalled that when they did report the crime, they were believed to be too young to testify, and therefore it was dismissed. In other instances, such as sibling abuse, adults recalled that as children they were too afraid to make an accusation against a family member.

Ms. English collects much of the research data through the use of polygraphs, or lie detector tests, which measure an individual's physiological responses to certain questions. During these examinations, adult offenders, anticipating their internal reactions to undisclosed offenses, may come forward with a multitude of confessions. A vast majority of these confessions involve a long history of undetected sexually abusive behaviors that began when the offender was quite young. As a result of these disclosures, Ms. English postulates that the number of children who sexually abuse other children, and the quantity of victims they have amassed, are far greater than what is reported by various government agencies. Through her department's research, she estimates that sexual offenders report fewer than 10 percent of their victims. She has also estimated through her collection of research data that 90 percent of victims under the age of twelve don't report sexual assault until much later in their lives, and that figure is even higher when the victim has been sexually assaulted by someone in the family.

LEGAL RAMIFICATIONS FOR SEXUALLY ABUSIVE YOUTH

Despite the different descriptors that professionals may use to mitigate the circumstances that lead to juvenile sex crimes, the judicial system often treats juvenile sex offenders in a similar fashion to adult sexual offenders. And because of this, the legal ramifications for sexually abusive youth can be quite severe.

Shana Cunnane is a parole officer for the Colorado Division of Youth Corrections and has a caseload of juveniles who are repeat sex offenders. She emphasizes that the legal consequences for children who are convicted for sexual assault are often harsh. In Colorado, where a child as young as ten can be tried and convicted for sex assault, it is feasible that this child could spend the rest of his or her childhood and adolescence on probation and in juvenile treatment programs.

Ms. Cunnane explains that sentences for these young offenders may involve incarceration in a juvenile facility or placement in a residential treatment center or a group home. In the case of sibling abuse, parents may be ordered to relinquish their parental rights over the juvenile to social services, who then place the child in a treatment facility or foster care.

Juveniles who are found guilty of sexual assault are sentenced to a two-year probationary period that may be extended if the juvenile breaks the conditions of the probation. Juvenile probation often involves similar mandates and constraints to those of adult probation. Convicted juvenile sex offenders are ordered to check in regularly with their probation officers. They are often mandated to take part in sex offender treatment, which often includes group, individual, and family therapy, and are submitted to regularly scheduled polygraph tests. Their terms of probation or the mandates of their treatment may include an order to inform landlords and employers of their status as convicted sexual offenders.

One of the most controversial issues that exists in regard to sexually abusive youth is the requirement that, in certain states, juveniles must list their names in the Sex Offender Registry. For example, in Colorado, children as young as ten are required to file their names with the local police department once they are convicted of a sexual assault, and their name will remain on the registry for some period of time, depending on the nature of their crime. One case in Colorado illustrated the dire consequences that can occur when a juvenile commits a sex offense. An eighteen-year-old boy who graduated with academic honors from high school faced a somber future. At the age of twelve he was sentenced as a sex offender, placed on probation, and was required to register his name and address with the local police department. For the next six years he received therapy; yet despite the fact that he never reoffended, this young man's name remained on the Sex Offender Registry and would stay there for fifteen more years, branding him a sex offender until he was thirty-three years old. This young man was likely to face obstacles when he applied for college, the military, or a job.

Not only do the consequences of juvenile sexually abusive behaviors last throughout childhood, they may remain with the offender for the rest of his or her life. In most cases of juvenile offenses, such as burglary, assault, and drug trafficking, their legal files are expunged or closed when the youth reaches adulthood. But in the case of a juvenile who has been charged with sexual abuse, their legal files *always* remain open and can be used as legal evidence against them for the *rest of their lives*. Most ten-year-old children can't comprehend the grave consequences of their sexually abusive behaviors, and this is what makes the situation so tragic, not only for the victims, but also for the child offenders.

This chapter will explore the characteristics of sexually abusive youth as well as the types of youth who commit these offenses. You will have the opportunity to meet a number of sexually abusive juveniles so that you can understand more about their personalities and the antecedents to their sexually abusive acts.

Baby-sitting may be a risky situation, especially for infants and toddlers, since it gives sexually abusive juveniles an opportunity to have unsupervised access to children. Unless you are fully aware of the risks involved and take the necessary steps to prevent abuse, your children may be placed in a dangerous situation whenever a baby-sitter comes to your home. Therefore, I have provided guidelines for safe baby-sitting to minimize the risk to your children.

GENERAL CHARACTERISTICS OF SEXUALLY ABUSIVE YOUTH

As in the case with adult sexual predators, sexually abusive youth can be found everywhere. They span the social spectrum from the popular gifted athlete to the social misfit and are just as likely to live in the lower-income housing of an inner city as in the upscale homes of suburbia.

Like their adult counterparts, they defy any attempt to place them into a certain religious or ethnic class. And to make matters worse, except for their sexually deviant behaviors, they are often indistinguishable from other adolescents. The majority of sexually abusive youth obtain average grades, are not mentally ill, and don't ordinarily engage in other delinquent behaviors. So how can they be distinguished from other juveniles who don't sexually victimize children?

Similar to the adult predators, certain characteristics can be found in youth who are sexually abusive. Yet unlike those used to describe their adult counterparts, these traits refer more to the juvenile's environment than to enduring personality traits. In this manner, the following characteristics can help us distinguish those circumstances that produce sexually abusive youth.

Children Who Act Out Sexually Are
Significantly More Likely to Have Been Sexually Abused

As noted in chapter 1, not every child sexual abuse victim preys on others. In fact, as you have learned, a majority of sexual abuse survivors do not sexually abuse others. However, when we look at those juveniles who do sexually abuse, we find that a majority of them *were* sexually abused. In fact, the younger the child offender, the higher the likelihood that he or she was abused. Statistics state that 72 percent of sexually abusive children under the age of six have been sexually abused.

Why is the tendency to sexually offend greater when a child has been a victim of sexual abuse? There are many explanations for this that run the gamut from conditional learning and role modeling to psychodynamic theories that examine the driving forces of unresolved conflicts. And, as is the case with most human behaviors, the explanation lies in a blend of these theories.

Conditional learning suggests that one of the most basic ways children learn behavior is through modeling their actions on those of others. For example, studies have shown that aggression is particularly susceptible to imitation, and that children who view an adult slapping a child will reenact the very same behavior on a doll, younger sibling, or a pet. Therefore, a natural consequence for a child who has been subjected to abuse, whether it be emotional, physical, or sexual, is to imitate the perpetrator's behaviors by abusing others smaller than themselves.

Social learning theories have illustrated an individual's inclination to identify with the aggressor, particularly if he or she has been a victim. Sexual abuse becomes a source of conflict for a child who has been rendered a helpless victim. Therefore, assuming the more powerful and controlling role of aggressor allows the child to conquer the fears and the overwhelming sense of helplessness that he or she experienced as a victim.

Theories that examine the powerful and volatile nature of sexual drive focus on the fact that sexual abuse is a terrible crime that floods a child with complicated, conflicting, and overwhelming feelings. For not only does sexual abuse destroy trust and self-integrity, it also can produce feelings of pleasure and stimulation. When young children are sexually abused, their "sexual thermostats" may be turned up prematurely, causing them to experience overwhelming and intense states of sexual arousal. And in this overstimulated state, these children are likely to engage in repetitive masturbation and sexual play with other children.

Sexually Abusive Youth Report a More Significant History of Family Dysfunction than Nonabusive Youth

Homes that are fraught with domestic violence, substance abuse, and emotional neglect are often breeding grounds for abusive youth. Adult offenders who see others as objects to meet their needs are likely to assume that their children are also available targets for them to discharge their sexual and aggressive drives. In this manner, not only do these children become victims, they may also learn to model the behaviors they observe in their homes and therefore interact with others in an aggressive, controlling, and hostile manner.

Many sexually abusive youth have also experienced parental loss. Children who have experienced a parent's death are dealing with significant emotional turmoil that may disrupt ordinary patterns of behavior. Acrimonious divorces that result in parent alienation or an abandonment of an estranged parent also produce significant conflicts in children that may be manifested in aggressive acting out.

Families in which parents neglect the emotional needs of their children also foster the tendency for aggressive behaviors. In families where parents may not have the time or resources to provide adequate supervision, children may be left on their own to resolve those conflicts that necessitate adult involvement. Lonely children, who receive little adult attention, are also likely to turn to each other to have their emotional needs met; and in this context sexual behaviors between siblings may result.

Case studies from professionals who treat juvenile sex offenders illustrate a compelling correlation between juvenile sex abusers and substance abuse in the family. Parents who abuse alcohol or drugs are certainly less available to their children. Drugs and alcohol cloud judgments, distort perceptions, and impair the decision making necessary to provide a safe and structured environment for children.

TYPES OF SEXUALLY ABUSIVE YOUTH

Not all sexually abusive youth are the same. Motives and patterns of sexually deviant behaviors differ considerably in this population. Therefore, it is critical that in evaluating sexually abusive youth and in planning appropriate treatment, they be categorized into different groups.

One of the most comprehensive distinctions among sexually abusive youth comes from two professionals who have worked extensively with juvenile sex offenders, Michael O'Brien and Walter Bera. They developed a classification system that placed young offenders into seven different groups depending on their personalities, family characteristics, patterns of sexual behaviors, and the number of victims they'd abused.

Naive Experimenters

These youth usually don't have a history of other behavioral problems and often come from relatively healthy families. They have few victims, and their sexual acts are driven mainly by curiosity. They may use little force, coercion, or planning; rather, they are likely to be presented with a situation that offers them the opportunity to engage in sexually abusive behaviors. Their sexual acts are often driven by exposure to sexually arousing stimuli, such as pornography, that peak their curiosity and drive them to experimentation. These youth are least likely to reoffend once they receive some basic intervention.

Undersocialized

These juveniles are isolated and socially inadequate, and they gravitate toward children to fulfill their needs for acceptance, attention, and recognition. These abusers will often have many victims and may use force, coercion, manipulation, and threats to gain compliance from victims. It may be hard to detect this type of abuser since he or she may not display other acting-out behaviors, such as truancy, substance abuse, or theft. However, they are likely to manifest low self-esteem, have below-average grades, come from unstable family environments, and have few age-appropriate friends or relationships with the opposite sex.

Pseudosocialized

These youth are most like the adult narcissistic predator you met in chapter 3. At first, they appear charming, intelligent, and confident, but prolonged contact with them will reveal more undesirable traits, such as untruthfulness, manipulation, arrogance, and imperviousness to others' feelings.

Because they are superficially charming, these juveniles find it quite easy to win the confidence of adults and therefore gain access to their victims. They are likely to use alcohol or drugs. They exploit others and will use other children as objects from whom they can derive gratification. They often have multiple victims and are likely to argue that their sexual contact with children was consensual. They have a high need for arousal and stimulation and a low tolerance for frustration. Therefore, sexually deviant behaviors are a way to raise their level of stimulation and, at the same time, provide them with temporary relief from tension.

Sexually Aggressive

Sexually aggressive offenders often come from dysfunctional families and display a number of sexual and nonsexual behavior problems. They have a history of acting out in socially inappropriate ways, such as lying, stealing, drug abuse, and truancy. They display poor impulse control and have significant problems with authority. These abusers will tend to use force, trickery, bribery, and threats to gain control over other children and will feel very little sympathy for their victims' plight. They are also likely to link up aggression with sexuality, and the use of violence can become sexually arousing. They are just as likely to sexually act out with younger children as with their same-age peers. "Date rapes" are more common among sexually aggressive youth than with the other types.

Sexually Compulsive

These young people engage in sexually arousing behaviors in a compulsive manner. They will plan out the offenses with the goal of achieving sexual gratification, and their behaviors are likely to become increasingly ritualized. They may engage in repetitive abusive behaviors that do not require direct physical contact with their victims, such as peeping, obscene phone calling, or exhibitionism. Their abusive acts are also likely to include touching sleeping victims or rubbing against others. These youth may have a vast collection of pornography or spend an inordinate amount of time on Internet pornographic sites. They often come from highly enmeshed families in which perfectionism and emotional constraint are valued.

Disturbed Impulsive

Disturbed impulsive youth have significant problems inhibiting their impulses. They may suffer from severe forms of mental illness that cause them to have disordered thoughts that lead to sexual acting out, or they may be intellectually impaired, which can also result in a lack of inhibition and increased impulsiveness. Impulse problems may also arise from other organic problems, like brain injury. At times, brain-injured youth may express severely aggressive and sexual acting-out behaviors with little external provocation. And last, problems with impulse control may also derive from medical complications from certain drugs, such as steroids. Consider the high school athlete who, in order to enlarge his body, took over-the-counter steroids and experienced a dramatic increase in aggressive and sexual behaviors.

For the most part, disturbed impulsive youth are often isolated and withdrawn from social contact with their peers since their peculiar habits and behaviors may appear offensive and strange. Therefore, this sexually abusive youth is often easier to detect than other types.

Group Influenced

These juveniles are driven by a desire for peer approval. They are likely to use poor judgment and are easily influenced by others. In order to win the acceptance of their friends, they will imitate others' behaviors despite their own sense of right and wrong. They usually have other behavioral problems that stem from poor judgment, particularly when they are in the presence of their peers. They tend to use drugs and alcohol on an experimental basis, and once again this is based on peer acceptance. These offenders, like the naive experimenter, are less likely to reoffend if they participate in treatment.

FOUR EXAMPLES OF SEXUALLY ABUSIVE YOUTH

You are about to meet four different types of sexually abusive youth. As you are exposed to their behavior, attitudes, and the thoughts that lead them to sexually abuse another young person, keep in mind the adult sexual predators you have already been exposed to in chapter 3. Remember that most of the adult sex offenders you met in the previous chapters began to sexually abuse children when they, themselves, were young. Some of the youth that you arc about to meet already display characteristics of certain adult sex offenders and may tragically live out their lives as sexual predators. You will meet Aaron and Blake, who began molesting children when they were quite young and have already amassed a substantial number of victims. They have a high probability of reoffending because they already display the pattern of sexual deviance that, as we have seen, is so difficult to break. You will meet Julie and Bobby, who, with the proper intervention, on the other side of the spectrum are likely never to sexually offend again.

Aaron: The Undersocialized Sexually Abusive Youth

Aaron is a slightly built, fair-haired boy. At thirteen, barely out of his own childhood, he was convicted in juvenile court for sexual offenses against twenty young children. At the time of his arrest, he was living with his elderly grandmother in a small home just outside the city limits of Chicago.

Aaron's father had abandoned the family when the boy was an infant, and for the next ten years Aaron and his mother shared a room in his grandmother's home. Aaron rarely saw his mother, who worked late-night shifts at a restaurant. By the time Aaron was in the first grade, he would awake next to his mother's sleeping body, still clad in her uniform, and get himself ready for school.

But there were occasions when his mother would bring home a male companion. Aaron would be awakened by the tinny sound of his mother's laughter mixed with the deep resonance of a stranger's voice. He would pretend to be asleep as a man with a sour smell would carry him to the living room and place him facedown on the couch. Aaron would lie awake well into the night listening to the strange sounds that emanated from the bedroom where he and his mother had slept just the night before.

Aaron never talked about those nights. The fear and shame that had eventually accompanied him to sleep were gone the next morning. But what remained was a foglike feeling that clogged his head, watered his eyes, and made his feet feel heavy.

Two years later, without any warning, Aaron's mother ran away. His grandmother told him that his mother had left with a man she had met at a bar and that she would never be coming back. His mother's name was never mentioned after that, and Aaron continued his life much as it was before she left. His grandmother was kind, but she was too old and tired to pay much attention to a little boy. In time she became just another lonely fixture in the old home that was filled with musty reminders of a family that had rotted away.

It was at the end of the fourth grade, a few months after his mother had left, that Aaron sexually molested his first child. His victim was a six-year-old boy who was a younger version of the forlorn and discarded Aaron. Their "special games," as Aaron referred to the abuse, took place behind the oak tree on the far side of a grassy playground. Aaron learned to entice other young children into sexual abuse by offering them special rewards of candy, comic books, and trading cards.

Aaron experienced little guilt. Rather, he relished these "friendships" since they offered him the opportunity to gain control and mastery over a world that had once made him feel so insignificant. The sexual gratification he derived from his abusive behaviors was only one of the many benefits he derived from the subjugation of those less powerful.

It wasn't long before Aaron moved on to other children. He found them in the schoolyards, in the playgrounds, and in his own neighborhood. He became adept at detecting those children he could easily control and intimidate; and as the years progressed, so did his mastery of seduction and abuse.

Aaron stumbled out of elementary school into junior high with weak academic skills and even poorer social abilities. He was ragged-looking and sullen, and he spent an inordinate amount of time skipping classes and avoiding academic responsibilities. Aaron was a below-average student who slipped unnoticed into the spaces between the seats and among the throngs of giddy adolescents who paraded up and down the halls.

When the final bell rang, Aaron would don his ragged jean jacket, and with his wan face exposed to the graying cold of the city, walk home. In the relative obscurity of his living room, he would sip on a can of soda and devour a bowl of cold cereal. After a short respite in front of the afternoon cartoons, he would get up from the couch and wander out the front door.

Aaron preyed on the unsupervised children who roamed the streets. He had detected potential victims in the four brothers, ranging in age from five to eleven, who had recently moved into the neighborhood. Like him, they had nothing better to do after school than to spend the afternoons unsupervised, watching television and eating junk food. The eldest boy, who effectively tuned out his brothers with the constant beat of rap music and video games, was impervious to Aaron's sinister maneuvers.

Sometimes Aaron would take one of the younger boys to his home on the pretense of playing a new video game. Aaron's ammunition had been assembled well before his victims ever set foot in his bedroom. He had carefully scattered several pornographic magazines on his dresser. Each one of the boys, when they discovered the pornography, would become sexually aroused, and it wouldn't take long for Aaron to coerce the child into sexual activity. It was in this manner that all three younger brothers were abused.

The sexual abuse went on for months until the boys' mother discovered her youngest son performing oral sex on one of his brothers. After being extensively questioned, the boys finally confessed that Aaron was sexually abusing them. After their mother called the police, Aaron was arrested, taken out of his home, and placed in the custody of social services.

Aaron is currently living in a foster home and attending a special treatment program for adolescent offenders. In his out-of-home placement, he is receiving a great deal more supervision and care than he ever had before. He has been placed in a special education program where he is receiving remedial help in reading. Yet even though the external realities of his life have improved, Aaron continues to be plagued with confusing feelings. He is angry with his mother for leaving him lost and lonely in a world where he can find no refuge. He has been prescribed an antidepressant medication that helps lighten his dark moods, but he still prefers to be alone in his room, sullen and withdrawn from a world that has so sorely disappointed him.

Julie: The Naive Experimenter

Julie was twelve when she was arrested on charges of fondling a two-year-old boy. When she was first questioned, she adamantly denied the allegations, and her parents stood steadfastly beside her. However, following a series of interviews with social workers, detectives, and a psychologist, Julie broke down and confessed. She wept tears of shame as she detailed her sexually abusive behaviors with the little boy for whom she baby-sat.

When asked about her motives, Julie was unable to explain why she had committed the abuse except to say that she was curious and that she didn't think it would do any harm to the child. Julie swore that this was the first time she had ever inappropriately touched a child.

Julie had begun puberty when she was only ten years old. Throughout the later years of elementary school, she struggled with a developed body that was at odds with the tiny, compact physiques of her friends. Yet despite her precocious development, Julie's kind and gentle personality gained her acceptance among her peers. She did well in school, had many friends, and was active in sports.

Julie loved younger children and hoped someday to be a teacher. When she was twelve she volunteered as a junior counselor at a local summer camp, and just last spring she completed a baby-sitting course and already had a few jobs lined up for the fall.

But that summer something happened to young Julie that pierced her innocence and sharply catapulted her sexuality to a new level. A handsome lifeguard had been hired to attend the outdoor pool. All of the young girls took notice of the bleached-blond hair that hung carelessly over his tanned forehead and his lean body as it effortlessly turned cartwheels off the diving board. What made the lifeguard even more attractive to the preteen girls was his status as an "older teenager." One remaining year of high school was all that stood between him and adulthood.

To Julie's amazement he began to focus his attention on her. His bright smile mesmerized her, and the fact that he openly flirted with her made her giddy with delight. Eventually he asked for her phone number; and during clandestine late night calls, he became forthright in expressing his attraction to her. He complimented her on her maturity and told her how exceptionally pretty she was. His desire for Julie made her body respond in an exciting way.

The sexual charge between them exploded one afternoon in

late August after Julie agreed to meet her admirer behind the recreation center. Pressed up against the cement blocks of the building, Julie allowed him to take her into his arms. She was nervous when he lifted her chin for a kiss. But she liked the feel of his lips on hers and even allowed him to push his tongue into her mouth. Julie experienced sensations she had never felt before, and she allowed him to press his body close to hers. In a matter of seconds, Julie felt his hands on her breasts. It was then that she became awash with fear and embarrassment. Pushing him away, she ran into the center, quickly dressed, and went home.

After that Julie stopped going to the center and spent the remaining two weeks of summer preparing for school. The lifeguard tried to phone her a number of times, but she always let the answering machine pick up so she wouldn't have to talk to him. Every time she heard his voice, a tingling sensation of fear and excitement would course through her body, and she would allow herself once again to relive the daring details of their encounter. After a while his calls ceased, and Julie sadly wondered if he had forgotten her.

Julie entered seventh grade preoccupied with what had happened that summer. She wondered if any of her classmates had had a similar experience, but she was too ashamed to talk about it. She was also afraid to confide in her mother. The previous year her mother had cautioned her about the effect her body would have on boys, and that she should be especially careful not to let them touch her. At the time Julie wondered why her mother was warning her since she was not even interested in boys. But now that she had actually kissed a boy and let him touch her, she knew her mother would be disappointed.

Left on her own to struggle with intense feelings of sexual arousal, Julie began to stimulate herself at night, which only intensified her sense of shame and guilt.

That fall Julie had been offered a job baby-sitting Jordan, a darling two-year-old boy who lived down the street. His parents had hired Julie for four hours each Saturday afternoon to watch their son while they went on errands and worked out in the gym.

One Saturday, as Julie was changing Jordan's diapers, the sight of his genitals unexpectedly aroused her. She decided to touch and kiss his penis to see what it would feel like. Immediately following this, Julie was filled with guilt.

She quickly diapered him and carried him into the kitchen. As she fed Jordan ice cream, she watched him closely for any reactions to what she had just done. Jordan smiled and laughed at her in much the same way as he had before, and she assumed that he was unaware of what had just happened. She rationalized that he was too young to understand her actions, and, therefore, he would forget all about it. She promised herself that she would never do anything like that again.

Julie kept her promise. She made up for her "act of indiscretion" by showering Jordan with attention and love. She stopped masturbating and focused her energy on her studies. Julie believed the incident was behind her.

A few weeks after the sexual fondling, as Jordan's mother was bathing him, he looked up at her with billows of soapsuds piled on his hair and asked her to kiss his penis. His mother was shocked and asked where he'd learned that. He replied that Julie had kissed his penis. Jordan's mother conferred with Julie and her parents and Julie adamantly denied touching the child. Jordan's mother took him to the pediatrician, and Jordan told the doctor what Julie had done. Eventually the police were notified.

For the next six months, Julie will attend a special treatment program for adolescent sexual offenders. She is also on probation and must complete a number of hours of community service. She has been banned from baby-sitting and is prohibited from having any contact with younger children.

In treatment Julie is learning that her arousal to sexuality was normal, but her decision to molest a child was not. She is being given a great deal of information about sex that satisfied her curiosity and calmed her anxiety. In individual therapy she shared her secret liaison with the teenage lifeguard. Her therapist made her feel less shameful about the incident and helped her realize that, although her body may have developed, emotionally she had not been ready for a sexual encounter with an older boy. She came to understand that the contact with him had stimulated her and created feelings she was not ready to handle. Had she been able to talk to someone about her sexual feelings, she may not have chosen to act them out on a defenseless toddler.

Despite the counseling, Julie continues to struggle with feelings of guilt and self-recrimination. She has vowed to herself that she will never again hurt a little child. She hopes that in the future she can be free of the gnawing shame and the prohibitions that now restrict her from interacting freely with children.

Bobby: The Group-Influenced Sexually Abusive Youth

For the most part Bobby was a good kid. Despite the fact that he came from a divorced family, he was well-adjusted. He received above-average grades and participated in sports. Friends were very important to Bobby, and his easygoing manner kept him in synch with the popular group. He ran for student council and was class president in sixth grade. His teachers liked him, but on occasion he could become rambunctious, especially when he was around certain friends.

One particular friend, Theo, was a big boy who used his bulky frame to intimidate others. He came from a wealthy family, and he lorded this over his peers. He had forced his way into Bobby's crowd, and once there he remained a central figure. Bobby, like the others, was intimidated by him and sought to win his approval.

Bobby's crowd remained intact through the transition from elementary school into junior high. At their new school, Bobby and the boys quickly established their pecking order and became the most popular group. They maintained good academic and athletic standings and, for the most part, kept out of trouble.

Although Bobby was good-looking, he had not yet reached the height of many of the other seventh-grade boys, and this made him insecure. He was shy and awkward with girls, and this lowered his status among his peers. On the other hand, the boys envied Theo's bravado and size, which made him popular with the opposite sex.

Kelly, a pretty seventh grader, moved in and out of Bobby's crowd according to her relationship with Theo. Bobby had a secret crush on Kelly; and during those times when she was at odds with Theo, he would take the opportunity to comfort her. They became friends, yet Bobby was always hurt when she and Theo would inevitably "make up" and he would once again lose her attention.

The sexual assault occurred during a surprisingly warm spring that brought the seventh graders to a premature anticipation of summer. The students' rowdiness escalated, and Bobby and his crowd were at the center.

One day, after a week of fighting between Kelly and Theo, Bobby and his peers had gathered on the top landing of the second floor preparing to go to lunch. Kelly found herself caught in the cross fire of the students who were rushing up to their next class, and those who were racing down to the cafeteria. She backed herself into a corner as Theo and the boys marched down. The bell sounded loudly, and, in a moment, the halls were swept clean of everyone except for the small group of adolescents who had gathered in the stairwell.

As Theo angrily confronted Kelly, the boys pushed in closer to watch the action. Kelly looked frightened, and this gave Theo the edge. The excitement in the air was palpable as the boys began to take part in the verbal assault. At first Bobby stood back, overwhelmed by what was happening, but the combustible power of the aggression and sexual arousal he was experiencing drew him closer toward Kelly. The transition from verbal to sexual abuse was so quick that, when later questioned, the boys weren't able to pinpoint just when it began.

Bobby, however, did remember. He told the detectives that after a few rounds of shouting, which had resulted in Kelly slapping Theo on the face, Theo had retaliated by exposing his genitals to Kelly and ordering her to perform oral sex. The boys, including Bobby, encouraged him with shouts and inappropriate sexual remarks. Bobby was among the boys as they pressed themselves nearer to their victim, thereby pinning Kelly up against the wall.

Fortunately for Kelly, a security officer had heard the commotion and came to her rescue, but not before a great deal of emotional damage had been inflicted. Kelly was traumatized by the event and moved to another school. The boys were suspended and were charged with sexual harassment. Theo received the harshest consequences. However, all the boys were ordered into treatment, placed on probation, and had to complete many hours of community service.

Bobby's life changed significantly after this incident. He was mortified by his actions and felt tremendous guilt for betraying Kelly. He admitted that he knew what he had done was very wrong, but he does not know how things got so out of control. Since the boys were prohibited from spending time with one another, Bobby was compelled to find a new peer group. He mourned the loss of his old friendships and found it difficult to associate with other students.

Bobby has had a difficult time in therapy. He feels embarrassed during group sessions, for his presence among the other juvenile offenders is a constant reminder of his own shameful behaviors. It has taken him awhile to believe that he is not so different from the other juveniles who sit beside him for, like them, he had made a decision to act out in a sexual manner that victimized another human being.

Even though there is a restraining order in place that mandates the boys not to have contact with Kelly, Bobby continues to miss her. He hopes that someday he will be able to see her in person and tell her just how sorry he is.

Blake: A Sexually Aggressive Youth

Blake was adopted when he was an infant, and two years later his mother gave birth to a baby girl. Blake is almost sixteen years old now and has been in a group home for the past two and a half years, following the sexual abuse of his sister and at least fifteen other children.

Blake is a heavy-set boy who seems rather impervious to his surroundings. Wherever he goes, he lumbers around with a set of headphones that continuously blare out angry messages to heavy metal beats.

His family consists of his father, a middle manager in a large corporation, his mother, who works as an interior decorator, and his younger sister. They continue to live in the upscale suburban Tudor outside of Cleveland that Blake once called home. Blake never wants to return to his family, and he doesn't claim to miss them. In fact he talks about them with open disdain. When asked

why he sexually abused his sister and the other children, he replies in a matter-of-fact manner, "I did it for my own pleasure
and to get back at my parents . . . and maybe also for power and
control."

Blake's anger is so tangible that it drifts about him like a fetid
cloud of smoke. He presents a litany of accusations against his
parents that reflects years of hostility and resentment. He argues
that he has never been in control of his life, and he resents the
fact that his parents "were control freaks and ran my life like I
was in a military camp."

By the tender age of ten, Blake was already notorious for his
bad behavior at school. He hated authority, and he was so defiant
and out of control at home and at school that he was placed in
a psychiatric hospital for an evaluation. Undeterred by the medications he was given for the diagnosis of attention deficit and
bipolar mood disorder, he continued his reign of defiance.

Blake has no memory of sexual abuse when he was a child;
however, he does recall being sexually aroused by girls when he
was quite young. He admits to being miserably unhappy as a child
and, at times, contemplating suicide. He began smoking mari-
juana when he was eleven, and he consistently shoplifted from
stores and stole money from his parents.

Despite Blake's behavior problems, when he was only eleven
years old his parents decided to leave him in charge of his
younger sister. He openly resented this, and he began to physically
abuse her. Even though he was punished, Blake was so resistant
to authority that his parents' admonishments only incited him to
further rage against his sister.

Blake was chillingly detailed in his description of how he
groomed his sister for the sexual abuse. By alternating verbal
threats and physical violence with bribes and offerings of candy
and toys, he kept her confused, distraught, and under his control.
Eventually the time was right, and Blake began the sexual molestation of his younger sister. This continued for almost two years
before Blake was finally caught.

Unfortunately, in those two years, Blake had already amassed
a number of other child victims, including relatives, neighbors,
and his sister's friends. One night, while his sister's best friend

was spending the weekend at the house, Blake took her into his room. Explaining to her that what they were about to do was a special game that he played with his sister, he violated this ten-year-old child in much the same way as he had been doing to other children over the past two years.

But this little girl was different because, despite Blake's threats, she went home that Sunday and immediately told her parents. When the sordid details of Blake's reign of terror on his sister and other children were revealed, Blake was immediately removed from the home and placed in residential treatment.

Blake is at high risk for reoffending. Although he is superficially compliant with his treatment, he shows little remorse for the pain and anguish he has caused his sister and his other victims. Instead, he continues to focus on his own misery and wraps a blanket of anger so tightly around himself that it is impossible for anyone to gain access to his thoughts.

The therapists are aware that Blake suffers from an attachment disorder that has disabled his ability to bond with others. The normal process of attachment that should have occurred in the infancy of his life was severely disrupted. Because of the early abandonment of his biological mother and his relatively short-term placement with impervious foster parents, Blake was never given the opportunity to bond with another human being. By the time he was placed with his adoptive family, an inner sense of emptiness had been formed that only anger and frustration could fill. Blake will need to be consistently supervised throughout the remaining years of his adolescence, and it is highly questionable whether he will ever be able to develop the sufficient empathy with and attachment to, others that will mitigate his antisocial impulses.

Although the four adolescents you have just met are very different from one another, it is feasible that they could attend the same sexual offender treatment program and be subject to similar restrictions and treatment mandates for their commonality lies in that fact that they each made a decision to act out in sexually deviant ways.

In all of the above situations, the youth did not have the proper support or open communication with their parents that might have prevented their sexually abusive acts. They were left unsupervised to act out sexually deviant behaviors on innocent children. And all of this could been prevented if they had had the opportunity to share their feelings with a sympathetic adult, been closely supervised, and evaluated as at risk for harming other children well before any damage had been done.

SAFE BABY-SITTING

What you are about to learn concerning the risks involved with baby-sitters may shock you and cause you to more closely examine your decisions about who should take care of your children.

The most recent report from the Bureau of Justice Statistics regarding sexual assault revealed that 77 percent of all child sexual abuse committed by juveniles occurred in the victim's home. Further, children under the age of six are most likely to be sexually assaulted in their home by a juvenile. When you couple these statistics with the fact that juveniles commit approximately 40 percent of all sex offenses against children, hiring an adolescent to take care of your children is risky.

Very young children are the most vulnerable population for sexual abuse since the largest percent of sexual assault committed by juvenile offenders is with children below the age of six. Infants, in particular, are most defenseless against sexual abuse because of their total dependence on others and the fact that they cannot tell you in words what has occurred; therefore some professionals advocate that infants never be left in the care of a baby-sitter.

An adolescent who wishes to engage in sexual experimentation may assume that fondling an infant will do no harm because the infant will not remember what has happened. However this is not true. Infants can be traumatized, and they will manifest this through observable changes in their behaviors. Listlessness, prolonged crying, inability to be soothed, a refusal to drink or eat, and a lack of eye contact are classic symptoms of infant trauma.

Although infants cannot verbalize what has happened to them, they are still able to store memories. Memories that are created before language develops are experienced as physical sensations. Often called *body memories*, these early trauma memories are likely to resurface throughout an individual's life. Feelings that can't be explained in words and seem to arise "out of nowhere" can seem strange and frightening. Yet these sensations that have no verbal correlates may be our earliest memories. An uncomfortable tingling in the stomach, a paralyzing restriction of the throat, or a feeling of being smothered by a looming object are just some examples of body sensations that may signify early trauma.

When you consider the statistics that reflect a young child's vulnerability to sexual assault by an adolescent, hiring a baby-sitter may appear to be too risky. Yet the reality of the modern-day family, where both parents work and juggle busy schedules, often necessitates the use of a baby-sitter. So how can parents set up baby-sitting situations that will ensure the safety of their children?

Keep in mind that sexual predators are counting on parents to misinterpret a child's refusal to be left in their care. They will seek out those situations in which they can abuse a child without being caught. Therefore, if a child says that he or she does not like a particular baby-sitter, a parent should always listen. Assuming that your child just doesn't want to be left in the care of others because he or she misses you is not always accurate. Your child may be sad that you are leaving, but this should always be distinguished from negative feelings that are directed at the baby-sitter.

Setting up a safe situation when an adolescent baby-sitter is hired to watch children is crucial and is the sole responsibility of the parents. Parents should always be in complete control of the baby-sitting experience, and this control begins long before the baby-sitter is ever left alone with the children. The process that parents must go through to ensure the safety of their children while in a baby-sitter's care may seem extensive and too burdensome; however, when you consider the risks involved to your children, it becomes an important step in preventing child sexual abuse.

Step One: The Decision to Hire a Baby-Sitter

The *age* of a child is an important factor in the decision to hire a baby-sitter. As we have seen, infants are extremely vulnerable to sexual abuse, and it is almost impossible, unless there are physical injuries, to interpret the infant's change in eating, sleeping, or emotional patterns as evidence of sexual abuse. For this reason certain mental health professionals advocate that a baby-sitter not be hired until the child can directly communicate experiences through words, can identify dangerous situations, and is able to protect the privacy of his or her body. However, this may be too restrictive for those parents who have no other option but to hire a baby-sitter for their very young children. Therefore, if parents can arrange the situation to minimize the risks to their children by following the essential steps that are outlined in this section, hiring an adolescent baby-sitter before a child is four might be an acceptable option.

Another important factor is the baby-sitter's gender. While most parents tend to hire female baby-sitters, some may believe that an adolescent male would be a better choice, especially if they have sons. Parents may reason that their ten- and eleven-year-old boys would rather spend time with an older male who could take them to the park and play football. And while there are certainly many adolescent boys who are responsible, caring, and genuinely enjoy children, hiring a male baby-sitter may be considerably more risky than entrusting your children with a female baby-sitter.

Let's examine why this is the case. First and foremost, the majority of sexually abusive youth are males. While females do represent a formidable percentage of sexual abusers, they still fall far short of the preponderance of males who sexually abuse children. Therefore, hiring a male baby-sitter increases the chance of sexual abuse.

Another important aspect to consider is the developmental stage of the male adolescent. Adolescent boys are often at the height of their sexuality, and thus it is a major preoccupation for them. While they are grappling with intense physical needs, they may find that caring for a young child's physical needs, such as diapering, bathing, and changing clothes, is too stimulating. Adolescent males are also striving to meet societal expectations for masculine behaviors, and being a baby-sitter is not seen in our society as a typical role for a teenage boy.

For adolescent girls, on the other hand, who are channeling issues of sexuality through maternal identification and romantic relationships, baby-sitting allows them to express this maternal inclination. During this stage of her life, an adolescent girl is much more likely to obtain satisfaction from caring for children, and, therefore, finding a responsible female baby-sitter is encouraged, particularly if very young children are involved.

Another aspect of baby-sitting that warrants careful consideration is *where* the baby-sitting takes place. Some baby-sitters, such as women who have their own children, may prefer to have children come to their home; and while some of these situations are acceptable, others may not be safe environments for children.

Placing your child in an unfamiliar environment is definitely more risky because, in another person's home, there are unknown variables that a parent can't control. First and foremost, if you use out-of-the-home day care, it is important that it be licensed. While this is not by itself a guarantee of safety, it does indicate that the day care has been inspected and the provider has been given a list of requirements that he or she must follow in order to stay licensed. Often, a requirement of licensure as a day-care facility involves presenting the board with a report that the day-care provider, and anyone associated with the facility, has never been accused of sexual abuse. This report comes from the Central Registry for Child Abuse, which is *different* from the Sex Offender Registry. The former is a confidential record that is protected by social service agencies and law enforcement. It lists the names of those who have had allegations of sexual abuse made against them. While parents will not be able to access these records, they may ask the day-care provider to furnish a report that will state whether or not his or her name appears on this list.

Yet despite obtaining a license, there are certain considerations that parents must make before leaving their children in the home of a baby-sitter. Foremost, are there other children who may be present in the home? If there are older children who will be unsupervised with your child, then you should seriously evaluate this situation. An unfortunate number of children have been molested at a baby-sitter's home by an adolescent who had unsupervised access to children.

Once you have made the decision to hire a baby-sitter, finding an appropriate one requires a great deal of preparation and thought. It should be done with as much care as choosing a pediatrician, a dentist, or a preschool. Never allow an adolescent into your home to watch your children until you have successfully completed the following steps.

Step Two: Hiring a Baby-Sitter

Hiring a baby-sitter involves a number of important steps:

Get a recommendation from people you trust, such as family, friends, and neighbors. While these recommendations are important, you should never assume that your friends or neighbors have a complete understanding of the issues involved in sexual abuse. You must assume *full responsibility* for screening recommendations before you allow any of these recommended adolescents into your home.

Carefully check the references of a potential baby-sitter. You should always get a list of the sitter's past employers and other professionals who know the adolescent. Contact families who have used the baby-sitter and be prepared to ask them questions about the sitter's level of maturity, responsibility, and knowledge about children. Some teens have completed a Red Cross baby-sitting course, and a consultation with the instructor may shed light on the adolescent's level of responsibility. You can also check the Sex Offender Registry, which includes names of juvenile sex offenders, to ensure that the baby-sitter has not been formerly charged with child sexual assault.

Interview the prospective sitter in person. Initial impressions are critical for they often tell us a great deal about a person. How a teen dresses, the language she uses, and the manner in which she relates to you will tell you something about her. But don't make a hasty decision based on an initial impression. Remember that some sexually abusive youth can be deceivingly charming, and therefore it may be difficult to initially detect these individuals.

During the interview ask the prospective sitter why she wants to watch children. Is she interested in the money? Is she too young to be employed in jobs that mandate a minimum age? These reasons, as valid as they may appear, should not be the sole reason for baby-sitting. What is important is that the prospective sitter should voice satisfaction and real enjoyment from being with children.

Find out about the adolescent's interests, academic pursuits, and relationships with parents and siblings. Teens who come from healthy families will obviously be at less risk for deviant behaviors. Don't be afraid to ask a potential sitter if he or she has ever been in trouble with the law or about possible drug or alcohol use. Though you may not get an honest answer, it lets the sitter know that you are aware and concerned about these issues.

Last, ask questions that will give you a measure of the adolescent's maturity level. Pose some difficult problems that may arise in the course of baby-sitting and evaluate the sitter's answers. Do they reflect an adequate knowledge of child development, and are her problem-solving abilities developed sufficiently so that the sitter could handle a crisis?

Arrange to meet the parents of the potential sitter. A visit to the sitter's home can tell you something about the environment in which she was raised. A home that is organized and well taken care of is a positive sign. However, don't forget that sexual offenders come from every walk of life, so don't be lulled into thinking that a teen from a nice neighborhood is always a safe candidate. The parents of the baby-sitter should be willing to discuss their adolescent. They should be supportive of their child's desire to watch children and understand the responsibilities involved.

Don't automatically assume that if a teen has younger siblings she is qualified to watch your children. Remember that siblings can have abusive relationships with each other that may not be readily apparent. Asking the adolescent's parents about sibling interactions is another critical piece of information that will tell you what kind of relationship the sitter will establish with your child.

Plan for a time when the sitter can come over to your house while you and the children are home. This is an important prescreening measure that will tell you a great deal about the comfort level the sitter has with children and the quality of her interactions with them. Plan to do an activity that will require the sitter to cooperate and supervise the children, such as baking cookies, playing a board game, or doing an art project.

This is also a good time to allow the children and the sitter to be alone for a period of time while you move to another area of the house. This will provide an opportunity to assess your children's comfort level with the sitter. Remember to take seriously any concerns that your children have. Vague feelings of discomfort that are reflected in statements such as, "She's weird, I don't like her," may be important warning signs.

A final meeting should be set up with the prospective sitter so that you can explain the rules and expectations you have when she is caring for your children. If all of the above five steps have led to a decision that the adolescent is an appropriate choice for a baby-sitter, it is imperative that you arrange for a final meeting prior to the sitter being left alone with your children. During this meeting the rules of the house should be explained, as well as your expectations for her role as a baby-sitter. Do you expect the sitter to actively participate in the children's activities? Do you want her to help the children with their homework and read to them? Remember that the more you clearly outline your expectations with the sitter, the less likely she is to engage in activities that may not be in your child's best interest.

Be prepared to establish behavioral limits involving the physical care of your children. This includes bathing, toilet behaviors, and dressing. Except for the care of infants and young toddlers who are not toilet trained, a sitter should not be put in the situation where she has to bathe or dress children. Showers, baths, and changing clothes should be completed before the sitter arrives, or, if the children are old enough, done on their own.

Let the prospective sitter know that you value your children's need for privacy. You should tell her that your children have been taught how to protect themselves from inappropriate touching and that there are no secrets in your home. *The more you communicate to the prospective sitter your awareness and concerns for these issues, the less likely that sexual abuse will occur.*

You should also inform the sitter that you will be monitoring her behaviors and questioning your children about what went on during her stay. Let her know in advance that you are going to drop in unexpectedly to check on things. By periodically monitoring the situation, you are preventing the possibility that secret activities will take place.

While all of this may seem excessive, it will significantly lessen the chance that your child will become a victim of sexual abuse. As noted previously, predators are expert at detecting those children who are the most vulnerable to abuse. Therefore, if your children can identify sexually inappropriate behaviors, will not keep secrets, and know that you will be monitoring their activities, they will be less susceptible to a sexual predator.

N ow that you have learned what factors increase the likelihood of your child being sexually abused by a juvenile, and you have met a number of these sexually abusive youths, you are ready to evaluate the many situations that will place your child in close proximity to other children, such as baby-sitting. And most importantly, you can establish a home environment that will not tolerate child sexual abuse.

I n the next chapter we will turn our attention to one of the more devastating forms of juvenile sexual abuse, sibling abuse. Tragically, the availability of siblings makes them easy targets for sexually abusive youth; and as you will witness, the devastation that this form of abuse causes extends far beyond the boundaries of abuser and victim.

Sibling Abuse

Sibling sexual abuse is not a rare phenomenon. We are aware that in almost 90 percent of child sexual assault cases, the child knows and trusts the perpetrator. If you couple this with the fact that *availability* is the number-one factor that most consistently determines who will become a casualty of sex abuse, you will realize the potential for sexual abuse among siblings.

Sibling abuse is perhaps the most underreported form of child sexual abuse. According to certain research estimates only 2 percent of sibling abuse is ever reported to the authorities. Children are less likely to report sexual abuse if it happens within the family for the victim often feels ashamed, fearful, and conflicted about telling others that a sibling has been sexually abusive. The child may feel intimidated by the threats of an abusive sibling; and in some cases, the rewards that the child may receive, such as attention and gifts, may keep him or her in a conspiracy of silence. Children may also fear the consequences to the perpetrator if the abuse is reported, and their attachment to this family member may overshadow their own pain.

Sexual abuse by a sibling often causes more damage than abuse by a nonfamily member. Because children are dependent for years on their families, sibling abuse traps the victim in a cycle of shame and betrayal that can last a long time. Furthermore, the seriousness of the sexual abuse is often greater in those situations where the victim is continuously available to the abuser. The Vancouver/Richmond Incest & Sexual Abuse Centre cited studies on sibling abuse that demonstrated sibling offenders committed more serious acts of sexual abuse over a longer period of time on their siblings than those committed by other sexually abusive youth.

In our culture all forms of child sexual abuse are considered taboo. Yet the harshest judgments are handed down to those who have experienced sexual abuse within the family. Because sibling abuse threatens the very foundation upon which we build our ties to one another, victims of sibling abuse and their parents often suffer from undue criticism and social stigma.

This is especially true for the young victims of sibling sexual abuse, for they often suffer peer ridicule and ostracism when knowledge of their assault is made public. Since children are, themselves, grappling with sexuality, they may find it easier to attack a sexual abuse victim than to deal with their own unacceptable impulses. Classmates may hurl sexually pejorative terms, such as "whore" or "slut," at the victim to ensure their separateness from him or her. And tragically for these victims, their rocky road to healing becomes even more insurmountable.

Although sibling sexual abuse occurs in all types of families, a higher incidence is found in *blended* families, where stepsiblings are brought together to live under the same roof. Stepsiblings, since they are children of divorce, are likely to come into their new family with old wounds. These children are vulnerable to loss and abandonment, and creating a new family with stepparents and stepsiblings may initially intensify their sense of displacement. Children in a blended family may be in combat as they jockey for position in their new environment. If they are left without parents to act as the officers in charge, they may fight the battles on their own by taking the weaker stepsiblings as hostages.

A number of critical factors are present in blended families that could lead to sibling abuse. First, the natural bonding process that attaches siblings to a new baby in the family is usually not available to stepsiblings. Therefore, stepsiblings will not have the internal protective measures that are established between biological siblings that normally prohibit them from abusing each other. It takes time to establish the necessary attachments and bonding that will ensure that family members protect one another. Therefore, combining families in a hurried fashion is often a prescription for disaster.

In a blended family, stepsiblings may resent one another. Children in a new family are bound to vie for attention and feel indignant about a stepparent who seems to be taking the place of the missing parent, or a parent who seems to be spending an inordinate amount of time with the "new kids." In this atmosphere, it is not uncommon for children to express this resentment and jealousy through abusive behaviors with one another.

It is critical that when joining families, parents be aware of the potentially dangerous interactions between the stepsiblings and afford sufficient time and the opportunity for family members to establish bonds with one another. Parents should be willing to identify and intervene when they see unhealthy patterns of behavior developing among the stepsiblings. Initially the children will need a great deal of guidance, structure, and support in order to ensure healthy patterns of communication.

The disruption that sibling abuse creates, whether it takes place in an intact family or in a blended family, is devastating. Family members may spend the next few years trying to find a reason for the sexual abuse, and in this search they often get lost in an endless maze of self-recrimination and blame. The family members become estranged from one another as they drift away from the ambushed sanctity they once called their home.

However, the real tragedy in sibling sexual abuse is not in the number of victims it lays asunder—it is the sobering fact that it could have been prevented. Once parents understand the necessary precautions and the early warning signs of sibling abuse, they can prohibit it from occurring.

The blended family you are about to meet has experienced the cataclysmic force of sibling abuse. Despite the turmoil that was building between the stepchildren, the parents did not recognize this as an early warning sign of sibling abuse. They chose to keep their family intact without providing the necessary supervision and intervention that would have ensured the safety of their children. When they were finally forced to infiltrate the dangerous war zone that had once been their home, it was too late. The sexual abuse of one of their children had blown away the last bastion of safety and had left no survivors.

THE HILL FAMILY: A STORY OF
SIBLING SEXUAL ABUSE IN A BLENDED FAMILY

Marianne and Carson Hill and their two children, Amber and Troy, lived in a suburb of a large midwestern city. Ten and a half years ago, Marianne had met Carson, a single father who was raising his six-year-old son, Troy. Carson, who was widowed shortly after his wife gave birth to Troy, worked as an engineer in a large manufacturing plant. Marianne was a speech therapist and was raising Amber, her three-year-old daughter, on her own. Her ex-husband had had no contact with his daughter since he'd left the state when Amber was a little over a year old.

Marianne and Carson were delighted to meet one another. Well before they married, they spent hours planning a future that would ensure a life of comfort and security for themselves and their children. What they had not counted on was that, despite their best intentions, a troubled child would turn their dream into a nightmare. Troy responded with anger the moment Marianne and Carson brought their families together. He was defiant, prone to temper tantrums, openly hostile, and jealous of Marianne and Amber. Yet even though there was chaos and frustration when they were together, Marianne and Carson decided to marry and join their families under one roof. They sincerely believed that their love and their intact family would have a positive impact on Troy.

Amber, on the other hand, was responsive to Carson, easy to please, and quite manageable. She did complain about her unruly new stepbrother, and her mother's only response was to assure her that, in time, things would improve.

Family dynamics often focus on the most challenging member, and such was the case in the Hill household. Even though Amber was a delightfully easy child, most of the attention had to be directed toward Troy. His antics always demanded center stage.

In frustration, Marianne and Carson sought out a series of well-meaning professionals who diagnosed Troy with almost every disorder that is applicable to children. One year his defiance was interpreted as jealousy and difficulty bonding with Marianne, and family therapy was prescribed. Yet when his behavior worsened, he was sent for an evaluation to a clinic that labeled him with attention deficit disorder. This resulted in trials of Ritalin. The year he entered middle school he began fighting with peers, disobeying teachers, and falling behind in his reading. He was diagnosed with a learning disability and placed in special education classes.

In the following years, as Troy careened out of control, his parents were told that he had a bipolar disorder and needed mood-stabilizing medication. When the medication failed to subdue his increasingly aggressive behaviors, the professionals suggested residential treatment. However, the Hills were unwilling to remove their son from the home, and therefore they continued a round of trials with psychiatrists, play therapists, family counselors, and behavior specialists. The Hills even enrolled in parenting classes and sat patiently while therapists picked apart their own childhood histories as well as their marriage.

While this drama was unfolding, Amber was silently sitting behind the scenes. She was slowly withdrawing into a world of sullen resentment and anger. Maybe if she were good enough, her parents would notice her. But somehow that never happened. Acquiescent and well-behaved, little Amber never did receive the attention she desperately craved. Instead, she learned to seek out sustenance from her books and the imaginary world she created behind the closed doors of her room.

Amber's years of withdrawal resulted in her inability to communicate effectively with others. And because she had spent so many years being ignored, her parents did not hear her complaints or interpret her increasing withdrawal as warnings of mounting danger in their home.

Years later, following the arrest and removal of Troy from the home, the Hills would lament that they had not been able to decipher Amber's warnings. "She never really articulated her concerns about her brother," Mrs. Hill would argue. "She just said that she didn't like to be with him, but we could never get her to tell us what was wrong."

Yet if Amber's repeated statements that she disliked her brother were not sufficient to communicate danger, her behavior was a red flag that something was terribly amiss. Amber's isolation and withdrawal from the rest of the family spoke of a traumatized little girl who did not feel protected in her own home. Tragically, Mr. and Mrs. Hill were not able to decipher these messages in time to prevent the catastrophe that was slowly edging toward their daughter.

As the years progressed and the problems with Troy intensified, Amber's fear of her brother heightened. While the violence between the two had escalated to a dangerous level, Amber's attempts to tell her parents remained futile. They themselves were overwrought, and their emotional resources were so depleted that they continued to interpret Amber's complaints as a by-product of stepsibling rivalry.

By the age of twelve, Troy had become a master of manipulation. He began to feign acceptable behaviors that would distract others from seeing the deviant schemes he devised. Since his outward compliance improved measurably, his parents gloried in the prospect that maybe their errant son had finally come to his senses.

Unfortunately for Amber, the occasional allegations that she dared make about Troy were now met with disbelief and even scorn. Her teachers and parents admonished her for making up terrible stories about her brother, and slowly feelings of anger were added to her already traumatized existence.

As Amber moved into puberty, her brother's abuse took an even more dangerous turn. Troy began to groom his sister for sexual abuse. He had collected an assortment of pictures that graphically depicted deviant sexual behaviors, and he began to expose his sister to this pornography. Warning her that one day they would do what was shown in the magazines, Troy kept Amber in a hypervigilant and anxious state.

The sexual subjugation of a sibling can take on such a monstrous shape that a victim often finds it impossible to describe. Therefore victims of sexual abuse will often use symbols of their lost innocence as a way of expressing the unspeakable horror that they are experiencing. For Amber, the puppy that she received on her thirteenth birthday was her symbol of the vulnerability of innocence that is so easily torn apart by those who seek to destroy it. Amber cherished and protected her puppy, and that little ball of fur was perhaps the first object upon which she could bestow her devotion and have it returned.

But for Troy, Amber's puppy represented just another opportunity to intimidate his sister. Threatening to harm the dog was a way to get Amber to acquiesce to his demands, and ironically it became the final pathway to the sexual assault.

Every Thursday evening, following a recommendation from a family therapist, Mr. and Mrs. Hill would go out for dinner without the children. The therapist had reasoned that they needed to focus on their relationship so that they could be unified and supportive of one another in the face of their family difficulties. Amber always resisted this. She would beg to come along or entreat them to stay at home. She didn't want to be left alone with her brother because she knew the reign of terror that would begin as soon as they left. But Amber's pleas were never heard, and she was left to fend for herself.

It was during one of these Thursday nights that Troy sexually assaulted his younger sister. With a knife in one hand and the puppy's neck held in another, Troy threatened to kill the dog if Amber did not cooperate. She acquiesced, and the sexual act perpetrated on her destroyed the last vestige of armor she had so valiantly erected around herself.

But what Troy had not counted on was that ultimately Amber's devotion to her puppy would supersede the fear she felt for her own safety. She was determined this time to be heard, for she would never again take the chance that her puppy might be destroyed. When Amber's parents came home that night, she asked her father to take the puppy out in the backyard. Running to her mother, who had gone upstairs to change her clothes, Amber told her about the sexual assault. Something in Amber's voice, perhaps the way she said what had happened or the manner in which her body was rigid with fear as her voice rang out in determination, made her mother stop and listen. And this time she heard.

Sitting with the Hills two years after this incident, a therapist looks sadly upon a fractured family that is still reeling from shock. Marianne and Carson are struggling to survive a trauma that has resulted in the removal of their son from the home, the acknowledgment that their daughter harbors deep resentment toward them, and the sense of guilt and failure that accompany them wherever they go.

Marianne and Carson continue to toil through every last detail of the previous few years in an attempt to compile the evidence that would explain how this happened. They point fingers at the therapists who had not warned them of Troy's potential for harm, at the doctors for prescribing medication that was ineffective in curing their son, and even at Amber for not telling them in words the inexplicable horror she was experiencing. However, as much as they would like to absolve thoughts of blame, inevitibly they do experience shame and regret.

To ameliorate their culpability, Marianne and Carson decided to come forward to discuss sibling sexual abuse. Eager to do anything they can to prevent this from happening to other families, they hope their story will teach parents how to recognize the signs of sibling abuse. They see themselves as examples of caring, loving, and devoted parents who were blinded by what was happening under their own roof. They caution that if this could happen in their family, it could happen to anyone.

Throughout the probing interviews and the numerous counseling sessions, Amber sits silently between her parents until she is asked to speak. Her statements resound with prophecy and wisdom. Her insight is probing, and her scope is vast. Beneath her slight frame is a large and courageous girl who fought hard to survive. Although she sees herself as a damaged person who will never again trust another human being, she continues to reach out to parents with a message that only a survivor can so poignantly communicate.

"Listen to your children," she warns. "Children will always tell you, in one way or another, what is happening to them, and *please*, believe what they are saying."

While this may seem elementary for most parents, in practice it is complicated. Listening to children requires an understanding of child development, in particular cognitive growth and language acquisition. It mandates that parents be aware of how children of different ages express their thoughts. For example, young children under the age of six will not have the words to associate with many of their experiences. They are unable to communicate abstract terms such as time and frequency, and their memory is limited to those things they *can* understand. Therefore, very young children may not be able to tell you how many times something happened or where it occurred. They are also likely to speak in simplistic terms that may appear too vague for parents who are searching for more details. Statements such as, "I don't like him," or, "He is mean," may be the most that a two-year-old child can send as a plea for help.

Remember that young children may also be too intimidated or too traumatized by the abuser to effectively communicate danger. Therefore, their messages may be cryptic, and the only way to decode them is through noticeable changes in their behavior. Children who have altered the course of their normal routine in any area of their lives are sending a message that something traumatizing has occurred. A change in sleeping or eating patterns, a regression in behavior, such as baby talk, a loss of toilet training, a disruption in speech, or a sudden fear of separation should always be taken seriously as they are often signs that a child is in distress.

Four-year-old Amber didn't have words to describe the abusive relationship with her brother; however thirteen years later, as she speaks clearly about her memories, it is obvious that Amber understood much more about what was happening to her than her words at that time could convey. Amber knew that her brother's abusive behaviors were escalating, and it was only a matter of time before she would be seriously harmed. She lived in constant fear, which intensified when her parents left her alone with Troy every Thursday evening. The fact that they minimized her complaints and misinterpreted them as "typical sibling rivalry" demonstrated their inability to acknowledge that Amber was being abused by her stepbrother.

Fear should never be a part of a sibling relationship. Consistently hiding or withdrawing from an older sibling, or persistently complaining about being left in an older sibling's care, is a warning sign that sibling abuse may be occurring.

Like many parents who have disturbed children, the Hills focused most of their energy on Troy at the expense of Amber. Troy was able to manipulate his parents into believing that he had changed. But Amber knew that her brother hadn't changed, and she attempted to tell them this. Because Troy was able to display two very different faces, he effectively alienated family members from one another. In this manner he severed the lines of communication and left Amber defenseless and alone. When he was given responsibility for Amber on a weekly basis, his destructive power over her was given free reign. It was in this context that the final ambush was allowed to occur.

Hopefully, you have learned from the Hills that sibling sexual abuse emits warning signs well before it ever arrives. Yet all too often, other events and actions may obscure these signals. It is the parents' responsibility to pay close attention to what their children are doing and saying.

Often warning signs of sibling sexual abuse will go unheeded because they land on ears made deaf by denial. It is natural for parents to not want to hear terrible accusations made about one of their own children. Parents want so much to believe in the sanctity and healing powers of their home that they may effectively tune out any cries of danger within the family.

To avoid denial it is important to examine the relationships within your own home. In general, healthy sibling relationships are often the product of a well-rounded family that has demonstrated the ability to effectively solve problems, communicate openly with one another, and allow for the healthy expression of feelings. In families where children's emotions are repressed or sibling aggression is used to dominate and control, children are most likely to isolate themselves from their parents and interact with one another in abusive ways.

WARNING SIGNS OF SIBLING ABUSE

The following is a list of factors that contribute to sibling abuse. Examine each one carefully, and determine if your family is displaying any of these characteristics. If these factors can be eliminated, the chance that your children will engage in destructive sexual acting out will be significantly lessened.

An Older Sibling Has Too Much Responsibility

Siblings normally take care of one another and assume responsibilities that reflect genuine attachment. An older sister feeding a bottle to her newborn sibling or an adolescent boy walking his little brother home from school are healthy displays of bonding. However, when one child assumes too much care of younger siblings, a distortion in roles may occur. A child, no matter how responsible, is never capable of assuming a parental role. And therefore, if children are assigned this role, they will use whatever limited resources they have to manage the task. They may resort to physical retaliation, verbal abuse, and intimidation to force their will on the other children. For these reasons children should never be given the assignment of carrying out the parents' dictates, and never under any circumstances should one sibling be in charge of disciplining the others.

Single-parent families may be more susceptible to sibling abuse when their situations necessitate older children assuming responsibility for siblings. Many children of divorce are dealing with their own issues of abandonment and loss and need extra support and guidance. Yet in those situations where a newly divorced parent must work full time to meet the economic needs of the family, children are expected to take more responsibility for each other. Left on their own, siblings who have experienced a loss will turn to one another as outlets for aggression as well as repositories for emotional needs. And it is in this context that sexual abuse can occur.

Physical or Verbal Abuse Takes Place Between Siblings

A child who displays any form of aggression or intimidation of others should never be allowed to care for siblings. The Hills made an egregious error in judgment when they allowed Troy to watch Amber. The fact that he was capable of aggressive and manipulative behaviors made him un-suitable for assuming responsibility for his sister. However, the Hills wanted desperately to believe that he had changed, and allowing him to care for his younger sister would have been one way that they could demonstrate their newly found trust in Troy.

While a certain amount of sibling disputes is normal, physical displays of aggression, verbal abuse, intimidation, and threats should never, under any circumstances, be tolerated. These behaviors only foster domination and seed the ground for sibling sexual abuse. Remember that if a family does not tolerate aggression in any form, it is less likely to occur between siblings.

A Disturbed Child Has Power over the Other Children

Troy Hill was a very disturbed child, and in hindsight his parents agreed that he should never have been left in charge of Amber. Any child who is currently displaying aggression or has in the past demonstrated uncontrol-lable anger should never be left unsupervised with siblings. There are times when it may seem like the "difficult child" has been cured, and like Troy, his behaviors may have improved noticeably. However, there is always a risk that once in charge of a younger or weaker sibling, dangerous incli-nations and impulses may resurface.

Children who have been diagnosed with a mental disorder or a cog-nitive impairment that affects their reality testing, problem solving, and judgment should never be left in charge of other children. Diagnoses such as attention deficit disorder, nonverbal learning disabilities, and bipolar mood disorder can significantly affect the way in which a child will handle a crisis. These disorders can result in poor judgment and impulsive acting out, particularly when the child is under stress. Even if that child appears stabilized on medication, there is always a risk that the stress of taking responsibility for younger children will cause a relapse in behavior.

Children Have Witnessed or Experienced Sexual Abuse

A number of the adult perpetrators and sexually abusive youth you have met so far have themselves been victims of sexual abuse. Since children are the most susceptible to sexually acting out when they have been sexually abused, additional care should be taken if a member of the family has been abused. Child victims of sexual abuse may be at an increased risk for manipulating or forcing younger children into the same sexual behavior to which they were exposed. And never, under any circumstances, should this child be put in the position where he or she is responsible for younger siblings.

Educating children about sexual abuse is an important preventative step. It is imperative that guidelines be set for appropriate behaviors between siblings; and if one of the children has been sexually abused, it is important that parents reinforce to that child appropriate boundaries and behaviors. Parents must explain to a child who has been sexually abused that he or she may feel the urge to touch other children the way that he or she was touched, but that this type of behavior is unacceptable. And most important, parents need to provide sufficient supervision and guidance to monitor a sexually abused child's behavior.

Children Have Access to Pornography

Pornography will overstimulate children and may lead them into experimental sexual behaviors with one another. Therefore, parents who have pornographic videotapes, magazines, and other sexual paraphernalia in the home run the risk of exposing them to their children. Children's curiosity will often lead them to discover pornography despite a parent's best attempts to conceal it. Therefore, it is prudent to keep all pornography out of the home.

Pornography on the Internet is a growing concern since children can easily access these sites. Unmonitored activity on the Internet is therefore very risky, and parents need to supervise their children's use of the computer. In a later chapter, you will learn more about pornography on the Internet and how parents can monitor and block their children's access to inappropriate material.

Children Live in a Highly Sexualized Environment

Children who act out in sexually abusive ways often come from homes where there are unsuitable displays of sexuality. Parents who don't respect the privacy and physical boundaries of other family members are modeling sexually inappropriate behaviors for their children.

While a certain amount of affection is encouraged between family members, explicit displays of sexual behaviors between parents can be highly stimulating. While exposure to hugging and kissing helps children learn about love and affection, other behaviors such as fondling and prolonged kissing are overwhelming for children.

From an early age, children need to learn appropriate boundaries, which means that the privacy of their bodies and those of family members are respected. Family members who parade around without clothes and don't close doors when they are showering or going to the bathroom are displaying immodest behaviors that may confuse children and lead to over-stimulation and sexual acting out.

Children Do Not Have Adequate Socialization Skills or the Opportunity to Socialize with Peers

The ability to make and sustain friends is an important skill that begins early in life. Children who are isolated from social contact outside the family or don't have the necessary skills to effectively interact with others are more susceptible to sibling sexual abuse. Peer relationships are essential for the development of self-esteem, socialization, and sexual identity. If children are denied access to peer relationships, by either parental constraints or peer rejection, they are more likely to turn to their siblings to meet their needs.

While siblings may form their own subgroup within the family, they should never totally rely on one another for friendship, acceptance, and intimacy. In many instances it may seem easier for parents to allow an ostracized child to stay at home and play with siblings. However, it is critical that parents carefully evaluate the causes of a child's isolation from other children and take the appropriate steps to remedy the situation.

Children Lack Sex Education

Our youth live in an age where sex permeates almost every aspect of their lives. In order to balance children's exposure to sex in movies, music, and video games, realistic information about sex is offered as early as elementary school. Yet despite the public schools' attempts to educate children about sex, many children continue to have misconceptions about sexual behaviors, particularly when it comes to sexual abuse.

It is critical that parents assume a central role in their children's sex education for, despite what children learn at school or from one another, they need the opportunity to discuss sex freely with their parents. When parents try to shield their children from information about sex, children's naïveté may lead to sexual experimentation. Further, if children are not allowed to discuss sex, they will come to believe that this subject is taboo and find other ways to satisfy their curiosity.

Parents should always provide their children with honest and age-appropriate information about sex. Educational books, videotapes, and articles about sexual development can be made available in the home for children and used to stimulate healthy discussions between family members.

Parents often worry that discussing sex will stimulate their children's curiosity and incite them to engage in sexually inappropriate behaviors. Yet just the opposite occurs. When parents approach their children about sex in an open and honest manner, it actually *reduces* the likelihood of sexual acting out.

Empowering children with the information they need to prevent sexual abuse is critical. Knowing what parts of their bodies should be kept private, distinguishing "good" from "bad" touch, how to avoid dangerous situations, and how to say "No" should be a part of every young child's education.

Although children may be taught to respect the privacy of their bodies and are told that they shouldn't touch the genitals of another child, they may still engage in certain prohibited behaviors, especially if they don't think they will be caught. Very young children who are at the stage of moral development where they cannot internally differentiate right from wrong are likely to hide unacceptable behaviors merely because they fear the consequences. Therefore it is crucial that parents supervise and monitor young children's interactions with one another.

A child's sex education should include information about the legal ramifications of sexually abusive behavior. For children who may inhibit responses because they fear the consequences, the strong arm of the law may serve as a further deterrent. Many of the young offenders I interviewed for this book stated that they were not aware that a child sexually abusing another child was against the law. One young man, after being sentenced to a juvenile detention facility, placed on probation, and given numerous hours of community service, explained his astonishment at the seriousness of his consequences: *"I knew what I was doing to my sister was wrong, and that my mother would be very angry at me if she found out. But I thought that getting in deep trouble with my mom would be the most that would happen. I never knew that I could get in trouble with the law for what I did."*

NORMAL VERSUS ABNORMAL
SEXUAL INTERACTIONS BETWEEN CHILDREN

Now that your awareness has been heightened as to the existence and the impact of sexually abusive youth, it is important to be able to distinguish between those behaviors that define sexual abuse and those that reflect normal sexual curiosity between children.

Children are sexual beings and normally engage in sexual experimentation with themselves and one another. This does not mean that children's sexuality is similar to that of an adult. Rather, a child's sexuality begins at birth and goes through developmental stages until it reaches adult forms of sexual expression. Deriving pleasure from suckling at a mother's breast or cooing with delight when rubbed with lotion are an infant's early expressions of physical intimacy. When parents allow for a healthy expression of sexuality, their children are likely to grow up with a healthy attitude toward sex.

However, when sexual abuse occurs, it can severely damage a child's sexuality. Therefore, it is critical that parents identify normal sexual play between children and intervene in those situations that are sexually abusive.

Sex play between children is always consensual and involves no force or intimidation and differs depending on a child's developmental level. In preschool children, normal sex play takes place with similar-age children of both sexes and is usually limited to the exploration of genitals and masturbation. Prior to puberty, sexual interaction between children is more often with the same-sex friends of similar age and usually involves exploratory games such as "playing doctor." During adolescence, sexual interactions are about exploring the social and interpersonal aspects of "adult" forms of sexuality. These interactions begin to be more selective and are more likely to involve opposite-sex peers who are in exclusive relationships.

The following are guidelines for differentiating behaviors that reflect normal sexual play between children and those that are sexually abusive. When a parent is aware that sexual contact has taken place between children, the following questions can help distinguish if sexual abuse has occurred.

Is there a significant age difference between the children? Children usually engage in sexual play with children who are of similar age. The wider the age range between the children engaging in sexual activities, the more likely that sexual abuse is taking place.

Many states have guidelines that define whether sexual abuse has taken place. For example, Colorado has an age differentiation of four years as a determination of whether sexual abuse has occurred.

Despite legal guidelines, when young children are involved, a difference of just one year can be problematic. For example, the difference between a two and a three year old in social, language, and cognitive development is significant, and, therefore, sex play between them may not be totally consensual.

Is there an inequality in the social relationships between the children? Normal sexual play between children usually involves friends and is, as noted previously, always *voluntary*. Whenever one child has the advantage over another due to social status, age, size, or position within their family, sexual abuse can occur. In this way older siblings and baby-sitters have a distinct advantage over younger children, and they may use their influence to coerce younger children in sex play.

Is there an aggressive and/or submissive manner in which the sexual contact takes place? Normal childhood sexual contact is explorative and mutual. Children are often giddy and playful during this time even though they may be embarrassed when caught. However, sexual contact is no longer considered normal if there are aggressive behaviors that place one child in a subordinate position, even if the children are close to the same age. Therefore, displays of anxiety and fearfulness during or after the sex play are signs of sexual abuse.

Is the sexual contact between the children frequent? Sex play between children occurs periodically. Initially, when they first discover the pleasure and fascination of their bodies, children may focus their play on sexual exploration. However, their attention spans are brief, and after a while, they are likely to turn their focus to other activities. However, if sex play keeps them from engaging in other play, then it should be considered problematic.

Does the type of sex play displayed by the child reflect a knowledge about sex that is concerning to the parent? Children's sex play usually remains consistent and is limited by their knowledge of sex. Therefore, sex play in preschool children, who are not aware of adult sexuality, usually involves genital exploration and does not ordinarily advance to mimicking oral sex or intercourse. If sexual play between children reflects a premature knowledge of sex, it should be questioned by the parents. As noted previously, children who have been exposed to sexual abuse are more likely to demonstrate sexual activity that is too sophisticated and extreme for their age.

We live in a culture where sexual information is easily accessible to children. Television, movies, advertisements, videos, and popular teen idols expose our children to a vast array of sexual stimuli that has dramatically increased our children's knowledge about sex. Most children today know a great deal more about adult sexual activity than ever before, and therefore it is difficult to discern just when, where, and how a child may have been exposed to sexually stimulating material. Therefore if a child is demonstrating adult sexual behaviors during sex play that is confusing and troubling to the parent, ask the child where he or she has learned this behavior.

Is there fear, intimidation, or secrecy involved in the sex play? Although children will be private in their sex play with one another, it should not take on the dimensions of "keeping a secret." If asked about sex play, children will usually respond with embarrassment but are able to talk about it with an understanding parent. However, a child who displays fear about telling may be sending a warning sign that he or she has been intimidated or threatened by an abuser.

Do other children complain about a certain child's sexual behavior? Children will be the first to sound a warning signal when they are exposed to another child who is sexually intrusive. They are likely to tell an adult that a child is exposing himself, touching others, or imitating sexual behaviors in front of them. It is important that adults listen to these complaints and consider them to be warning signs of abnormal sexual behavior.

Does the child continue to engage in certain sexual activities despite being asked to stop by an adult? Children who are discovered enacting problematic sexual behaviors, such as public masturbation, and are asked to stop are likely not to repeat them. However, children who, despite the interventions of adults, continue to act out in sexually inappropriate ways are sending warning signs that they can't control their behaviors and need more serious intervention.

Knowing the difference between sexually abusive behaviors in children and those behaviors that reflect normal sexual development is critical, not only in protecting your child from abuse, but in establishing a foundation for the development of healthy sexual attitudes and behaviors. It is important that parents not overreact when they see their children engaging in normal sexual behaviors because that can cause undue anxiety and shame that could have a negative impact on a child's sexual development. If you do witness behaviors between children that you assess to be sexually abusive, it is important that you react calmly and decisively. Redirect the behaviors immediately and, later, spend some time alone talking with your child. When you talk to your child about what has occurred, try to remain as neutral as possible. Children are often unduly impacted by witnessing a parent's intense reactions to their behaviors; and if they experience the parent as overwhelmed or very angry at what has occurred, they are less likely to talk about the experience. Children may be more traumatized by a parent's reactions to their behaviors than by the sexual abuse itself. This is why I recommend that if a parent has strong reactions to their child's sexual behaviors, they take time out for themselves to process their emotions. Talking to a spouse, friend, relative, or a counselor is often a good way to work through your reactions. However, it is important that you get advice from a trained professional and not follow the recommendations given by well-meaning friends or relatives who may not be trained in this area.

Now that your are aware of the issues involved in sexually abusive youth and, in particular, sibling abuse, you are ready to move on to another type of sexual predator. This predator can arrive unannounced in your home via the vast network we call cyberspace. Internet sexual abuse is on the rise; and unless we prepare for this foe, it will steal into the sanctity of our homes in the time it takes to boot the computer.

Cybersex: Child Abuse on the Internet

The Internet is exciting new territory for a multitude of young people. According to the June 2000 report from the National Center for Missing and Exploited Children on *Online Victimization: A Report on the Nation's Youth*, nearly twenty-four million of our nation's children from the ages of ten to seventeen surf the Internet regularly, and millions are expected to join them in the near future. For many of these youth, cyberspace presents endless possibilities for learning, fun, and worldwide communication. However, not every on-line adventure is a happy one. Just like the real world, cyberspace can present risks and threats of real harm to children. An increasing number of young people are experiencing the effects of exposure to on-line sexual abuse in the forms of sexual solicitations, exposure to unwanted sexual material, and threats or harassment by on-line sexual predators. The most tragic victims are those who are sexually assaulted or murdered when they encounter their on-line predator face-to-face.

For most of my career, I have taught parents how to detect and avoid child sexual predators. In the past decade, as I heard more and more stories about children being exposed to pornography on the Internet and being lured into meeting on-line acquaintances, I realized that the virus of abuse had mutated to an advanced technological stage. Therefore, I had to teach parents different skills to identify this cunningly adaptive cyberpredator.

In the following story, based on an actual case in my clinical practice, you will see how one young girl was subjected to overwhelming sexual stimuli that began as a seemingly innocent on-line relationship with a "young man" she had met in a chat room.

Thirteen-year-old Moira came into my office happy to see me after a summer break. I took note of her transformation. Over the summer she had begun to wear makeup, cut her once long blonde hair into choppy layers, and wear tight cotton shirts and oversized jeans. Moira had hit adolescence. As a child psychologist, I had seen many such transformations. I anticipated, however, that crossing the chasm from childhood to adolescence might be more precarious for Moira because she had been a victim of sexual abuse when she was ten years old.

> Moira had been referred to me shortly after the uncle of her best friend fondled her during a weekend slumber party. It took months to cure her of her nightmares and chronic stomachaches, but what lingered on was her pervasive sense of shame. She blamed herself for the abuse because, although there were three other young girls who were spending the night, the offender had singled her out for the abuse.
>
> Moira told her mother about the abuse, the authorities were notified, and the perpetrator was arrested. To make matters worse for Moira, her sexual abuse was treated like a tantalizing scandal. Her best friend accused Moira of lying and turned the other girls against her, and Moira was forced to walk the halls of her junior high school alone.
>
> It took a long time to resolve Moira's sense of shame and her grief over the loss of her innocence, her best friend, and her self-esteem. But no matter how hard we both tried to minimize the impact of the abuse on her life, the premature exposure to sexuality created a great deal of turmoil. Shunned by her girlfriends, Moira had begun to focus on boys, and her sexual experimentation accelerated. Her precocious sexuality was heightened by the onset of puberty, and, eventually, the force of her anger and sexuality reached a combustible high.
>
> For a few months prior to the summer break, Moira and I had been working on reestablishing her sexual equilibrium. Moira's mother, aware of her daughter's vulnerability, supervised and monitored her activities; and together we provided enough safeguards for Moira to prevent her from further exposure to sexual abuse.

In the spring Moira's mother, intent on aiding her daughter's healing, planned a summer vacation away from home. She believed that a two-month respite from her peers would give Moira a better chance to heal.

I was curious to see Moira after a summer's absence; and after we'd exchanged pleasantries, she told me about her vacation. She complained that at first she had been lonely and missed home. She was angry at her mother for making her leave and for taking her to a place where there was "nothing to do." But Moira was resourceful; and since she had taken her laptop with her on the vacation, she soon found companionship on the Internet. She confessed to me that during the summer, she had met a "sixteen-year-old boy." In the span of eight weeks they had fallen in love, married, honeymooned, and had sex; and this had occurred entirely on the Internet. As Moira described the sequence of communication with her "cyberhusband," I became concerned. He appeared too sophisticated in his seduction, and I was suspicious that Moira's "teenage husband" was actually an adult predator who frequented the chat rooms of young people in order to snare a child victim.

As I learned more about the events that had led to Moira's cyberrelationship, I was appalled at how it paralleled the basic stages in predator-victim relationships. I was almost certain that the cunning predator had *detected* Moira's vulnerability. Still deeply affected by her earlier abuse, she was an easy target. And because Moira was unable to recognize this new form of sexual abuse, she believed that her suitor was merely an innocent young man who, like herself, was searching for a confidant. Secrecy was no problem since Moira knew that her mother would never approve of this cyberrelationship. In fact, her mother was led to believe that Moira was engaging in harmless exploration of information and innocent "chats" with hometown friends and therefore left her alone when she was online.

After the predator had identified Moira as a suitable victim, he began to *groom* her. Her predator paved their Internet relationship with false pretenses, promises, and endless compliments about Moira's special qualities. Her cybersweetheart told her that he, too, had been lonely for a long time and that she made him "feel alive again." They shared their most intimate secrets, and Moira confided in him that she had been sexually abused. He said all the right things and assured her that he would never hurt her and he would always take care of her. As he navigated Moira into the *approach stage*, he enlisted her trust and secrecy. He isolated her from the rest of the chat-room subscribers and devised special codes that they could use to communicate in secret.

Before the predator took Moira to the *abuse stage*, he and Moira exchanged messages that were increasingly sexual in content. He would ask her to describe her body in detail, and he, in turn, would paint with words the landscape of his "perfect" physique. He became privy to her innermost fantasies and seduced her with his promise to fulfill her every desire.

Three weeks went by before the on-line predator proposed to Moira. With a wonderfully executed love poem, complete with graphic designs of butterflies, flowers, angels, and two interwoven hearts, he asked Moira to be his cyberwife. Moira accepted the "proposal," and they arranged to be "married" online.

After the "cyberwedding," her articulate predator wrote with beautiful precision of a romantic honeymoon on a deserted Caribbean island. The message read, *"We'll roam the deserted beaches and comb the white sands for lovely coral-colored conch shells . . . picnic in the sun, swim naked in the turquoise water and rub exotic oils over our already tanned bodies."* As he led Moira into their secluded beach hut, he carefully prepared her for their "first sexual encounter." The words that appeared on Moira's computer screen thrilled her; but for the first time since she'd met her cybersweetheart, she became alarmed. Anxious for a respite, she claimed that her mother was entering the room, and Moira disconnected from her predator. But the next evening, Moira once again joined her cybernewlywed online as they recreated their honeymoon suite amid the sand, surf, and starlit night of the island sky. He then asked her to "consummate" their love by simultaneous masturbation.

As Moira detailed to me the on-line sex she had had with her cyberhusband, I realized that what she was describing was the tragic transformation of sexual abuse in the new millennium. These technologically advanced predators are now able to enter the homes of thousands of vulnerable youth like Moira. The multitude of children who each night seek to fill empty spaces by anonymously keying words onto a screen have now become potential victims for these cyberpredators.

Even though Moira was superficially excited by her cybermarriage, she was, in reality, frightened and overwhelmed by having cybersex. She told me that the last time she had had contact with her cyberhusband was when he had asked her to meet him in person. When I questioned Moira about whether she thought her cybermarriage was cybersexual abuse, she protested, "No, it couldn't be. It wasn't real; it was only on the Internet." But, unfortunately, her emotional responses to her Internet experience were real. Moira had once again become sullen and withdrawn. Her nightmares had resurfaced, and she had begun to miss her classes; all symptoms of sexual abuse.

Fortunately for Moira, she never actually met her cyberhusband. Moira's encounters on the Internet were eventually reported to the FBI, who later confirmed that this "young man" was in actuality a forty-nine-year-old repeat sex offender. Moira was already in therapy, and although her experiences over the Internet had set her back, Moira would eventually recover. But for many children, the symptoms of cybersexual abuse will go unidentified and therefore untreated.

Moira's experience is not unique. According to the *Online Victimization* report, one in five children who regularly used the Internet are exposed to unwanted sexual solicitations, and one in four of these children view unwanted pornography. These children had encountered sexual stimuli by surfing the Web, clicking onto links, or misspelling a web address. Some had opened an instant message or an unknown E-mail that resulted in exposure to unwanted pornography. And while not all of the children were upset or frightened, some of them did suffer from anxiety and depression due to undesired exposure to pornography. The following are just some examples of distressing experiences that youth have encountered on the Internet that range from exposure to inappropriate sexual stimuli to a face-to-face encounter with a sexual predator:

> ➤ A twelve-year-old girl complained that someone in a chat room had asked her bra size.

➤ A thirteen year old was sent, via E-mail, a drawing of a man having sex with a dog.

➤ A fifteen-year-old boy came across a bestiality site while he was researching wolves for a homework assignment. He was exposed to a picture of a woman having intercourse with a wolf.

➤ A sixteen-year-old boy said he was talking about the problems he was having with his family with an on-line acquaintance in his thirties. The man suggested that the boy run away and offered him a place to stay. The boy reported this to his parents.

➤ A fifteen-year-old boy met a young man online who was requesting help in designing a web site for his new business. After the boy designed a web page for him, they became on-line friends. They eventually met in person, and the man propositioned the boy. The boy refused and reported the incident to the police.

➤ A fourteen-year-old girl met a twenty-two-year-old high school coach in a chat room. After exchanging messages several times, she finally agreed to meet him in person, and they began to have sex on a regular basis.

TYPES OF SEXUAL EXPLOITATION OF CHILDREN ON THE INTERNET

Children, easily captivated by the seemingly innocent and adventurous spirit of technology, can be lured into dangerous territory on the Internet in a number of ways. By becoming actual subjects of Internet pornography, viewing sexually explicit material, or by actually meeting a sexual predator, children can become victims of Internet sexual abuse.

Viewing or Becoming Subjects of Child Pornography

According to Cyberangels, an on-line group that educates people about how to protect children from predators on the Internet, there are "tens of thousands" of web sites that currently promote child pornography. Child pornography, as defined under the federal law, is a visual depiction of a minor engaged in sexually explicit conduct. Child pornographic material may include photographs, films, and magazines of children in sexual poses and acts. Children can become victims by viewing child pornography or by becoming subjects of this material.

Child pornography can have devastating effects on children who view it as well as those who are exploited in the X-rated material. Children who are forced into posing for pornographic material are at high risk for harm. Many of them have contracted sexually transmitted diseases or have been subjected to rape, assault, torture, and murder.

One of the most valuable possessions in a pedophile's life is his or her collection of child pornography. To acquire their collection, prior to the Internet they had to obtain this material through exchanges among themselves, mailings, or visiting vendors who carried child pornography. Unlike commercial adult-obscenity dealers, child pornographers rarely, if ever, openly advertise or solicit new business. Because their operations are illegal, they go underground. However, the Internet now makes it possible for pedophiles to obtain child pornography anonymously and also provides an avenue for easy exchange of pornographic materials between pedophiles.

Child pornography is not only used for the pedophile's sexual arousal, it is also a way in which to seduce children into participating in sexual activities. The pedophile may show intended victims pictures of other children performing sexual acts in an attempt to lower their inhibitions and to make them believe that sexual acts with children are normal and acceptable. Pedophiles may also take pornographic pictures of a child and then use them to blackmail the child into secrecy. The visual documentation of a child's exploitation causes a sense of deep shame and guilt in the victim as well as fear that family and friends will discover his or her abuse.

There are a number of dues-paying organizations that are considered by the FBI to promote and condone pedophilia over the Internet, such as the North American Man-Boy Love Association (NAMBLA) that provides material that can be easily downloaded to a pedophile's computer.

Exposure to Adult Pornography

An article in *Time* magazine on May 10, 1999, reported the results of a CNN poll in which 82 percent of the teenagers questioned replied that they regularly used the Internet. The same poll asked, "Have you ever seen Web sites that are X-rated or have sexual content?" and 42 percent replied that they had.

Pornographic sites may also be programmed to make them difficult to exit. In fact, some of the sites are designed so that the exit button takes the viewer into other sexually explicit sites.

The ease in which pornographic sites can be accessed has made them available to underage Internet users. According to a study done by Net-Value, children intentionally spent 64.9 percent more time on pornography sites than they did on game sites in September 2000. They also cited that over 3 million minors had visited pornographic sites and that over 20 percent of them were under the age of fourteen.

Sexual Solicitations

While it is illegal to transmit child pornography on the Internet, and the mere possession of such pornography is illegal, talking about sex online, although it can expose a child to overwhelming sexual stimuli, is *not* a crime. Therefore, unless the perpetrator asks the child to travel for the purpose of sex, obscene verbal exchanges on the Internet are not illegal.

The Youth Internet Safety Survey, which was conducted by the Crimes Against Children Resource Center, confirmed that a large number of children are sexually propositioned by offenders who go into chat rooms frequented by youth. These propositions run the gamut of seemingly innocuous questions about their bodies to direct invitations to meet them for sex. Sexual solicitations online may occur from strangers in a chat room, anonymous E-mail senders, or from on-line "friendships" that have developed over time.

Like Moira's experience, some sexual solicitations are propositions for cybersex. This type of sexual interaction, like phone sex, is likely to include detailed descriptions of sexual activity and orders for the child to disrobe and masturbate.

It is important to realize that many of these cybersexual predators will disguise their identities as they spend time searching the chat rooms for their next victim. They will look for those children whose writings reflect loneliness and alienation from parents, teachers, and friends. They are adept at spotting those who have low self-esteem and are searching for attention and recognition. They will also recognize those children who may not be receiving the proper guidance at home, such as a young girl who is on the Internet all night. It is these vulnerable youth who are more likely to fall prey to the skillful manipulation of an on-line sexual predator.

Much like Moira's cybersweetheart, on-line sexual predators will take their victims through the same stages of abuse that occur when a victim is seduced in person. They may spend a great deal of time communicating with their intended victims in the chat room, playing on-line games, or teaching them more about the computer, all in an attempt to groom them for sexual abuse.

Some chat rooms are actually run by child sexual predators. They are often so cleverly disguised that young people, in search of attention and companionship, may innocently enter these sites only to find themselves hooked into an on-line relationship with a dangerous sexual predator. These sites utilize language that justifies their sexual interest in children and attempts to normalize and legitimize their behaviors. They claim that sex between adults and children is "pure," "kind," and "gentle," and they believe that it is an adult's responsibility to teach children about sex. They also tend to see themselves as being persecuted by the rest of society and will rationalize their sexually abusive behaviors with young people in well-written arguments. One particular site that caters to pedophiles states that "our goal is to end the oppression of men and boys who have consensual relations."

Internet relationships pose a complex problem. Since a large majority of them are indeed genuine and have no taint of sexual exploitation, this form of communication can be a healthy way to become acquainted with another person who may live in a different location. Yet because of the danger that can befall an innocent youth who is surfing the Internet in search of new friends, it is important that cautions be used to help a young person detect sexual predators in the vast territory of cyberspace.

Harassment

Although it is often less publicized and does not occur as frequently as unwanted exposure to sexual material or sexual solicitation, threats to assault or harm a youth and his or her family and friends can create significant emotional turmoil. Often harassment comes from perpetrators who are known to the victim, making the threats seem more real. An example of this is a twelve-year-old girl who found a note posted in a chat room about her that included sexual name-calling. The source of these notes was eventually traced to a group of her peers who wanted to ostracize her from her classmates.

Some forms of harassment, however, do come from anonymous sources. This was the case in an incident involving a fourteen-year-old boy who was home alone. He received an Instant Message from someone who said that he was hiding in the boy's house with a laptop. The boy's fear was acute. Similar to the stalking behaviors of an unknown assailant, this type of cyberharassment can cause undue anxiety and hypervigilance in the victim.

Traveling

Traveling, or arranging to meet an on-line sexual predator, is the most serious type of exposure a child can have to a sexual predator. The National Center for Missing and Exploited Children, along with federal, state, and local law enforcement, were able to identify 785 "traveler" cases in 1999 where on-line sexual predators had arranged to meet a victim in person. By empathizing with youth who are unhappy at home or at school, these on-line predators can seduce their intended victims into believing that they can offer them comfort and sanctuary if they run away from home. The factors that heighten a child's vulnerability to a sexual predator can easily be detected online. A few exchanges in a chat room with an unhappy, isolated, neglected, emotionally disturbed, or insecure young person can easily be decoded as a green light for a crafty predator intent on meeting his next victim.

Children who frequent chat rooms often feel that they have the protection of anonymity that can lift the burden of their silence. Using an on-line pseudonym, they can be free, in relative obscurity, to unleash the emotions they may have kept hidden from the rest of the world. They may even create a new persona: one that is more daring, exciting, and desirable than their ordinary selves. In fact, this new cyberimage may enhance their sense of adventure, lower their inhibitions, and create lapses in their judgment. In this manner the creation of an inflated on-line persona may actually cause an ordinarily well-behaved adolescent to act out in an uncharacteristically dangerous way.

The following is another example of on-line victimization that occurred in my practice. It involves a vulnerable young girl whose on-line relationship led her into a near miss with disaster.

Ashley came from a deeply religious family. She was the oldest of two girls; and when she was just a toddler, the family had moved to an isolated farming community. Ashley's parents preferred the secluded atmosphere of this small town because it offered them an opportunity to protect their daughters from the distracting influences of modern-day life.

In the beginning everything seemed fine. The family was close-knit, and all they ever needed could be found in their church, friendly neighbors, a multitude of animals that ran wild in their backyard, and the quiet evenings that smelled of wood-burning fires and home-cooked meals. Yet as Ashley grew, her insulated world began to close in around her. She longed to break free from her parents' constraints and experience a part of life that she felt she was being denied. She wanted more exposure to friends her age than the handful of familiar neighborhood youth who sat beside her in the small brick building that served as their school.

Ashley began to rebel. She didn't want to attend religious services with her family, and she began to question their beliefs. She spent more and more time alone in her room daydreaming about the time she could run away to the city and really begin her life. Her grades plummeted, and her isolation from friends and family continued.

The year Ashley turned fifteen, her father surprised the family with a computer. Unbeknownst to him, he had just handed Ashley her "way out." She quickly learned how to use the computer and talked her father into obtaining an on-line service. Her parents never took the time to learn how to use the computer, and thus it fell into the sole proprietorship of Ashley. They left her alone with her computer, naively believing that the Internet had rekindled her interest in her schoolwork.

Ignoring her schoolbooks, which she hid under the bed, Ashley traveled through cyberspace, learning about things that her parents had kept hidden from her. She craved her time on the Internet; and with the speed of her nimble fingers, she keyed into places and people around the world until her wanderings landed her right in the middle of a chat room for teens.

With an adventurous screen name, she entered the room with the confidence of a seasoned player and sought to fill the empty spaces in her life with the exchanges of newly found confidants. She typed in confessions, wrote a plea for understanding, and inadvertently exposed her vulnerability as a misunderstood, lonely, and isolated adolescent.

Unbeknownst to Ashley, a sexual predator in his mid-twenties had skillfully executed his way into this chat room. He spent time reading her exchanges, and within a week he set the bait. He gave himself an appropriately youthful screen name and posed as an eighteen-year-old boy. He skillfully designed an adolescent who was strikingly similar to Ashley. Soon they were corresponding solely through E-mail, and over the next few weeks he maneuvered Ashley into believing that she was infatuated with a high school senior who, like herself, had been "jailed in a prison of small-town minds and rigid beliefs." He catapulted their on-line exchanges out of cyberspace into Ashley's bedroom when he requested her phone number so that he could call her late at night.

Eventually, during a long phone conversation that lasted well into the early hours of the morning, he asked Ashley to run away from home and join him in search of a "new life." With "love in her heart" and anger at her life of restrictions, she packed her bags in preparation to meet her "boyfriend" at a train station in the next state. They then planned to board a train East where they could "live together in blissful freedom."

Ashley ran away on a cold and wet spring night, but her plans didn't go as expected. Somehow their correspondence had gone awry, and Ashley arrived at the train station a day early. By that morning Ashley's parents had found her empty bed and had already notified the police. Fortunately, an experienced detective asked to see Ashley's room and noticed the computer sitting on her desk. When he questioned her parents, they admitted that she spent a great deal of time on the Internet. The detective searched Ashley's computer; and within the next hour, the contents of her secret life were revealed. Ashley had saved her E-mails from her on-line paramour, and thus her parents and the police learned of her plan to run away.

The police were suspicious of the screen name used by Ashley's boyfriend and quickly recognized the type of communication that on-line predators use to lure teens. They informed her parents that, most likely, their daughter had been corresponding with a sexual predator who frequented the chat rooms of young people. After a few hours, Ashley's parents were finally notified that the police had found her in the next state, alone, frightened, and cold, waiting at the train station. The predator, on route to meet her, had been apprehended.

Despite the fact that she ran away from home only to find herself stranded in a unfamiliar train station, Ashley's story had a good ending. Fortunately, she never met the on-line predator; and because of her drastic actions, her parents were finally forced to take notice of her pain. Her attempt to run away from the restraints of her family and community was a cry for help. With the support of a family counselor, her parents were able to understand the needs of their adolescent daughter. The family was able to renegotiate their rules and allow Ashley to make certain decisions about her life. Ashley learned of the potential danger she had placed herself in by agreeing to meet a stranger, and rules were set up for future Internet use.

Most of us will never hear about stories like Ashley's for tragically, the ones that we will hear about will be cases when children actually do meet a sexual predator and abuse occurs. In order to prevent these crimes from occurring, parents need to be active in understanding how their children can become victims on the Internet and the various ways in which they can prevent this from happening.

Before we look at preventative measures, you need to be aware of the laws that relate to the protection of children on the Internet and the prosecution of on-line predators.

LAWS AND PROSECUTION OF INTERNET SEXUAL ABUSERS

Federal laws that protect children from sexual abuse have been in place before the widespread popularity of the personal computer. The Sexual Exploitation of Children Act, enacted in 1977, prohibits the use of a minor in the making of pornography, the transport of a child across state lines, and the production and circulation of materials advertising child pornography. Furthermore, transportation, importation, shipment, and receipt of child pornography by any interstate means, including the computer, are illegal.

The Child Protection Act of 1984 specified the definition of a "child" as anyone under the age of eighteen. Therefore, sexually explicit photographs of anyone seventeen years old or younger is child pornography. In 1986, the Child Sexual Abuse and Pornography Act banned the production and use of advertisements for child pornography. This act also raised the minimum sentences for offenders who repeatedly violate these laws from a two-year prison sentence to five years.

Following the above legislation, additional laws have been enacted that specifically relate to child pornography and computers. The Child Protection and Obscenity Enforcement Act of 1988 made it unlawful to use a computer to transmit advertisements for child pornography or any visual depictions of child pornography. It prohibited the buying, selling, or otherwise obtaining custody or control of children for the purpose of producing child pornography.

In 1990, Congress declared that it was a federal crime to possess three or more depictions of child pornography that were produced using materials that were mailed or shipped by any means, including the computer. The Telecommunications Act of 1996 made it a federal crime for anyone using the mail, including the computer, to persuade, induce, or entice an individual under the age of eighteen to engage in any sexual act.

The Child Pornography Prevention Act of 1996 amended the definition of child pornography to include that which appears to be the depiction of a minor engaging in sexual conduct. This definition takes into account computerized images that have been "morphed" to look like children.

A number of children have been harassed as a result of messages that have been posted on the Internet. In Illinois, a nine-year-old girl's name and telephone number had been posted on the Internet, along with a statement that she was available for sex. To address this problem, The Child Online Protection Act prohibits the use of a facility of interstate commerce, such as a computer connected to the Internet, to transmit information about a minor for criminal sexual purposes. This law also applies to those sex offenders who communicate online with another sex offender and share personal information about a minor.

Children's web sites have been known to collect information from children. As a requirement to enter a web site, children may be asked to become a "member" by filling out an application that will reveal their ages, addresses, phone numbers, family names, and other personal information. This type of information can then be sold to other web sites. The Federal Trade Commission surveyed 212 commercial children's web sites in 1998, and they reported that 89 percent of these sites collected personal information from children, and only 1 percent of them required parental consent for the collection and disclosure of children's information.

The Children's Privacy Protection and Parental Empowerment Act addresses this issue. Also known as "The Polly Klaas Bill" (Polly Klaas was a twelve-year-old girl who, in October of 1993, was abducted from her home in the small town of Petaluma, California, and later found murdered), this act makes it illegal for commercial web sites to obtain personal information from children under the age of thirteen without parental consent. Businesses that obtain lists to sell to vendors must, under this law, release all information that they have to parents if they request it, and they must also release names of all those to whom the broker has distributed the list.

The overwhelming majority of states have also established laws pertaining to child pornography. Unfortunately, there are some states that still have not enacted laws that prohibit the possession of child pornography. Some Internet sites will provide more information about your state's laws relating to child pornography. For more information about these, check the resource section at the end of this chapter.

Most of the legal prohibitions against child pornography on the Internet involve the *visual* depictions of a minor engaging in sexually explicit behaviors. Yet it is legal for web sites to make pornographic writings available to minors who use the Internet. In response to this concern, a Federal Communications Decency Act was proposed, which sought to prohibit material on the Internet that was inappropriate for children. However, in 1994, the U.S. Supreme Court reviewed a case that declared it unconstitutional.

FBI AND INTERNET SEX ABUSE

In 1993, a ten-year-old boy was abducted from his house in Baltimore. An investigation led to a couple who had been using the Internet to lure young boys in the mid-Atlantic region into having sex with them. They were also using the Internet to transmit child pornography.

In 1995, as a result of this incident and others like it that had come to the attention of law enforcement, the FBI began The Innocent Images Program. This program provides central operations and multiagency co-ordination of cases for all FBI investigations that involve on-line child pornography and child sexual exploitation. It focuses on sex offenders who are willing to travel for the purpose of engaging in sexual activity with a minor and those persons who are producing and distributing child pornography. In 1995, Innocent Images was responsible for 562 arrests nationwide of pedophiles who either were transmitting child pornography on the Internet or had arranged to physically meet a child they had met online. They have an outstanding conviction rate of 95 percent.

The FBI believes that on-line sexual predators are not a new breed. They are the very same offenders who would once hang around play-grounds or schools, and who now find their victims online. They are also some of the most sophisticated computer users the FBI has encountered.

According to Pete Gulotta, an FBI agent specializing in media rela-tions, the *average* on-line predator is a white male who is above average in intelligence, between twenty-five and forty-five years old, and is usually upper-middle-class with no prior criminal history. Yet Gulotta cautions that while this describes the "average" on-line predator, these predators, like other sex offenders, can be found in all ethnic, socioeconomic, and pro-fessional groups and can also be women and even children themselves. In February 2000, a sixteen-year-old Michigan boy was charged with distrib-uting child pornography on the Internet. He was arrested following a seventeen-month investigation that began when the German National Police came across his child pornography site on the Internet.

The FBI has over fifty field offices throughout the country, and each office has a trained professional who can spot child pornography traffickers and travelers. Agents assigned to Innocent Images may spend as many as ten hours a day online. FBI agents go undercover in chat rooms and pose as children in order to catch those on-line predators who are prepared to travel to have sex with a child or are transmitting child pornography over the Internet.

In 1999, a top entertainment executive was arrested in Los Angeles and charged with crossing state lines for the purpose of engaging in sex with a minor. The predator met someone he thought was a thirteen-year-old girl on the Internet, only to find out that she was an FBI agent.

The traffickers of child pornography are often harder to detect than those who lure children to travel. Child pornography, like any other message or picture, may be transmitted through private electronic mail, and many Internet services, such as America Online, do not monitor private communications. If a willing sender sends an image to a willing receiver, the transaction is virtually undetectable because of the on-line service's policy of privacy of communications. However, an undercover FBI agent, posing as a pedophile, will attempt to attract a sexual offender who is interested in obtaining child pornography. As soon as the pornography is exchanged and downloaded, pedophiles can then be apprehended.

These types of operations have come under much criticism from civil libertarians. They argue that many offenders might not have committed the crimes for which they are charged were they not approached online by authorities masquerading as children. These groups argue that the federal agents are entrapping otherwise innocent people into committing crimes.

Despite these criticisms, the FBI and other agencies worldwide continue to work together to apprehend on-line predators. Many of these organizations provide web sites that the public can access and provide information about illegal sexual activity on the Internet.

The U.S. Customs CyberSmuggling Center was established in August of 1997 and, as of September of 1999, it has resulted in well over four hundred convictions. The center forwards all leads, tips, and complaints of child pornography to the area FBI offices and also conducts its own investigations. Operation Cheshire Cat was a joint investigation of U.S. Customs and the English National Crime Squad that targeted an Internet-based organization called the Wonderland Club. This name was derived from Lewis Carroll's *Alice in Wonderland,* a symbolic favorite of the pedophile underworld. According to Mark Gado in *Pedophiles and Child Molesters: The Slaughter of Innocence,* this club was responsible for the distribution of the most vile child pornography, including child rapes. It was said that in order to be a club member, a person had to possess over ten thousand images of child pornography on his or her computer's hard drive. In 1998, U.S. Customs officials arrested over two hundred suspects from fourteen different countries who were involved in this pedophile ring. Evidence gathered in the search warrants indicated that the club had members in forty-seven additional countries.

The Postal Inspection Service has also conducted more than 3,500 child-exploitation investigations since 1984 that have resulted in the arrest and conviction of close to 3,000 child molesters and pornographers. This service has undercover operations that place contact advertisements in sexually oriented publications via the Internet.

Thanks to the efforts of the FBI and its Innocent Images, as well as the other agencies that have joined in the fight against on-line sexual abuse, the prosecution of Internet-related sex crimes is increasing. A March 2000 report of the president's Working Group on Unlawful Conduct on the Internet reported that since 1995, the prosecution of these types of cases has increased 10 percent.

PREVENTION

Prevention programs that are sponsored by the FBI and the National Center for Missing and Exploited Children advocate that parents take responsibility for monitoring their children's activity on the Internet. The *Online Victimization* study revealed that, while a majority of parents reported that they talked to their children about Internet use and established rules for the safe use of the computer, less than half of them regularly checked their child's activity on the Internet. In addition, over half of the children surveyed did not need parental permission to use the Internet and didn't have any restrictions as to the number of hours they could spend on the Internet.

Many parents have a false sense of security regarding Internet use because they view the computer as a safe educational tool. They believe that because their children are at home, and often in their own rooms, they are safe from harm. But as you have just learned, this is not always true. As in all other areas of your child's life, you need to stay involved, keep the lines of communication open about Internet activities, and develop rules for safety.

Like all other household rules, you need to make sure that computer safety rules are made clear to your children. Explain the rules to your children because they may not be aware of all of the dangers involved on the Internet. Don't assume that because your child is computer savvy, he or she knows about these. Children should learn about the specific dangers involved in all aspects of the Internet, such as E-mail, newsgroups, and chat rooms, so that when they are given the rules about safe computer use they will have a better understanding of why they are essential.

> E-mail is like regular mail, except that the mail is sent via the computer rather than the post office. Once someone has your E-mail address, you can receive unwanted mail. Sometimes the messages request you to buy something or link you up to an Internet site. Messages can be sent to thousands of people at a time in a mass mailing, which is called "spamming." Some messages may contain viruses that can destroy your computer files, while others may be harmful to children because they contain sexually explicit material.

  Every E-mail that is sent or received has a return address. However, a return address may be false. For instance a message from friend@home.com may actually be from a sexual predator whose real E-mail address is sex@pornography.com. Messages may also give you false headers about the true content of the material.

> Newsgroups, which are also called bulletin boards or forums, are places where individuals can post and read messages or download or upload files. Newsgroups are not "live" like chat rooms. Instead, any posted message remains on the bulletin board for people to review later. Newsgroups are also used to post files, computer programs, stories, and pictures, and usually include E-mail addresses so that other people with common interests can respond. While newsgroups can be a great place to share ideas and information, they can also be dangerous. When a child posts personal information on a bulletin board, it is there for everyone to see. That child, therefore, may be sent sexually explicit stories, illustrations, or photos. Be aware, that, like E-mail messages, certain newsgroups may hide their real intent with misleading information and thus lure a child into a pornographic site.

> Chat rooms are probably the most dangerous areas on the Internet. Being in a chat room is like being on a "party line." Instead of talking on the phone, however, the person is typing messages on a keyboard, and everyone in the chat room can see what is being typed. You can never be certain who is in the chat room. Some chat rooms have monitors or chaperones who make sure that people are acting properly. If someone is acting inappropriately, they can

ensure that this person leave the chat room, but only after the fact. There are also private chat rooms that are available, and monitors can't prevent users from entering these. And because these are un-monitored, they can be dangerous.

It is important to realize that in a chat room, people can pose as someone else. Chat rooms that are for "teens only" may be visited by unscrupulous adults who are posing as teens. Adolescents may wish to meet someone who seems sympathetic and understanding and who will offer them advice and friendship, and they may be tempted to unknowingly arrange a meeting with a sexual predator. Obviously, this is extremely risky, and meetings should never occur unless they take place in a public area and a parent accompanies the adolescent.

ESSENTIAL TIPS FOR PARENTS TO HELP PREVENT INTERNET ABUSE

- ➤ Become computer literate. When parents know little about com-puters or the Internet, they are likely to be unaware of the potential risks involved. Therefore it is essential that parents understand how to check their child's web site activity and how to access their E-mail. They should also be able to select and use software that will block or restrict their child's access to certain web sites.
- ➤ Most computer users gain access to the Internet by using either an Internet service provider or an on-line service. These services set up an account for the computer user that allows access to web sites, E-mail, chat rooms, and newsgroups, as well as the ability to listen to music and watch videos. Consider using a service provider that pro-vides special child accounts with restricted access and ask your ser-vice provider how to best protect any personal information that your child may submit to an Internet site. Yet be aware that while on-line services may exercise some control over the type of content that is displayed on their service, they have no control over what goes on in cyberspace as a whole.
- ➤ Consider software programs that will block access to certain sites and help parents decide which Internet sites their children may visit. These services will rate web sites for content and allow parents to block sites that contain objectionable material. Certain programs

can prevent underage Internet users from entering information such as name and address or prevent a child from entering chat rooms. Still others can restrict the ability to send or read E-mail. Cyberpatrol and Net Nanny offer software to help protect your child from cyberabuse.

The *Online Victimization* study found that, despite the high levels of concern among parents, only a third of the families in their study were actually employing any filtering or blocking software, including software made available by the Internet providers themselves. However, no software program can possibly block out every inappropriate site. According to Enough is Enough, an organization that has joined the fight against pedophilia online, the United States has over twenty thousand outlets selling hard-core pornography over the Internet. In fact, they state, "There are more outlets for hard-core pornography in the United States than McDonald's restaurants."

Therefore, if you do decide to use a blocking program, discuss this decision with your child so that he or she will understand why it is necessary. Even with these safety programs in place, continue to emphasize the basic Internet safety rules and monitor your child's on-line activities. The following recommendations will greatly increase your child's safety on the Internet:

> ➤ Spend time with your child on the computer. Put the computer in a place that can be easily accessed by the entire family. Use the Internet with your child to play games, plan for a family vacation, or learn about new places and people. Ask your child to teach you more about the computer and to show you certain tricks he or she may have learned. Not only will you gain computer knowledge, you will also get valuable information on just how savvy your child is on the computer. Make sure to ask your child what he or she likes on the Internet and to show you favorite sites.
> ➤ Let your child know that you will be periodically watching and monitoring his or her on-line activities.
> ➤ Share an on-line pseudonym, password, and E-mail account with your child. In this way, you can monitor on-line correspondences and the Internet sites that your child has accessed.
> ➤ *Never, under any circumstances,* allow your child to have face-to-face contact with someone they met online without your permission. If

you agree to the meeting, accompany your child and arrange for it to take place in public.

➤ Don't allow your child to go into *private* chat rooms without your permission and supervision.

➤ Monitor your credit card bill. Many pornographic on-line vendors require credit cards in order to have access to their sites.

➤ Alert your Internet provider if you or your child come across sexually obscene material. You can also notify the National Center for Missing and Exploited Children's Cyber Tipline, your local police, or the FBI.

➤ Visit on-line web sites with your child, such as Cyberangels.com, that educate families about how to protect themselves from predators on the Internet.

While many of the above rules can be easily applied to younger children, they may be more difficult to implement with older adolescents since they have more experience and are striving toward independence from their parents. To regularly check their Internet and E-mail use may be seen as a real invasion of privacy, much like reading their mail. However, even for older teens, it is essential that you talk openly to them about their Internet use because older teens are actually more likely to get into trouble than younger children. They are more apt to explore the out-of-the-way nooks and crannies of cyberspace and reach out to people outside of their immediate peer group. Therefore, if you do suspect that your older teen is engaging in dangerous behavior on the Internet, it is important that you intervene as quickly as possible.

While I am not advocating searching your child's computer every time you feel uncomfortable about a situation, parents need to be informed about their child's Internet use. No matter what age, your children's use of the Internet should never be done in total seclusion or complete privacy. You should be able to share their Internet activities and talk about what they are experiencing online.

Rules for Internet Use:

The following rules should be given to your children when they are using the Internet.

Children Should:

- ➤ Never give out personal information on the Internet, such as their address, telephone number, the name or location of their school, or their parents' names. Web sites or other on-line services may ask children for information in order to enter special contests or to obtain free gifts. Other web sites won't allow access unless the user gives them personal information. However, once personal information is given, it is important that your children understand that their privacy can be compromised. Their names could end up on a sales database, or worse, the information could be used to harm or exploit them.
- ➤ Be cautious when developing a web site. Children should know never to post a home address, telephone number, or personal photograph on the site. If children wish to have people contact them, they should post an E-mail address. However, children should be aware that once an E-mail address is posted, they may receive unwanted messages. Children should be very cautious when opening any E-mail from an unknown address. If children receive messages that are threatening or sexually explicit, they should immediately inform their parents.
- ➤ Always inform their parents when they come across anything online that makes them uncomfortable. Parents and children can alert their Internet provider or the National Center for Missing and Exploited Children hot line.
- ➤ Never, under any circumstances, agree to meet face-to-face someone they have corresponded with online without a parent's permission. If a meeting is arranged, make sure that it takes place in public and that parents always accompany the child.
- ➤ Avoid chat rooms that discuss sex or cults. While these topics may seem interesting at first, they could put a child in danger.
- ➤ Be suspicious of anyone they meet in a chat room who tries to turn them against their family, friends, teachers, or religion.
- ➤ Choose a gender-neutral on-line name in a chat room to avoid harassment.
- ➤ Never respond to messages or bulletin boards that are sexually obscene, threatening, or make them feel uncomfortable in any way.

➤ Never send any personal materials to an on-line friend, such as an address, telephone number, or photograph, without first informing parents.

➤ Always be reminded that the people they meet online may not be who they say they are.

RESOURCES

There are many organizations that address the issues of child sexual abuse on the Internet.

1. The Federal Bureau of Investigation has an extensive web site that offers parents and children a great deal of information about Internet safety and where you can learn more about Innocent Images. Their web site address is www.fbi.gov.

2. The Federal Trade Commission hosts a web page for parents and children to help them understand the provisions of the Children's Online Privacy Protection Act that relate to the collection of personal information online from underage users. Their web site is www.ftc.gov/kidsprivacy.

3. The National Center for Missing and Exploited Children (NCMEC) provides reports for families about on-line safety. You can contact them at 1-800-843-5678 or online at www.missingkids.com. The NCMEC also offers a Cyber Tipline that has information about reporting on-line abuse. You can log onto their web site at www.cybertipline.com.

4. The Children's Partnership organization educates parents about the Internet as well as issues pertaining to children's use of computers. They can be reached at 1-310-260-1220 or at www.childrenspartnership.org.

5. Enough is Enough is an organization that focuses on making pornographic material unavailable to children. It encourages community efforts to guard against pornography. Their phone number is toll free, 1-888-2-ENOUGH, or you can log onto their web site at www.enough.org.

6. SafeSurf is an organization that is working toward creating

an Internet rating standard that will allow web browsers to detect the content of web sites before it is displayed on the screen. Their telephone number is 818-902-9390 and their web site is www.safesurf.com.

7. The on-line Public Education Network is a partnership of the Internet Alliance, the National Consumers League, and the leading Internet and on-line services such as America Online, AT&T, CompuServe, Microsoft, Netcom, and Bell Atlantic. It addresses privacy issues, and works to educate consumers about safe and responsible on-line use. For more information contact their web site at www.internetalliance.org.

8. At www.childlures.com there is a program that informs children, parents, and educators of safety issues regarding children on the Internet. It also offers an Internet safety pact that children and parents can read and sign.

9. Cyberangels promotes child safety and abuse-prevention methods on the Internet. Their web site is www.cyberangels.org.

10. PedoWatch is one of the oldest web sites in existence that works with law enforcement to combat child pornography and child seduction on the Internet. Their address is www.pedowatch.org.

11. Inside PANdora's Box offers a wealth of information regarding children and Internet access. They can be found at www.prevent-abuse-now.com.

12. www.officer.com provides hundreds of links to a wide array of police agencies in every state in America. No matter where you live, you can find a police agency near your home to report on-line sexual abuse.

13. Safety Net in Pacific Bell Internet Services offers a guide to safe Internet use for families. Copies of Safety Net brochures can be obtained at public.pacbell.net.

*For Information on Your State's Laws on Child Pornography,
Contact the Following Organizations:*

1. National Clearinghouse on Child Abuse and Neglect
   P.O. Box 1182
   Washington, DC 20013-1182
   Toll-free: 1-800-FYI-3366
   Web site: http://www.calib.com/nccanch

2. National Center for Prosecution of Child Abuse
   American Prosecutors Research Institute
   Suite 150
   99 Canal Center Plaza
   Alexandria, VA 22314
   Telephone: 703-739-0321
   Web site: www.jus.state.nc.us

3. National Conference of State Legislatures
   Suite 700
   1560 Broadway
   Denver, CO 80202
   Telephone: 303-863-8003
   Web site: http://www.ncsl.org

4. Washburn University School of Law
   1700 College
   Topeka, KS 666621
   Telephone: 913-231-1088
   Web site: http://www.washlaw.edu/

The Following Web Sites Are Designed for Parents and Children:

1. Bess is an Internet retriever for kids, families, and schools.
2. Cybersitter is a family Internet site.
3. i-SAFE America offers Internet safety training for children
   and teens.

4. <u>MegaGo</u> is designed for children and offers a one-click service for searching the Internet.

The Following Offer Software for Safe Internet Use:

1. <u>Cyber Patrol</u>
2. <u>Net Nanny</u>

D espite the warnings you have just read about concerning the dangers of sexual abuse on the Internet, keep in mind that, for the most part, cyberspace can be an exciting and adventurous territory for the entire family. The potential for learning is endless, and Internet use should not be forsaken because of potential harm. Just like a modern city, with its wealth of cultural resources, the Internet provides a wonderful opportunity for exploration and growth. However, similar to a city, the Internet has its caverns of decadence and dimly lit avenues of dark intentions. With the knowledge you have gained in this chapter, you and your child can now navigate cyberspace with a sense of purpose, challenge, adventure, and safety.

Now that you have learned about the potential dangers that may be in your own home, your neighborhood, or on your child's computer, what further steps can you take to ensure that your child doesn't come in contact with a sex offender? In chapter 8, you will discover another important preventative tool, the Sex Offender Registry. If used properly, the registry can provide you with valuable information about the identification and location of sexual predators in your neighborhood.

Sex Offender Registries and Community Notification

It was a hot evening on July 29th, 1994, in Hamilton Township, New Jersey. Seven-year-old Megan Kanka had just had dinner, the sun was setting low in the sky, and she was eager to go outside. Megan lived on Barbara Lee Drive, a pleasant tree-lined street in a middle-class neighborhood. Maureen and Richard, Megan's parents, allowed Megan to go outside that fateful evening, unaware that danger lurked in their neighborhood. Jesse Timmendequas, a thirty-three-year-old, twice-convicted pedophile, also lived there. He was a parks worker for a nearby town, and he shared a house with two other single men. Unbeknownst to Megan or her parents, Jesse had been secretly watching Megan and had detected his next victim. The tragic events that followed would propel Megan Kanka's parents to launch a crusade that would culminate in a national debate over how society should protect itself from convicted sex offenders who were released back into the community.

Shortly after Megan left her house, Jesse lured her into his home on the pretense of seeing his new puppy. By 7:40 P.M. Megan had not returned home, and her parents began to worry. A search of the neighborhood began, and by 8:45 darkness was settling in and Megan had not been found. The police were called, and they went door-to-door on the street and talked to neighbors, including Jesse Timmendequas. He denied any knowledge of the disappearance of the little girl, but the police were suspicious. He refused to make eye contact with them, and he appeared nervous. Search dogs were brought in, but they failed to find a trail that led to his house. Efforts to find Megan continued without success throughout the night.

The next day, the police discovered scraps of Megan's clothing buried in the trash outside of Timmendequas's house. After hours of questioning, Timmendequas eventually admitted to raping and strangling Megan. He had stuffed her body in a plastic toy chest and dumped it among the weeds at a nearby park.

The Kankas had just suffered an unimaginable loss, but they were determined to give meaning to the senseless act of violence that had taken their daughter's life. They believed that something was very wrong with a system that would release a Jesse Timmendequas on an uninformed and defenseless community. The Kankas began to lobby for legislation that would require registration and public identification of convicted sex offenders.

Almost a year later, in the neighboring state of New York, on June 9, 1995, fifty-eight-year-old George Miller raped and murdered four-year-old My Ly Nghiem. Miller was a three-time convicted child molester, and he was the caretaker in the apartment building in which My Ly lived with her family. Her death, along with Megan Kanka's and other child victims across the United States, was a catalyst for the passage of laws that would attempt to protect children from dangerous sex offenders.

Megan's parents believed that they were not given the opportunity to protect their daughter from a violent sexual predator because they didn't know that one was living nearby. Therefore, in an attempt to protect other children, they lobbied for a law that would inform citizens if a high-risk sex offender was living in their community. The Sex Offender Registration Act, appropriately named Megan's Law, was first enacted in New Jersey. Megan's Law attracted media attention and gained considerable political momentum. On May 17, 1996, President Clinton signed a national version into law that required all fifty states to have a Sex Offender Registry and a community notification plan. For the Kankas and other parents whose children were victims of heinous sex crimes, the passage of federal and state laws mandating the release of information necessary to protect the public from high-risk sex offenders would protect other children from the terrible fate that had befallen their own.

The information you are about to learn carries with it a weight of responsibility. You will learn how in some cases you can search the Sex Offender Registry and identify certain individuals who may be living in your community. What you do with that information is critical. Sex abuse is a frightening topic, and fear can distort perceptions and alter judgments. Moreover, fear is contagious, and it can spread through a community like wildfire and affect even the most reasonable among us. The laws that you are about to learn are very controversial because they deal with the identification of sex offenders who may then be subject to a great deal of suspicion, fear, and retaliation from others. The knowledge you will gain can either fan the flames of fear, in which case, it can be misused as retaliatory ammunition, or it could be assimilated judiciously as one preventative measure used to protect your child. Later on in this chapter, I will discuss in greater detail the controversies that exist with Megan's Law. For example, you will become aware that some professionals caution against the accuracy of the Sex Offender Registries since innocent people have been misidentified as sex offenders, while certain convicted sex offenders' names were never found on the registry. You will learn how to handle the information you receive from the registries in a responsible manner in order to avoid vigilantism.

MEGAN'S LAW

There are three federal statutes that serve as the foundation for the sex offender registration and community notification plan in the United States. Although these statutes are commonly referred to as Megan's Law, in actuality, Megan's Law is only one of these laws.

1. *Megan's Law* requires the states to release sex offender registration information that is "necessary to protect the public."
2. *The Jacob Wetterling Crimes Against Children and Sexually Violent Offender Registration Act*, enacted in 1994, is named after Jacob Wetterling, an eleven-year-old Minnesota boy who was abducted at gunpoint on October 22, 1989. This crime is still unsolved. The act provides financial incentive to states who establish ten-year registra-

tion requirements for persons convicted of certain crimes against minors and sexually violent offenses. The law establishes strict registration requirements for a subclass of highly dangerous sex offenders, characterized as "sexually violent predators." A *sexually violent predator* is defined in the act as "a person who has been convicted of a sexually violent offense, and who suffers from a mental abnormality or personality disorder that makes the person likely to engage in predatory sexually violent offenses." States that do not establish the registration requirements within three years risk reduction in certain government funding, which will then be disbursed to states that are in compliance with the act. The Jacob Wetterling Act is a government attempt at establishing nationwide compliance with certain registration requirements and encouraging states to maintain or expand their registration requirements.

3. *The Pam Lychner Sexual Offender Tracking and Identification Act* mandates a creation of a national sex offender database to be available to the FBI. Pam Lychner, a Texas real estate agent, was attacked in a vacant house by a twice-convicted felon. Lychner survived the attack because her husband arrived at the house and intervened. Pam and her husband helped lobby for the act to be passed. This act also requires the FBI to maintain sex offender registration and community notification in states unable to establish a minimally sufficient protection program of their own.

Adoption by States

While the national version of Megan's Law called for a Sex Offender Registry and a community notification plan in all fifty states, each state differs in the implementation of this law. Some states have a very strong notification program while others are weak. (Refer to the tables at the end of this chapter for information about the Sex Offender Registry in each state.) At a minimum, the registration aspect of Megan's Law requires offenders to register so that law enforcement is aware of their presence in the community. Community notification means that, at the very least, schools, daycare centers, and other vulnerable entities will be alerted when a registered sex offender moves into the community.

Robert Scott, a private investigator, provides a comprehensive guide to

Megan's Law in each state in his book, *Sexual Predator: How to Identify Registered and Unregistered Sex Offenders.* (However, since the book was published in 1999, it is important to investigate if there have been any changes in your state's laws since that time.)

Scott compares Megan's Law in several states in order to illustrate the states' different interpretations of this law. In 1990, Washington was the first state to permit community notification of sex offenders. Washington adopted its notification law after a recently released sex offender lured a seven-year-old boy into a wooded area, raped him, and then severed his penis. Washington allows local law-enforcement agencies to develop their own procedures for disclosure of information to their communities.

In Louisiana, convicted sex offenders, at their own expense, must send a notice by mail to residents within one mile of their residence in rural areas, and within a three-block radius in urban or suburban areas, as well as to the superintendent of the school district in that community. The offender must also publish two separate notices of his or her presence and past conviction in the local paper. Louisiana also reserves the right to require other publicity of the offender's presence.

Oregon's sex offender notification law is probably the most public. The agency that supervises the sex offender is allowed to use any means of communication it deems appropriate. For instance, high-risk sex offenders may be required to post a black-and-yellow poster shaped like a stop sign in the front window of their home, which reads SEX OFFENDER RESIDENCE.

New Jersey's notification law is the most extensive and far-reaching. The law allows dissemination of a convicted sex offender's likeness, place of employment, a description and identification of his or her motor vehicle, address, nature of crime, and conviction. New Jersey uses a three-tiered approach to notification. If the offender poses a low risk of reoffense, only law-enforcement agencies are notified of his or her presence in the community. If there is a moderate risk, officials notify schools, religious groups, and youth organizations. Individual residents in the community where the offender lives are notified if there is a high risk of reoffense. New Jersey's laws have been recently broadened to allow an Internet registry of convicted rapists, child molesters, and other sexual predators.

Texas requires sex offenders convicted in that state over the past thirty years to submit to having their names, addresses, and photographs available on the World Wide Web. Sex offenders must also renew their driver's licenses every year, and their sex offense data will appear on the license's magnetic strip. Serious offenders are also required to mail postcards to prospective neighbors (within three blocks in urban areas and two miles in rural areas).

In California, community members can go to any local police station and use a CD-ROM that reveals profiles of 72,000 registered sex offenders. One can search the CD-ROM by name or zip code. Other states, like Florida and Nevada, have an Internet site with offenders' photos and a hot-line number. Many states do not have Internet access to their registries, and notification is only allowed through local law enforcement. Some states, like Pennsylvania, only publicize the names of high-risk sexually violent predators convicted after April 21, 1996. Appendix B at the end of this book will give the reader a state-by-state analysis of Megan's Law. It is important to note that each state is different regarding the access allowed to their registry, the methods of obtaining information (i.e., mail, phone, Internet), and when they began to require sex offenders to register.

IMPLEMENTING THE SEX OFFENDER REGISTRY

The goal of a Sex Offender Registry is to ensure that accurate and complete information about released sex offenders is made available to protect the public and prevent further victimization. Specifically, the program will ensure that the state's sexual offender registries identify, collect, and properly disseminate relevant information that is consistent, accurate, complete, and up-to-date.

Registration laws generally require that persons convicted of certain sexual offenses must register with local authorities where they live and must update their registration whenever they change addresses. Most states and communities have enacted this law.

Some states have review procedures to determine the level of public notification. In most cases a three-level system that ranks sex offenders according to their perceived risk of reoffending is used to determine what type of information is disseminated and how that information will be made public.

Level 1, which is the lowest risk, requires that the information on the sex offender be shared with other law-enforcement agencies. Level II, which is moderate risk, provides information to schools, neighbors, and community groups. Level III, which is high risk, may allow for residents in the community to be notified by press release or posting information, in addition to the other requirements in the lower levels.

To further understand how the registry operates, let's look at Wisconsin and examine the process that takes place when a sex offender registers. In Wisconsin, every convicted sex offender has to register with the State Department of Corrections once a year. Department computers send each registrant an address verification letter close to his or her annual registration date, and the offender has ten days to respond. As soon as the response is received, the computer will generate a letter to the offender's reported address to verify whether the person actually lives there. If Corrections doesn't receive anything back or receives a "return to sender" notification, the system identifies the offender as noncompliant, and an investigation will follow.

The computerized registration system will keep track of how many registered sex offenders there are in each county and which ones have not complied with registration requirements. Because the Sex Offender Registry is connected to the state's computerized Crime Information Bureau database, police officers checking on criminal histories and arrest warrants will also know whether someone they have arrested has failed to register as a sex offender or is a registered sex offender.

Now that you understand what the Sex Offender Registry is and how it operates, you need to know how to access this information.

SEARCHING THE REGISTRY:
NAME VERSUS COMMUNITY SEARCHES

Not every state allows public access to the Sex Offender Registry. However, depending on the implementation of Megan's Law in your state, you may be able to conduct either a name search or a community search.

Name Searches

The following are examples of situations that would be applicable for a name search of the Sex Offender Registry:

➤ You are in the process of hiring a new baby-sitter. Julie Marie *Smith* has applied for the position, and before going any further with the interview process, you would like to see if Julie Marie *Smith* is registered as a sex offender.

➤ You have joint custody of your two daughters, who come to spend every weekend with you at your condominium. Just recently, a middle-aged man, Robert P. *Smith*, moved into the building. He seems aloof and unapproachable. You have questioned the neighbors, and no one seems to know anything about him. You notice, however, that he spends an inordinate amount of time talking to the children. He meets them at the condominium's recreation center and has been known to buy them candy and gifts. Is Robert P. *Smith* a registered sex offender?

➤ You are a single woman with small children, and you have met an interesting man named Richard L. *Smith* on the Internet dating service you recently joined. You have been trading E-mails for a few months, and you have also chatted on the phone a number of times. He seems promising, and he is interested in meeting you. You are concerned about the safety of yourself and your children. Is Richard L. *Smith* registered as a sex offender?

Steps Involved in Conducting a Name Search

1. Look up your state's version of Megan's Law and determine how your state has implemented this law.

2. It is critical that when doing a name search, you obtain a *second* means of identifying that person, such as a middle name or initial, date of birth, a photograph, last known address, or a social security number. These types of identifiers can often be found through application forms, voter registration or motor vehicle records (if they are made available to the public), phone directories, and court records. *These are essential to ensure positive identification of an offender.*

3. If your state allows you access to a Sex Offender Registry, check to see if the name of the person you are investigating is on the list. It is important, however, that you take careful note of the limitations of the Sex Offender Registry in your state. Some of the registries list

only those sex offenders who were convicted in the past three years, while others may include those individuals convicted of a sexual offense as far back as the mid-eighties. Therefore it is possible for a person to have committed a sexual offense twenty years ago and not be listed on your state's registry.

4. Compare the personal identifiers provided by your state's Sex Offender Registry with the personal identifiers of the person you are investigating. It is only when *two or more* personal identifiers match that a positive identification can be made.

Community Search

A community search will tell you if there are sex offenders living in your immediate neighborhood, town, county, or zip code, and might be helpful in the following situations:

- ➤ Your daughter's youth group has just voted to raise money by selling candy. Besides parents, teachers, and family friends who will donate money, the children will be going door-to-door to sell the candy. You are concerned about the safety of your child and whether there are any doors that you don't want her to knock on. Is there a registered sex offender living in your area?
- ➤ You have recently moved into a new home, and your twelve-year-old son wants to distribute a notice that he is available to care for lawns. You encourage his desire to earn extra money, but you are concerned about the strangers who populate your new neighborhood. Are any of them registered sex offenders?
- ➤ Your daughter has been a victim of sexual abuse in the past, and you have just moved to a neighborhood to start a new life. You are fearful of this occurring once again, and you find yourself hypervigilant and overly cautious about your new neighbors. To ensure your peace of mind and to give you a greater sense of control and safety, you would like to conduct a community search to see if there are any registered sex offenders in your area.

Steps Involved in Conducting a Community Search

1. Look up your state's version of Megan's Law to determine whether your state allows community searches.
2. If your state has a Sex Offender Registry that allows community searches, you must follow the state's guide to receiving information on the registrants in a particular geographic area.

Besides accessing the Sex Offender Registry yourself to determine the presence of a registered sex offender in your community, your child's day care, school, youth sports camp, community organizations, and houses of worship may also be able to provide you with this information. According to the law, schools and other vulnerable entities may disclose or further disseminate information about a registered sex offender at *their discretion.* You may want to check with your child's day care, preschool, or school to see how they are managing high-risk sex offender notification. But once again remember that mistakes can be made by putting innocent people on the list. Therefore checking with the police department for verification of criminal reports may be helpful in assuring that the listed individual *is* a sexual offender.

Parents for Megan's Law, an organization that is easily accessed on the Internet, provides information for parents on how to effectively use name and community searches. They have also developed regulations and sample letters that help parents check with schools, superintendents, or persons in charge of a facility for information about registered sex offenders.

Technology has helped make the community notification process easier in certain states. Megan's Mapper is a software program that uses geographic mapping to notify residents when a sex offender moves into their area. The Reno, Nevada, and Huntsville, Alabama, police departments use this program, which is able to generate thousands of notification letters in minutes. With the push of a button, a police computer can print out address labels, flyers, and the locations of sex offenders. The program also tracks where sex offenders live and creates databases of sex offenders who are not required to register.

Before this software was developed, police had to drive to the communities where sex offenders were located and look up the addresses of schools and child-care centers to notify them. In the case of a high-risk offender, some police had department officers go door-to-door alerting everyone living within 2,500 feet of the offender.

The software also alerts police if a sex offender is living too close to a prohibited location, such as a child-care center, school, or even to their victim. Pinellas County, Florida, uses a similar software program they call "The Enforcer," which is a mapping program that uses county tax records and state licensing information to track sex offenders. Soon, "The Enforcer," like Megan's Mapper, will be able to print mailing lists and address labels for community notification.

DO THE REGISTRY AND COMMUNITY NOTIFICATION WORK?

According to the Bureau of Justice's Statistics report, in 1997, almost 60 percent of the 234,000 convicted sex offenders were living in the community on parole or probation. However, do the Sex Offender Registry and community notification plan establish a greater degree of protection for our children from these sex offenders?

An important determinant regarding the effectiveness of the registry and community notification is the rate of reoffenses committed by sex offenders who are subject to these laws. However, there exists controversy in regard to the entire issue of the recidivism rate for sex offenders.

Certain research studies indicate that sex offenders have a high rate of recidivism, while others suggest that, with proper treatment, their recidivism rate is actually lower than that of other criminals. Yet despite the controversy that exists over recidivism rates in sex offenders, the fact remains that, due to the overcrowded conditions in our prisons and the often insufficient funds for implementing effective treatment programs, many sex offenders are released back into the community with the same problems that first led to their arrest.

The Sex Offender Registry and community notification plan are designed to increase public safety by warning citizens of a sexual offender in their community, and the increased surveillance of the sexual offender will presumably deter his or her future acts of violence. But does this occur?

A study done by the Washington State Institute for Public Policy, prepared by Donna Schram and Cheryl Darling Milloy in 1995, examined how the community notification laws were being implemented in the state of Washington and the impact of community notification on the recidivism rate among 150 sex offenders. The study found that in the state of Washington, community notification had little effect on recidivism, yet it may have had an effect on the timing of new arrests. The study found that offenders who were subject to community notification, because of the police surveillance and public awareness, were arrested for new crimes quicker than offenders who had been released into the community without notification.

In the same year, two other studies of sex offender community notification programs were done in Oregon and Wisconsin. The Oregon study found that the supervised sex offenders had a recidivism rate of approximately 5 percent, and that overall there were benefits to the community and the offenders when a responsible and well-planned notification program was put into effect. The results of the study done in Wisconsin revealed that while the notification program may have had a benefit for the general public, the impact on the sex offender was more questionable. Although there were no published statistics on recidivism, interviews with sex offenders revealed that most of them believed the notification laws wouldn't prevent reoffending. In fact, they felt that these laws would have just the opposite effect because they placed a tremendous pressure on sex offenders that could drive many of them back to prison.

It is important to be aware, however, that these studies were limited by the relatively small number of offenders who were included in the research. Comprehensive studies need to be conducted with larger numbers of subjects and longer follow-up periods to more accurately assess the impact of community notification on recidivism.

Similar to the sentiments described by the sex offenders in the Wisconsin study regarding recidivism and community notification, there is concern among many critics of the notification program that the Sex Offender Registry could actually *increase* the likelihood of reoffense. A December 19, 1999, *Austin American-Statesman* article, written by Mike Ward, voices a concern about the impact of these laws on the sex offender. "Publicly branding them for life makes their successful, law-abiding reentry into society much more difficult — in low-paying jobs, in cheap apartments in bad neighborhoods, in seclusion."

As you have been made aware, there also exists concern about the validity of the Sex Offender Registry, for inaccurate information can have dire consequences if it leads to the identification of an innocent individual. Sex offender registries have been found to have misinformation and, in some cases, were incomplete. The accuracy of the registry depends upon the compliance of all released sex offenders to register. While it is a crime in most states for an offender to fail to register or to give false addresses, follow-up on these cases can be costly and time-consuming for already overburdened police departments.

Michael Ward found that a spot check of ten offenders' files on the Texas Department of Public Safety web site revealed seven of them had erroneous information related to the address of the offender, the gender and age of the victims, and the crimes that had been committed.

Some critics also believe that the Sex Offender Registry appears to classify all sex offenders in a similar category and may be unfair to certain types of registered offenders, such as juveniles, mentally retarded individuals, or persons convicted under statutory rape laws. For example, an eighteen year old who had had consensual sex with his fifteen-year-old girlfriend could be required to file with the Sex Offender Registry. Should this individual be listed with other offenders who may have committed a number of sexual assaults on young children? This calls into question whether the public is sufficiently informed to discern the potential risk of a particular registered sex offender.

Along with the many concerns that exist in regard to the Sex Offender Registry, community notification programs are also under attack. Monica Ratchford in her publication, *Community Notification of Sex Offenders*, talks about the constitutional, ethical, and practical issues that categorize the controversy over community notification laws. She states that constitutional challenges to community notification statutes have included a number of arguments claiming that it is a form of ex post facto punishment, denies equal protection, violates due process rights, impinges upon the right to privacy, and constitutes cruel and unusual punishment.

The courts have generally concluded that the notification laws, while they may impinge on a person's privacy under certain circumstances, are necessary to protect the rights of society's children. Yet ethical dilemmas do exist with regard to the government's release of selected information. In the future could public notification extend to all adolescents who have AIDS? Ratchford questions why community notification laws only target sex offenders. For if the public has repeatedly voiced concerns about violent crimes, why not extend the legislation to include all forms of violent offenses?

Many of the critics of the community notification laws believe that once the public is aware of an offender's location, the offender has limited chances of reintegrating into society because sex offenders are likely to be treated much more adversely than other criminals. And this is particularly relevant when it comes to the juvenile offender. As noted previously in chapter 5, labeling a young offender could significantly impact his or her future development.

Critics argue that community notification may also negatively affect the offender's treatment. Sex offenders who are actively engaged in changing their lives may feel that the cards are stacked against them when the public is aware of their presence. They may believe that they will never be given the chance to interact in a normal fashion in society and will be forced into low-level jobs and live in run-down apartments far away from the protected middle-class communities that will decry their presence.

While many sex offenders have trouble managing stress and handling their anger, the added pressure that comes with public identification could force some to leave treatment and choose obscurity. Certain professionals who treat sex offenders argue that the offenders need a stable, consistent, and supportive environment in which to live, and the vigilantism and harassment that could result from public awareness of their presence could easily destabilize the sex offender in treatment. Many offenders claim that the community notification process adversely affected their transition from prison to the outside world. Sex offenders interviewed in the Wisconsin study on community notification revealed that loss of employment, exclusion of residence, and the breakup of personal relationships were three deleterious consequences of the expanded notification action. Twenty-three out of the thirty who were being interviewed for the study told of being humiliated in their daily lives, being ostracized by neighbors and lifetime acquaintances, and of being harassed or threatened by nearby residents and strangers.

An important ethical dilemma in the notification program involves those offenders who have committed incest, for public notification will inevitably lead to public identification of the victims. If the last known address of the offender was their own home, or they have been reintegrated into their family, the identities of the offender's family will therefore be exposed. This could lead to further victimization of the child and the family. While child sex abuse is commonly believed to be underreported because victims fear being exposed, notification laws may serve to further prohibit victims from reporting abuse. *The National Institute of Justice: Research in Brief on Sex Offender Community Notification: Assessing the Impact in Wisconsin*, by Richard Zevitz and Mary Ann Farkas, cited a number of instances where sex offenders' family members were harassed. One interviewee talked of his mother's anguish and depression following the newspaper accounts stemming from the notification that he was a sex offender, while another talked of his son's decision to quit his high school football team because of the ridicule from teammates. A third adolescent offender talked about how his sister's victimization became public knowledge at the school following the notification that he had committed sibling sexual abuse.

Does public notification create a false sense of security, or does it create panic and terrorize a community? Critics of the notification laws state that it does both. While community members may feel safer in being able to avoid a particular offender, released offenders have been known to give false addresses or not register at all, and, therefore, their whereabouts are completely unknown. *STOP IT NOW!*'s publication *Child Sexual Abuse: Facts About Abuse and Those Who Might Commit It* reported that despite the lawmakers' attempts at making sure convicted sex offenders register with the police, 84 percent of them never registered. It is also possible that registered sex offenders will travel to an uninformed community in search of victims. Therefore parents may be lulled into a false sense of security by believing that they know the locations of every sex offender in their community and may relax some of the preventative measures they had once instilled in their children. Parents need to understand that accessing the Sex Offender Registry *does not guarantee absolute protection*. The following case illustrates how sex offenders could fall through the cracks of the system and be in the community without the residents' awareness.

> In June of 1998, Miami school bus driver Cesar Gonzales-Rubio was arrested for lewd and lascivious acts on a child. Megan's Law should have stopped him from ever working with children again, but it didn't. Less than a year following allegations that he had assaulted a child, Rubio was back at work driving a school bus.

Why was this offender allowed, once again, to interact with young children?

It happened because the eleven-year-old girl who initially accused Rubio of putting his hand down her skirt and fondling her changed her allegations. Initially, Rubio was arrested and charged with a felony sex offense that, if convicted, would have forced him to list his name on Florida's Sex Offender Registry. However, before Rubio's trial, the girl revised her story and said that Rubio had never touched her privates. Prosecutors were afraid that Rubio would escape all punishment, so they offered him a plea bargain. He pled to misdemeanor child abuse and was placed on probation. Unfortunately, his conviction did not require him to list his name on the Sex Offender Registry. No follow-up treatment was mandated, and Rubio was released. No one in the community knew about his previous offense, and Rubio continued to drive a school bus. On March 17, 1999, he was arrested again for child sexual assault. Since that date, approximately twelve children have come forward and revealed that Rubio had sexually molested them.

The above scenario is not an isolated incident of how sex offenders can slip through the cracks of the legal system. Accused sex offenders plea bargain to lesser offenses to keep their names from appearing on the Sex Offender Registry; and prosecutors, often eager for a conviction, are accepting these plea bargains. In response to this problem, a New York State legislator has sponsored a bill that would prevent plea bargaining in sex offense cases down to a non-sex-related crime. The problem is not only that these offenders are avoiding the registries; but when they plead to a nonsex crime, they don't get the treatment that they need, making it more likely that they will commit another sex offense.

On the other hand, knowledge that a sex offender is living in the community may not always foster a sense of security; it may, instead, generate a sense of anxiety and fear. Child sexual abuse is every parent's fear, and the knowledge that a sex offender is living in the neighborhood may transform generalized fear into an identifiable enemy. Fear often leads to many irrational behaviors that may be expressed through acts of violence.

There have been several instances of violence against sex offenders and their families when the community has been notified of their presence.

Some states have enacted statutes to prevent violence against a sex offender, yet despite these laws, some offenders have been forced to move to avoid harassment. Mike Ward cites an example of a vigilante attack on a man who was not a registered offender but who lived at the former address of a sex offender.

Robert Freeman-Longo, who is a nationally acclaimed expert on the prevention of sexual abuse and the treatment of sex offenders, has been an outspoken critic of the sex offender registries and community notification plans. His web site, Sexual Abuse Prevention and Education Resources International, includes a number of his commentaries regarding legislation for sex offenders. Freeman-Longo states in *Commentary: Challenging Our Thoughts* that the media's focus on high-profile sex crimes and sex murders gives the American public a "biased, distorted, and unrealistic view of sexual abuse," when, in actuality, violent sex crimes compose less than 3 percent of all sex crimes. According to Freeman-Longo, community notification laws foster an angry public who want to indiscriminately punish sex offenders regardless of their type, frequency of their crimes, or the actual risk they pose to the community. He emphasizes that not all sex abusers are alike, and they should not be handled in a similar fashion.

CAUTIONS IN USING THE SEX OFFENDER REGISTRY

Now that you are aware of the limitations, problems, and controversies of the Sex Offender Registry and community notification plan, it is important that you use the information from the registry in a *responsible* manner. The following cautions should be observed when using the registry:

- ➤ Never, under any circumstances, harass a registered sex offender. Remember that not only is this ethically wrong, but any type of harassment or vigilantism is likely to drive a registered sex offender underground. It is also important to be aware that an innocent person may be mistakenly identified as a registered sex offender and that not every registered sex offender poses the same risk. A sex offender may have been rehabilitated long ago and is now leading a normal life.
- ➤ Every situation is unique and should be handled differently. However, if you do believe that your children's safety is in danger, *do*

not handle the situation on your own. Contact your local police department for assistance.

➤ Once you have identified a sexual offender, it is critical that you take the necessary precautionary steps to make your child aware of this individual in order to protect your child. However, never allow your child to harass a known sex offender.

➤ Decide whether or not to share the information about a registered sex offender with other community residents. Once again, it is highly advisable *to first contact your local police station for guidance before taking matters into your own hands.* If the police believe that the offender is in danger of harming other children, they may decide to post flyers or have an informational community meeting.

STOP IT NOW!, an organization that promotes the prevention of sexual abuse of children, offers the following recommendations when you have been notified that a sex offender lives in your community:

➤ Share what information you feel would be helpful to your children about the sex offender in order to ensure their safety. Remember that you should never encourage your child to harass this individual.

➤ Ask the police whether the sex offender is being supervised by a probation or parole officer. You should be able to get the name and telephone number of the supervising officer. This person may be able to answer some more questions about the risk the offender poses to your family.

➤ Depending on how receptive the offender is to the community, you might consider talking to him or her. If the offender is open and honest, he or she may be really trying to change and live a different life and therefore would be willing to talk to you. You can show your support of the offender's recovery process, yet make him or her aware that you will protect your children.

➤ Notify the police if you see this person in a suspicious situation such as: spending time alone with a child, buying gifts for a child, talking to a child on a deserted street, or asking a child into his or her home. Most sex offenders on probation or parole will be restricted from contact with young children; and during their course of treatment, they learn that contact with young children is a trigger for them and to avoid these situations. Your watchfulness may help the abuser monitor his or her behaviors. Be mindful, however, that *never*, under any circumstances, should you make threats or harass an offender.

The presence of Megan's Law, and specifically the community notification plan, will continue to receive a great deal of attention as we struggle to find the most effective ways to protect our children from sexual predators. Because it is a national movement that relates to our greatest concern for the safety of our children, it will generate controversy over the moral, ethical, and constitutional rights of both the victim and the offender. However, if used responsibly and with the perspective and knowledge that you have learned in this book, Megan's Law can be another resource in protecting your child from harm.

As you have been made aware throughout this book, there exists a great deal of controversy over the question of whether or not a sex offender can be *cured*. The fear that is generated in our society about sexual predators often stems from the fact that we tend to see them as incurable individuals who are distinctly different from other criminals. However, as you will learn in the next chapter, this is not always the case, for in many instances sex offenders have been known to benefit from treatment and go on to live productive lives without ever harming another individual again. But how can you tell if a predator has been rehabilitated and is therefore safe to interact with your child? In the following chapter, you will meet sexual offenders in treatment in order to better understand the nature of their treatment and what exactly constitutes the definition of *cured*.

C h a p t e r 9

Can a Predator Be Cured?

The meeting room is small and crammed with two large couches, an old wooden coffee table, and mismatched chairs. Some of the men recline on overstuffed cushions, while others perch at the edge of their seats with notebooks balanced on their knees.

The fluorescent lights on the ceiling paint the walls a sallow green as an overhead bulb flickers to an uneven beat. Men's voices heat the air as fragments of conversation collide into one another.

"Did you see the game last night? I couldn't believe we pulled it out in the last quarter."

"No, didn't have time. I had to prepare my taxes and finish tonight's homework. Was it a good game?"

"Unbelievable, the offense was really in synch. Well, at least someone is on a winning streak 'cause it certainly isn't me."

"I know what you're saying. I had a fight with my girlfriend yesterday. I tried to call her all night, and I kept getting her answering machine. I'm sure she was home and screening her calls. I don't need this kind of stress right now."

"Talk about stress, I just came from my ex-wife's house. She's hitting me up for more child support. Great timing. I'm spending so much money on my treatment, I can barely afford food."

The men laugh in an attempt to temporarily ward off the grave realities they soon must face. The conversations cease as a tall man with glasses and an older woman enter the room. The man is wearing khaki pants and a striped cotton shirt that has come loose from his belt. Even though it is the end of the workday for many professionals, he strides to the center of the room with eagerness and intent. His coworker has on a long skirt that swirls gently around her feet as she walks to her chair. In her arms are stacks of printed material and an appointment book.

The therapists greet the twelve group members and take their seats among them. They scan the room for missing people and mark the names of those present. After the participants' fees are collected, they sit back in their chairs and begin the process.

The male therapist takes out a sheet of paper and taps a pen rhythmically on his knee. "Okay, let's start with check-ins. Who wants to go first?"

A heavy-set man in his late forties speaks out. "I will."

"Go ahead, Sol," the leader prompts. "How was your week?"

"Well, the week went fine except I couldn't see my probation officer. We had an appointment on Tuesday afternoon, and I just got a job. I can't tell my boss on the first day of work that I have to leave to see my probation officer."

John, a new group member who was convicted of assaulting his stepdaughter, becomes noticeably anxious. "Hey, do we have to tell our bosses that we're on probation? I haven't told mine yet. I can't afford to lose my job right now; my ex is hounding me for more child support."

The woman therapist looks at John and releases an audible sigh. "Yes, you should already have told your boss."

She then turns to face Sol. "But you have been in the group long enough to know that we expected you to inform your new employer of your status as a sexual offender *before* you were hired. Why have you set yourself up like this?"

Sol shakes his head and rolls his eyes. It is unclear whom he is the most disgusted with: himself or the group leaders.

"All right, I guess I just didn't want to take a chance with this new position. It took me so long to get it. I finally found a job that I'm proud to be doing. I can actually sit in my own office in the light of day and design software programs instead of cleaning up someone else's dirty office building at night. But I have no choice. If I have to do it, I'll tell him tomorrow after the company meeting. I think everything will be okay. He thinks I'm doing a great job."

The counselor continues her confrontation.

"I hope it goes okay, Sol. I know how much you wanted that job, but I also want you to look at how you set yourself up for disappointment and failure. Telling the truth up front is much better than hiding behind false pretenses."

She turns to face the group. "Many of you have been doing that your whole lives, and now it's time to come clean and present yourselves to the world as you really are."

She sits back in her chair, satisfied that she has made an important point. "So let's move on Sol. How was the rest of your week?"

"Pretty good. I'm writing in my journal everyday. In fact, I have last night's entry with me. Do you want me to read it?"

The group members voice their interest.

Sol opens a tattered notebook and begins to read out loud. "I used my safety plan last night when I was at the supermarket. I was standing in line, and this little girl was sitting in the cart right in front of me. Her mom was busy checking her groceries, and the little girl was squirming around. She was bored and wanted attention. She was so cute. She waved and offered me her hand. I smiled at her and reached out to take her hand. But then I remembered about my victims and how a few of them were the same age as this little girl. It's not as if I was planning to abuse her; but to be safe, I waved good-bye and went to another check-out line."

The room is silent for a moment until Jackson, a retired army officer with ten years of offender treatment under his belt, offers his feedback. "I think you did a good job, Sol. But then what happened? Did you have any sexual thoughts about this little girl later that night?"

The group members look at Sol, anticipating his reply.

"No. I know that I have to take my polygraph next week and I'll be asked that, so I can't lie. But honestly, I didn't fantasize about her at all. Besides, my tests say that I'm not sexually attracted to kids anymore."

Tony, a detective who had been with the police department for twenty-five years until his conviction for child sexual assault, takes this opportunity to challenge Sol. "Hey, I know that you claim not to have had sexual feelings for this little girl, but then why did you have to record in your journal that *she was cute.* Doesn't that imply that you were attracted to her? That's incriminating evidence, man."

"Come on, Tony, that's going a little too far. Like you never noticed that kids can be cute? Cute does not always mean something sexual." Sol turns to the group for support.

"Well, I know that I try to ignore kids as much as possible," offers Joe, a large and muscular man who once played on a professional sports team. "I can't take the chance that even being nice to kids will be seen as grooming them. I used to be around them all the time, signing autographs, giving talks to schools and Boy Scout troops. But now, no way! I'm out of that scene for good."

Sol is not convinced. "That's crazy. You mean, I should never see my sister's kids again until they grow up? Should I just ignore every kid I meet? That's pretty unrealistic. I thought the goal of this program was to learn to be around kids in a healthy way, not to run away from them every time we see them."

Once again the counselor intervenes.

"Sol, you know we don't advocate that. It's just that you need to be mindful of your intentions and actions every time you do come in contact with a child. I think that you did the right thing by moving away from that little girl, and obviously you did, too. You wrote in your journal about using your safety plan, so why are you being so defensive now?"

Sol nervously taps his heels on the carpet. "I don't know. I just feel that I'm always being accused of having sexual feelings for kids. I can't seem to make you guys understand that kids do not turn me on anymore. I just can't imagine that because of what I did four years ago, I'll always have to explain myself when I'm around kids."

B.J., a fifty-one-year-old auto mechanic who has been sitting silently with his arms crossed, comes alive with emotion. "You know, I feel the same way as Sol. I can't offer a kid candy, a pop, or even smile at them when they come into the station without thinking that I'm going to have to report this to my probation officer. I mean it's not like I'm going to groom every kid I meet. I know what I did to my girlfriend's kids was wrong, and I've learned a lot since then. But somehow I feel like I'm going to pay for the mistakes I made for the rest of my life. It's not fair."

Lance, a handsome, dark-haired accountant, shakes his head in agreement. "I know how you guys feel. Sometimes I forget what I did, and I just think that I'm a regular person who can go about my business like anybody else. Then I remember that I am a *sexual offender* in treatment, and because of that, I stand quite a few steps down the social ladder. Even if I never touch a kid again, I will always be branded as a sexual offender. I have these big scarlet letters that hang around my neck; but instead of an A they are an S and an O, for 'sexual offender.' "

The group's newest member, thirty-year-old Dennis, who is a hospital attendant, agrees with Lance. "It's difficult to live an everyday life. I have to think about everything I do. I can't even watch the tube anymore without having to switch channels when I see a young, sexy girl on a commercial or a kid in underwear. I even have to pick the movies I watch to make sure that they don't have young girls in sexy scenes. Well, I guess I won't be going to many movies from now on unless I stick with Disney."

The men chuckle as they nod their heads in recognition.

Tony, however, is not amused, and he continues to challenge the group. "Bottom line, guys. Whether we stay away from kids in the candy store or turn off sexy commercials, we do carry the signs of convictions with us all the time because all of us in here committed a sexual offense. We created victims, and we can't forget it. Our victims certainly can't forget it. And remember, once we forget who we are and what we have done, we could sexually offend again in a heartbeat."

"Tony's right. I mean we're all sexual offenders, and we may never live a normal life again," says Arnie, a college student and the youngest member of the group.

B.J. jumps at the opportunity to challenge Arnie.

"What do you know, Arnie? I don't know why you're here. I think it's bogus to have a guy in this group who had sex with a girl he met at a bar. She was just asking for it, hanging around there with a fake ID. You probably didn't even know she was underage. You're not a sex offender."

"Yes, I am, B.J. Do you think just because I'm young and in college, I couldn't have committed sexual abuse? Well, I hate to break it to you, but I'm no different from the rest of you. I knew all along that the girls I was meeting were too young to be at the bar. I could spot them at a glance. They thought I was so cool because I was a college guy, and I used that to get what I wanted from them. But I never felt good about myself. I knew that what I was doing was a scam just because I was too afraid to be with girls my own age. Even though it got me in this mess, I'm thankful to that girl who told her mother. Jeez, she was only fourteen, and she was really screwed up by the things we did. Who knows how far this would have gone if I hadn't been caught. My life would probably have been in a bigger mess than it is now."

Ian, another college student in the group, identifies with Arnie's situation. "You know, at first I didn't think that I belonged in this group either. I mean, I was just a freshman in college, and I really believed that the girls who claimed that I'd raped them were full of it. I thought they really wanted to have sex with me. This whole thing about 'date rape' seemed like a big hype to me that girls made up because they felt guilty about having sex. Even my attorney agreed with me. But being in the group has taught me something different. I know now that when a girl says, 'No,' she means *no*. But it took losing everything to learn that lesson — my athletic scholarship and a possibility to play with the pros. I just have to set other goals for myself and try to lead as normal a life as I can."

"Well, I don't know how much of a normal life any one of us can live," Lance retorts. "Other people don't see us as too normal, let me tell you. We're portrayed as monsters, and we don't stand a chance out there. Did you guys see that TV special on sexual predators the other day? The way they made those guys sound even scared me; until I realized, hey, no need to be afraid, I'm one of them."

The men laugh, once again leveling off some of the intensity that has built up in the room.

Joe, like Sol, has become quite restless throughout the discussion, and he pounds a fist on his knee to emphasize his point. "No, really it's nothing to laugh about. It scares me how people see us. The other day I was reading about some guy who had the windows of his house shot out because someone in the neighborhood found his name on the Sex Offender Registry. I'm in a group home now, but just wait until I have to find a place to live and register my name with the authorities. Lord knows what will happen to me."

Lance decides to join in for another round. "What I really hate is the rule that we have to tell the women we date about our sexual offenses. The other day at my gym I met this girl, and we started talking. We really clicked, and that hasn't happened to me in a long time. We went out for a bite to eat after our workout, and we had so much in common. I asked her out again for this weekend, but man, I'm just dreading telling her that I've been convicted of sexual assault. I'm sure that will go over big with her. Can you imagine me saying something like, '*Hey, I really like you and I would like to date you, but first I need to tell you that I'm a sex offender*'?"

The men take another opportunity to deflate their anxiety with shared laughter, while Lance continues. "Forget it. I don't think I want a relationship; it's not worth all the trouble. I'm branded as a sex offender, and that's what I'll be for the rest of my life."

The male therapist decides to shift the focus of the group.

"I know that this is tough on you guys. But remember, you put yourselves here. It was the choices you made that got you in this predicament in the first place. Your victims *had* no choice. Don't forget that. Your lives have to change as a result of that; and this is part of the group process, to help you adapt to a new way of thinking and living. All right, let's move on. Arnie, how about you? Have you completed your homework for this week?"

"Yeah, I did," Arnie complains. "But it was really hard. The questions about my childhood are tough. I'm not in denial, but my parents were good parents, and it's not their fault that I turned out this way. I mean, my dad hit us, but what dad didn't? My mom was a good mom; she stayed at home and was always there for us. We never did talk much in our family, but I know for sure that nothing sexual ever happened to any of us kids."

"Most of us thought that our families were great when we first came here," explains Michael, a slightly built, middle-aged man who, before his conviction for sexual assault on one of his students, had been employed as a high school math teacher. "It's not as if we're trying to blame our parents; but when you stop denying that you had a perfect family, you realize that a lot of things happened in your past that really affected you."

"I know what you mean," replies Joe. "Before this I thought that I grew up in a normal family, like *Leave It to Beaver*. My dad was the coach at the high school, and everyone looked up to him. But to tell you the truth, I never allowed myself to remember the bad things that happened, you know, the stuff we were taught to keep secret. And once those memories came back, I really had a rough time. But I guess it was worth it. That's what my counselors tell me anyway. At least now I know why I became so screwed up."

Arnie is overwhelmed as he searches for a reply. "Well, I don't know. I can't remember any bad things except for being afraid of my dad. I wrote here in my homework assignment that my dad always had to be in control, and when he came home from work, the whole feel of the house changed. My mother was scared, I could tell, and we kids were scared too because we didn't want him to be in a bad mood. But I could always help him out of his mean moods, and everyone in my family respected me for that. But all in all, we knew that Dad loved us and so did Mom."

Henry, a young, serious businessman who always wears a suit and tie to the group, decides that it is time for him to speak up. "The same thing happened in my family. My dad was so strict and ruled everyone. I hated it, though, because I always thought he was disappointed in me. I was always odd and I never fit in. Kids didn't like me at school, and I was ashamed that I wasn't athletic and popular. I began to abuse when I was in junior high. I remember exposing myself to little kids. I knew what I was doing was wrong, but I couldn't stop. I got a thrill out of it. The therapist told me that maybe I felt powerless and angry with my father, and this was one way that I could express it."

The room becomes silent. For the next few moments each member is lost in recollections of his past and how it affected the egregious choices he'd made.

Eventually, the leaders will refocus the group, continue the check-ins, and for the next ninety minutes, in a confrontational and direct manner, they will encourage each member to hold himself accountable for his sexually criminal behavior. Phrases and terminology, such as "objectification," "victim empathy," "safety plan," and "grooming behaviors," ring repeatedly in the air as the men try to understand the dynamics behind sexual offense.

A part of the group process requires that the men confess intimate sexual fantasies they may have had amid their moments of self-pleasure. It is as if a camera has been installed in their psyches that will bear witness to every action. They are allowed no "little white lies," "no intimate secrets," and no "private moments."

Weighted down with deeply rooted fears of intimacy, the next hour and a half will press heavily upon these men. They will struggle to share intimate fantasies, behaviors, and fears with one another. These men, who have lived most of their lives in isolation and angry withdrawal, are now expected to embark on a journey that will require cooperation, sharing, and a connection with each other.

When the time is up, the homework for the next session is distributed. Each participant will collect his notebook, bid the others good-bye, and head for the door, having made what is, hopefully, another small step toward rehabilitation.

When the last man has left, the therapists prepare the room for the next day. They rearrange the chairs into a neat circle and throw away the scraps of paper that have fallen between the seats. And tomorrow, instead of twelve men, a handful of women will occupy the seats to continue their process of rehabilitation. Their conversation will cover some of the same themes you heard in the men's group, as the women complain about the hardships of their lives and the consequences they must live with because of their sexual offenses. Some will deny their abusive actions, while others will take full blame for the abuse. The therapists will emphasize the same basic points that were given to the men and encourage each offender to take full responsibility for her behavior.

What you have just read is a small fragment of a group process that takes place in an offender treatment program. Each of the twelve men you have met has been convicted of child sexual assault. Depending on their court order, the men will spend between three to eight years in the program.

Although every group member has committed a sexual offense, as you have witnessed, some of them believe that they should be expunged of their labels as sexual predators. Sol alleged that his offense was in the past, and that he no longer has sexual inclinations toward children. And Lance certainly opposes wearing the label of sexual predator for the rest of his life. Both these men claimed they'd learned their lesson and that they were no longer in danger of harming children. Did you believe them? Would you feel safe if you knew that these men were released from treatment, living in your neighborhood, and had access to your children?

There is a chance that Sol and Lance will never again sexually abuse a child. Statistics about the effectiveness of offender treatment programs reveal that out of the twelve male offenders who participated in this group, approximately half of them will *never* reoffend. But are Sol and Lance two of them? Would you instead choose Arnie, Henry, Ian, or Tony as a predator who is most likely to benefit from rehabilitation? After all, they did say the *right things* during group, which should indicate that they are on the road to recovery.

Most of us would agree that you cannot measure a person's risk factor merely by what he or she says in treatment. Remember that predators are experienced in manipulating others in order to get what they want. Therefore, some offenders will comply with the program's mandates and superficially say all the right things in order to present themselves as "cured."

During the group discussion, Lance and B.J. complained that they will never be seen as cured. They maintained that they will always be labeled "sex offenders" even if they never commit a sexual offense again. If this is true, then just what should sex offenders expect from their treatment? Can they really hope to be cured from an ailment that has left them branded as sexual deviants for the rest of their lives? Or should they, at best, plan for a remission of symptoms that might last well into their old age?

Most professionals who work with this population agree that sexual predators do not have a disease that can be *cured*, and that in most cases, with the exception of severe mental diseases, committing sexual abuse on a child results from a *choice* that an individual makes to act on his or her deviant sexual urges. Once this choice is made, it can be made again and again until the predator learns appropriate coping skills so that, under similar circumstances, a different choice will be made.

Professionals also acknowledge that the urge to sexually act out is likely to resurface sometime in an offender's life, particularly during stressful periods; the goal of treatment is to teach the offender how to use internal controls and external resources to *prevent* acting on these urges. Therapeutic intervention aims for a remission of the sexually deviant behaviors, which does not automatically mean that the predator has developed different sexual interests.

An individual's sexuality begins early in his or her development and manifests itself over the years in deeply ingrained patterns of behavior. Sexual desires are therefore very difficult to modify, even more so if the individual has already acted upon them.

Because deviant sexual interests are seen as being strongly embedded in an offender's personality, society has viewed sexual crimes differently from other offenses. Sexual predators are viewed as more prone to relapse, less manageable, and therefore more dangerous than other criminals. As a result the legal system has become instrumental in establishing court-ordered offender treatment programs, and community warning systems, such as the Sex Offender Registry, to contend with sexual offenses.

RELAPSES IN SEXUAL PREDATORS

The notion that sexual offenders have a higher relapse rate than other criminals is not necessarily true. According to Philip H. Witt, a clinical psychologist who served as director of psychology and research at the sex offender treatment unit in New Jersey's Department of Corrections, the relapse rates for sexual offenders are actually *lower* than those for most other criminals, particularly if the offender receives treatment.

Dr. Witt identifies the factors that play an important role in relapses for sexual offenders such as: relationship to the victim, the number of prior offenses, the type of sexual offense, the use of alcohol or other drugs, and the amount of violence that is used in conjunction with the abuse. Thus a high rate of reoffending is likely to occur with sexual predators who have a large number of prior offenses, molested children at an early age, abused alcohol or other substances, victimized nonrelated children, and used force.

Incest offenders, on the other hand, have the lowest rate of reoffending, which falls between 4 to 10 percent. Because they abuse their own children, they are less likely to amass a large number of victims; and they are generally more motivated for treatment since they do have an emotional attachment to their victims. Pedophiles, specifically the ones who abuse boys and have been molesting children for a long time, have the most number of victims. They can have as high as a 40 percent chance of reoffending. And finally, exhibitionists, who often have no relationship with their victims and begin their patterns of abuse at an early age, have a relapse rate ranging from 41 to 71 percent.

There are a number of additional factors that contribute to a lower relapse rate in child sexual predators. A supportive family, stable residence, and long-term employment reduce the likelihood of reoffending. The more the child sexual predator can engage in meaningful adult activities and relationships, the less likely he or she is to turn to children to satisfy emotional and physical needs.

Predators who are engaged in treatment are less likely to reoffend. Therefore, mandatory participation in these special programs is usually a condition of the predator's probation.

THE BASIC ELEMENTS OF TREATMENT

Not all sexual offender treatment programs are the same. Some states, such as Colorado and New Jersey, have developed guidelines for offender treatment programs, and therefore programs certified in these states have a relatively uniform approach to treatment. Since not all states have certified guidelines for offender treatment, programs in these areas may vary in their interventions with offenders.

However, comparative studies have been conducted throughout the United States that reveal a high degree of similarity in the goals of offender treatment programs. The fundamental goal of a sexual offender treatment program is that the participant adhere to a lifelong commitment to evaluate, change, and monitor those thoughts, feelings, and behaviors that could lead to sexually deviant acts.

Comparative studies have also demonstrated that most offender treatment programs include group and individual therapy along with regular monitoring of deviant sexual patterns through polygraphs and plethysmographs (the physiological monitoring of erectile responses). Adjunct therapies often include family and marital counseling, alcohol or drug abuse intervention, and anger-management classes.

The following are the goals of most sex offender treatment programs. The first objective focuses on developing the basic motivation for treatment, and sets the stage upon which all other changes will develop.

Motivating Offenders to Engage in Treatment

Initially, compliance to treatment often occurs because the offender has been court ordered into treatment. If there is not compliance with the mandates of the program results in a violation of probation and usually a return to prison. Therefore, like children who do not steal from Mother's purse because they don't want to be punished, offenders' basic level of compliance to the program's mandates, such as attending group sessions and acquiescing to the polygraphs, often reflects their desire to avoid unpleasant consequences.

This facade of compliance may appear to be genuine motivation. But remember that many sexual offenders are experts at seducing, pleasing, and adapting to their environments in order to obtain what they desire; and therefore one must look well beneath superficial compliance to assess a predator's true motivation for treatment.

A basic level of compliance, however, is not always undesirable since this may be the first step in engaging an offender in a treatment. Change is a slow process; and if offenders can agree to the minimum degree of conformity that will ensure the safety of those around them, a deeper level of transformation may be possible.

In individual and group therapy, offenders must divulge a great deal about themselves, in particular, sexual fantasies and past behaviors that may have been hidden for decades. They must also be ready to give up those sexual acts that not only offer them a great deal of excitement and pleasure but also satisfy their needs for intimacy, love, power, and control. Because offender treatment requires considerable courage and sacrifice, an offender who is not truly committed to the process will view it as overwhelming, burdensome, and intrusive. The nonmotivated offender will complain that the homework takes too much time, there are too many restrictions placed on his or her life, check-ins and polygraphs threaten a sense of privacy, and exploring the past is worthless.

Initially, there will be many prohibitions placed on the offender, and acquiescence to these dictates is the first step in measuring an investment in treatment. Remember Sol, who resisted telling his boss about his criminal record, and B.J., who griped that he could not watch television commercials or movies that depicted young girls in sexually compromising scenes? And what about Lance, who complained bitterly that he had to tell a woman he was interested in about his status as a child molester? These men were voicing their anger at having a multitude of rules that restrained them from many ordinary activities.

Although these men may complain about the many rules and restrictions in their program, their compliance with those regulations is a measure of their basic commitment to treatment. A critical factor in successful rehabilitation, however, is that the offender moves beyond a mere compliance to treatment and develops a motivation to *change*. And for over approximately one-half of the participants in an offender treatment program, motivation to change will develop slowly and continue to grow throughout the course of their therapy.

The offender's decisions, such as where to live and work, with whom to be intimate, and in what recreational activities he or she should participate, reflect a commitment to change. For example, an offender who chooses to live in a condominium complex that caters to adults is certainly minimizing his or her exposure to children more than one who decides to reside in a neighborhood populated by families.

The motivation to change begins with an offender taking *full responsibility for his or her actions and defining those actions as abusive*. The well-publicized case of Mary K. Letourneau, the Seattle schoolteacher in her mid-thirties who was found guilty of having sex with her thirteen-year-old student, is an example of an individual who was not motivated to change because she never defined her actions as abusive.

> When Mary's actions were finally reported to the authorities, in compliance with her attorney's advice, she pleaded guilty to the charge of child rape. Mary was sentenced to seven and a half years in prison. However, because this was her first offense, and Mary was a married woman with four children who had dedicated her career to teaching, the judge granted a suspension of her prison sentence. Mary served eighty days in prison and was released on the condition that she not have any contact with her victim and that she be in an outpatient offender treatment program.

Although Mary had publicly told the judge that she knew what she had done was wrong and pleaded for her help, her motivation to change was significantly challenged in treatment. She never "bought into" the fact that she was a sexual offender and continued to present her sexual contact with a thirteen-year-old boy as an expression of love between two consenting individuals. Mary challenged many of the restrictions and mandates of the program, and she didn't comply with the basic requirements.

Within days of her release, Mary K. Letourneau violated the terms of her parole and resumed contact with her teenage "lover." As a result she was arrested and sent back to prison to serve her full sentence.

Mary has consistently resisted the notion that her love for her victim was sexual abuse; and therefore, as the prosecution will claim, she needs the confinement of prison to keep other children safe. Whether or not you agree with the conviction of Mary Letourneau as a sexual offender, she *was* convicted of child sexual assault; and the ramifications to her victim, the two children she bore with him, and her four children from her marriage have been severe. Until she develops the motivation to change, which requires defining her actions as abusive, she is not a good candidate for offender treatment.

Developing Empathy and Compassion for the Victim

Empathy was presented in chapter 1 in connection with the ten most common characteristics of a predator. A lack of empathy was described as one of the most prevalent traits found in predators. If one has empathy for another individual, it precludes the possibility of abuse. It is more difficult to intentionally hurt another human being if you understand the pain and suffering it will cause.

Developing empathy is an essential component of an offender treatment program. Yet empathy is very difficult to teach. As was explained in chapter 1, empathy is a complicated skill that requires both an intellectual understanding of another's needs and the ability to elicit appropriate emotional responses to those needs.

Empathy, while difficult to learn, is easy for predators to mimic. They may learn the behaviors that are required to feign empathy without ever experiencing this emotion. Writing an apology letter and sharing with the group tears of sympathy for a victim can appear to the untrained eye as empathy.

However, real empathy, like a motivation to change, will be demonstrated over time through the changes that the offender makes. True empathy will be exemplified in the quality of the predator's interactions with other group members, the facilitators, coworkers, friends, and significant others.

Building empathy in predators is based on a series of interventions that increase their awareness of the impact that their sexual abuse had on their victims. They review videotapes made by victims, read accounts of their victims' pain and suffering, and learn about the specific psychological damage of sexual abuse. In this way their victims become real people and not objects upon whom they acted out aggressive impulses.

A majority of offenders have themselves been victims of abuse as children, and a part of their treatment often involves an exploration of the effect that their own abuse had on them. A history of abuse is never offered as an excuse for an offender's decision to molest children. However, by exploring an abusive past, a connection can be made between an offender's childhood pain and the suffering he or she subsequently inflicted on others. In this manner predators' identification with victims' feelings can be strengthened.

Many offenders did not have role models in their early childhood to help them learn empathic behaviors. Therefore, when therapists offer compassion and understanding to offenders who have experienced childhood abuse, they are providing them with a template from which they can learn how to be empathic.

Some sexual offenders will claim that they did have empathy for their victims and that they truly cared about them. They will state that they became emotionally attached to the children they abused and believed that the sexual acts were an extension of their relationships with them. And, in some cases, when the abuse is exposed, certain predators will admit that they knew their actions were hurting others, and they may experience genuine guilt for the pain they have caused their victims. So can we assume that *all* predators have no empathy?

For some predators a sense of empathy can be elicited, but it is extremely conditional. Their empathic response is often motivated by their own needs. Sexual offenders may be able to feign empathic responses when they lead to desired outcomes. They may detect a child who is in need of companionship and use their empathic antenna to seduce that child into sexual acts. Therefore it is critical that, while in treatment, the facilitators confront these cunningly sophisticated predators who will use empathy like a magnet to attract their victims. Their tasks will be to strip that predator of his right to feign empathy and instead replace it with genuine care and compassion for others.

Another important aspect in creating empathy has to do with under-standing the specific needs of children. As explained in chapter 1, many of-fenders do not understand the emotional, cognitive, and social phases of childhood sufficiently to truly comprehend the impact of offenses on young people. They often assume that children don't remember, can't understand, or are not deeply impacted by the things that happen to them. Statements such as, "She's just a kid; she'll forget what happened," "He was so young, he didn't know what was going on," or, "She didn't resist when I touched her, so I didn't think I was really hurting her," reflect ignorance of child develop-ment. Therefore, teaching the offender in treatment about how children conceptualize what happens to them at different stages in their lives will pro-vide a firmer foundation for the development of empathy.

Finally, there are those predators who will never develop the capacity for empathy. They seem to lack the essential ingredients needed to identify with another's emotions, and these necessary components are very difficult to instill, even in a therapeutic environment. These predators are often the antisocial individuals who are likely to remain impervious to the impact that their behaviors have on others. However, antisocial individuals, al-though they may never develop empathy, can learn more appropriate ways of behaving that will minimize their danger to others. Therefore, to main-tain a proper level of safety, these individuals require lifetime supervision.

Increasing the Capacity for
Healthy Adult Interactions and Intimacy

Many child molesters live a lonely existence that is devoid of meaningful contact with people their own age. They describe a history of isolation and al-ienation from others. They talk about being ostracized and ridiculed by peers when they were in school, and as a result, they suffer from low self-esteem and a belief that they are inadequate and unacceptable. Those predators whose relationships with members of the opposite sex are overwhelming, unsatisfying, and chaotic turn to children as substitutes for intimacy.

A close connection with others is difficult for many sexual offenders who have lived their lives with silent fears, inner doubts, and darkly hidden recriminations. To share emotional pain with others is not only difficult for them, it is also something they may have never before experienced. But once the dark side of their nature surfaces, its power is startlingly diminished. Therefore the sexual offender who openly shares his forbidden self with the group will learn that his inner demons can be tamed. As one predator told me during an interview, "We all have our dark side, every one of us. I learned that in group therapy; and, although I know that mine may have been darker and scarier than others', and that I *acted on mine*, at least I am not alone."

Most offenders have not had satisfying adult relationships. Their connections to the opposite sex have often been fraught with domestic violence and sexual dysfunction. They have never been able to achieve healthy intimacy, and therefore they continue to engage in destructive relationships that leave them angry and unfulfilled.

Once an individual's identity as a sexual offender is made known, it may seem difficult to imagine that anyone would want to continue a relationship with him or her. And in many situations that is the case, since remaining in a relationship with an offender requires a considerable commitment from the nonoffending partner. He or she must be included in certain aspects of the treatment program in order to be fully aware of the expectations, goals, and methods of the treatment. This often means participation in couples therapy, where the offender must learn how to effectively communicate, empathize, and resolve conflicts within a relationship. Remember that the healthier and more satisfying a relationship the offender has with an adult, the less likely he or she will turn to children for fulfillment.

Improving Communication Skills

Learning effective communication skills is essential for the offender, who may never have had the opportunity to verbalize feelings. For many sexual predators, their destructive acts speak of years of anger and pain, and therefore they must learn not to act on their feelings but to express them safely in words.

Anger management is often an important component of offender treatment and a precursor to developing safe and intimate relationships. Many offenders have difficulty expressing their anger without it causing damage to themselves or others, and anger management teaches them how to deal with their anger in constructive ways. Anger does not always have to be a negative emotion that leads to the erosion of rational thought. It can serve as a healthy tool in helping offenders change those things in themselves and in the environment that are causing them frustration.

Anger management usually involves helping offenders identify those situations that lead to anger and developing different strategies for dealing with them. They learn how to recognize the early signs of frustration so that their anger does not build to a dangerous level. Techniques to reduce stress are offered as a part of this program, and specific exercises require the offender to engage in alternate ways of responding to anger.

Another critical part of effective communication skills is learning how to resolve conflicts. These extend to the offender's relationships at work and with significant others. Most offenders resolve conflicts through violence and other forms of intimidation. Learning how to handle problems in a constructive fashion is essential to establishing an atmosphere where the predator can safely interact with others.

Modifying Thought Distortions

Changing thought patterns is a crucial aspect of offender treatment. Thought distortions are the building blocks that the predator uses to construct a reality in which he or she can deny, justify, minimize, and perpetuate abusive acts. All sexual predators employ one or more of these thought distortions. Even though many predators would like to think that their offenses were caused by external circumstances, they *allowed* themselves to engage in thinking errors that justified the abuse.

The fundamental ways in which we see ourselves and the world around us are referred to as our *core beliefs*. For most offenders these core beliefs reflect the damaging ways in which they were taught to see themselves and others. Beliefs such as, "Others are always out to get me," "I am worthless," "Nothing has ever worked out for me," or, "I am helpless," are some examples of the deleterious thinking that can lead to abusive behaviors.

When a predator assumes the role of a "victim," it is often a result of the above negative self-statements. If offenders believe that they are worthless and that nothing they do makes a difference, it is inevitable that they will portray themselves as helpless sacrifices to the cruel whims of chance. The "victim stance" is not only a position from which offenders can deny responsibility for the abuse, it also increases the likelihood that others will sympathize with them. Perhaps if others find them *misunderstood, lonely, and unlucky,* they will not judge them to be at fault. In this manner they hope to be seen as "different" from other sexual offenders and therefore should not have to suffer the same consequences.

You witnessed this type of irrational thinking during the group session when Lance, B.J., and Michael complained about the unfortunate circumstances that rendered them helpless, unfortunate, and unduly punished for their "mistakes."

There are other types of faulty thinking that exert a great deal of influence on how a predator feels and behaves. Offender treatment programs help the participant identify these irrational thoughts and implement techniques to change them.

Denial. There are many forms of denial that predators use to avoid accepting full responsibility for their actions. They may range from denying the fact that sexual abuse occurred, such as, "The child is lying; I didn't do anything," to a denial of responsibility that is reflected in the following statement, "I didn't know she was underage until it was too late." Denial can also include obscuring the impact of the offense on the victim, such as, "She was sleeping; she didn't know what was going on." A refusal to accept responsibility can also be displayed in denying an awareness of committing the offense, which is communicated in the following: "I was so drunk, I didn't know what I was doing; I just sort of blacked out."

Excuse making and blaming. This involves justifying the abuse by finding reasons for it, such as, "I was abused as a child," or, "My wife was very ill for a long time and I was so lonely, I turned to my stepdaughter for love and support." When offenders blame someone else for their choices and decisions, they avoid taking personal responsibility for the sexual abuse. Offenders will often blame the victims, their parents, and, more commonly, "the System," for the terrible predicament they are in. A great deal of anger and resentment can be focused on the legal system and social services if the offender views him or herself as being unjustly punished. These individuals will repeatedly rail against a system that has made them remain in treatment long after they are "cured," leave their homes, separate from their children, register with the local authorities as sex offenders, and notify landlords of their criminal status. Unfortunately, their anger is misplaced, and unless they begin to take full responsibility for the suffering they have imposed on others, as well as the hardships they created for themselves, they will never be open to rehabilitation.

Objectification. This was reviewed in chapter 1 as a general attitude that the predator has toward his or her victims. It describes the ways in which the predator strips victims of all human qualities and reduces them to a "thing" to be used only for self-gratification.

Viewing others as a means to meet one's needs necessitates that the predator lower others to a subordinate status and transfer negative characteristics onto them. Name-calling, physical abuse, and other controlling and dominant behaviors are ways in which the oppressor places the victim in a status beneath him or her. It is always easier to abuse an object rather than a human being.

Projection. This is a powerful thinking error that can create significant distortions in the way in which a predator perceives his or her own behavior and the behavior of others. Projecting one's thoughts, feelings, ideas, and impulses onto others allows the predator to avoid personal responsibility for his or her behaviors. It helps justify abusive behaviors, since projection assumes that the other person is feeling what the predator is experiencing. Therefore when a predator tells himself that his stepdaughter sat on his lap because she was seducing him, he is projecting his own unacceptable sexual desires onto an innocent child.

Moderating Deviant Sexual Arousal

As you learned in previous chapters, not all offenders have deviant sexual interests. Some child sex offenders are not aroused by children, but they victimize them because they are accessible and easily manipulated. However, certain sex offenders are sexually stimulated by children and are therefore labeled pedophiles.

Deviant sexual patterns can be objectively measured through polygraphs and plethysmographs. By measuring a physiological response to a variety of sexual stimuli, the examiner can detect a pattern of arousal. If a deviant sexual pattern is detected, then interventions to alter this are implemented. Remember that a deviant pattern of sexual arousal that has existed for some time is highly resistant to change and is therefore one of the major factors in recidivism.

To change a chronic pattern of sexual arousal takes a great deal of time and motivation on the part of the offender. It requires constant monitoring and implementing specific exercises designed to break the link between the deviant stimuli and the sexual arousal. These interventions are not unlike the aversive-conditioning techniques used to break harmful habits, such as smoking or drinking. An undesirable image is repeatedly paired with the habitual response in an attempt to break the connection between the desire and the behavior. For example, visualizing being sent to jail and sexually assaulted by other inmates would be repeatedly paired with a pedophile's sexual stimulation by children. Over a period of time, the pairing of the negative image with the deviant sexual arousal would lessen the latter and ultimately condition the offender to avoid the deviant sexual stimuli.

Preventing Relapse

Rehabilitation, as noted previously, does not assume that an individual will never again have urges to sexually offend. During times of stress, deviant sexual feelings may resurface, and it is what the offender plans to do during these times to avoid acting on these impulses that will determine whether or not he or she reoffends. Therefore it is essential that while in treatment the offender construct sufficient *safety plans* to prevent a relapse.

Because access to probable victims is denied for a period of time, a perpetrator in treatment may initially feel "cured" because he or she does not experience the urge to commit a sexual offense. Predators may therefore falsely assume that they will not reoffend and that they no longer have deviant sexual urges. They are likely to argue that they are ready to reenter the community without any restrictions. But this can be a dangerous time for sexual offenders. To minimize their risks of reoffending, they must acknowledge that they will always be vulnerable to acting out sexually deviant impulses, particularly during times of stress. They must be able to identify those high-risk situations that place them in danger of reoffending and learn effective coping responses. These measures will constitute their safety plan.

When Sol wrote in his journal about not touching the friendly little girl he met in the supermarket and walking to another checkout line to avoid any further contact with her, he was referring to his safety plan. He learned in treatment to recognize his sexual vulnerability to children and the subtle grooming behaviors that prepared his victims for abuse. His safety plan included avoiding contact with children and removing himself from situations that would increase the likelihood of physical contact with them. However, even though Sol did implement his safety plan, he is not yet out of the woods. His resentment over having to ignore children and continuously being labeled a sex offender is a remnant of his faulty thinking that still needs to be addressed before he is considered at low risk for reoffense.

An offender must also be able to recognize when he or she is beginning to engage in an abusive relationship. Grooming behaviors that may appear subtle and habitual to an offender often need to be confronted early on, or they may eventually escalate to a reoffense. Without denying, minimizing, or excusing these behaviors, the offender who is truly invested in treatment will be able to identify these early signs of abuse and intervene quickly in order to avoid relapse.

Considering that the risk factor for reoffense of child sexual offenders who are in treatment averages between 40 to 50 percent, it is a wonder that any woman with children would decide to take the chance and become involved with one. If a woman is to become involved with a sex offender, not only must she continuously monitor his interactions with her children, she will also have to make a substantial commitment to the offender's treatment process. She will be asked to attend couples counseling, family therapy, and feedback sessions with the offender's therapist. Even the children may be required to take part in the treatment. This alone could drive a single mother away. Yet women do become involved with predators, and for many of them, they are hoping that their relationship with these men will make the difference.

Yet as we have seen, a relationship may not be enough to change a sex offender's pattern of abusive behavior. While supportive relationships are often critical to the progress that an offender will make in treatment, they should not preclude your children's safety. It is critical that a potential partner become fully aware of the issues involved with sexual offenders and their treatment before they ever decide to subject their children to the potential risks involved. In the following chapter you will meet Maggie, and through her relationship with Brian you will learn how to discern whether or not a sex offender can be considered safe.

Chapter 10

Should You Ever Become Involved
with a Sexual Offender?

A woman may be lured into believing that the sex offender she has met is different from the rest. You have seen how predators can seduce, manipulate, and distort their thinking to rationalize and justify abuse. Therefore it is critical that if a woman is thinking about becoming involved with a sex offender, she go beyond what he is saying and investigate the real nature of his pattern of abuse.

Checking the Sex Offender Registry and meeting with the counselors in his treatment program are more reliable ways to obtain an accurate picture of the offender. Most counselors will willingly talk to a significant other if there is an authorized release of information. If the offender is not willing to allow a woman to consult with the professionals in his treatment program, then something is awry. An offender who is invested in treatment should have a partnership with his significant other that strives for open communication, self-disclosure, and the prevention of reoffense against children.

Now I would like to introduce you to Maggie. She is a single mother of two school-age children, and she recently became involved with Brian. He has just confessed to her that he was convicted two and a half years ago of child sexual assault on his twelve-year-old niece.

Maggie is in a state of turmoil. She likes Brian, but she is vacillating between believing that they can work this out together and fearing that her children could be hurt if she continues her affiliation with him.

As you read Maggie's story, you will become aware of the issues that must be addressed if you are to enter into a relationship with a sexual offender. You will also learn what interventions should be implemented during a relationship in order to maximize the safety of you and your children, and, finally, you can help Maggie assess whether staying in the relationship with Brian would pose a threat to her and to her children.

Maggie's Story

Maggie was a precocious adolescent and, despite her parents' restrictions and warnings, she had two children out of wedlock before she was twenty-one. She set up residence with the father of her children in a small apartment in the city. Barely able to make ends meet, they struggled to put food on the table. When her children were not yet out of diapers, their father left with no intention of remaining financially responsible for his family.

Since that time Maggie has lived with her parents in their modest suburban home. She and her children occupy the basement rooms; and with the support of her mother and father, Maggie has been able to raise her children in moderate comfort.

While her parents assumed the role of day-care providers, Maggie was able to work full time and attend night classes for her college degree. She rarely dated, and her evenings and weekends were spent studying and spending time with her son and daughter. She was isolated from her peers and often lonely for companionship. It was in this context that she met Brian.

Maggie had taken notice of the tall, quiet, and unassuming young man who always sat at the back of her environmental studies class. When they were paired together to work on a research project, Maggie was secretly thrilled. For the next few weeks, as the study progressed, they became acquainted with one another over stacks of periodicals and coffee. They found that they shared a great deal in common, such as a love of animals, the outdoors, and jazz. Maggie told Brian about getting pregnant and marrying at a young age, and the father's subsequent abandonment of the family. She confided in him about how lonely and isolated she was living with her parents. Maggie was so grateful for the opportunity to talk to someone, she didn't notice that Brian shared little about his own life.

On their first date, Brian took Maggie to a concert. They had a wonderful time, and Maggie was reluctant to have the evening end. She suggested that they go for a drink after the concert so that they could talk to one another, but Brian declined. Instead, he invited her to a baseball game the following Saturday. After the ballgame, Maggie suggested dinner, but once again Brian refused. With a reassuring hug, he suggested that they meet the following afternoon for a picnic. Maggie asked if she could bring her children, and Brian suggested that they get to know one another better before he met the children.

Maggie told Brian that the children would love to come with them on a picnic. She argued that they had not met anyone else since their father had left, and that they were starved for attention, especially from a man. Even though they had their grandfather, Maggie reasoned, they needed to be around a younger man who could wrestle with them and play sports. Reluctantly, Brian agreed.

Yet as Maggie drove home that afternoon, she wondered why Brian had been hesitant about having the children join them at the park. She thought about his statement that they needed more time to get to know one another and how that was only half true. She had already shared a great deal about her life with Brian; however, except for his hobbies and preferences in sports, she knew little about him.

The picnic was fun and Brian appeared comfortable with eight-year-old Michael. They played soccer on the grassy fields of the park, and later they passed the football. Yet Maggie noticed that Brian kept a distance from her six-year-old daughter. When Stacy tried to jump on Brian pleading for a "horseback ride," he removed her legs from around his waist and redirected her to Maggie.

After the picnic the kids asked if Brian could come to their house to see their toys. Brian politely declined and told Maggie that he would call her later at home. As Maggie loaded the car and helped Stacy and Michael fasten their seat belts, she thought about Brian's reluctance to become more familiar with the children. Maybe he had been right, and she needed to know more about Brian before involving the children.

That evening, as promised, Brian phoned Maggie. They exchanged pleasantries about the day until Brian told Maggie that he needed to tell her something very important. The tone of his voice had changed noticeably. Maggie's anxiety increased as she sat down on the bed, held her breath, and waited.

During the next fifteen minutes, Brian confessed certain details of his past. And as he did, Maggie's idealized image of Brian came tumbling down. He told her that he had had sexual relations with his niece and, as a result, had been convicted of child sexual assault. He went on to explain that he had served almost a year in jail and was currently on probation. He also informed Maggie that he had been in offender treatment for the past twelve months and was court ordered to remain there for another six and a half years.

Maggie was silent for a few moments before she spoke. "Why didn't you tell me this before?"

"I wanted to, Maggie, but I couldn't find the right time. I had planned to tell you today at the park, but you insisted that the kids come along. I couldn't talk to you with them around. Besides, I really liked you from the beginning; and I was afraid that if I told you right away, you would never have seen me again."

"That's not fair, Brian. I had no idea that you wanted to talk to me about something this serious. I mean, I brought the kids because they have been so starved for attention. If I'd known what I know now, I would have never taken them to the park with us."

"Please don't judge me, Maggie, not until you know the whole story. I've changed. I know what I did was wrong. It was a terrible mistake, and I have been paying for that mistake everyday. After my arrest, I never thought I would be in another relationship again. I mean, who would want me after what I'd done? I just resigned myself to the fact that I would live my life alone and that was my just punishment for what I did. But then I met you. You were so friendly and sweet to me, and I allowed myself to have hope again."

"Brian, I can't believe what you're telling me. This is incredible. I would have never believed that you could have done something like that. What were you thinking?"

"I wasn't thinking and that's the point. Honestly, I just sort of fell into it, and I let myself get swept away by the situation. Let me tell you, if you had seen my niece at that time, you would never have believed she was only twelve."

"But she was twelve, Brian, and you knew that."

"I know, I can't deny it; and believe me, I beat myself up everyday for that."

"Brian?"

"Yes?"

"Have you done this before, I mean to other children?"

"No, not like that. I was never arrested on any other charges. But on our lie-detector tests, we have to tell everything about our past. I told them that when I was a kid, some neighborhood friends and I were playing around with each other, and we were caught by one of the parents. I got into trouble because I was the oldest, and they said I should have known better. But it was only kid games, you know, the kind everyone plays when they're young. Anyway, my counselor said that this was sexual abuse."

"I don't know what to say."

"Then don't say anything right now, just promise me that you will give it some time. You need to understand the whole situation. It's not like you think. When I got involved with my niece, my world had just fallen apart. My mother had died of cancer, and my father had gone off the deep end. All he did was sit in his house with the curtains drawn and a drink in his hand. I felt like both my parents had died. Then to make matters worse, I lost my job when the company I worked for was sold. They offered me a job back East where the business was relocating, but I just couldn't leave my dad in his condition. So I moved out of my apartment and in with him. I had no job, and I was at a low point in my life. Then my sister and niece kept coming over to help us at the house, and it just sort of happened. My niece and I began talking, and she told me she had always had a big crush on me. She was so mature and very seductive. I was lonely, confused, angry, and too caught up in my own grief to see that what we were doing was wrong."

There was silence at the other end of the line as Maggie's thoughts twirled around in her mind and settled deep in the pit of her stomach.

"Maggie, are you still there?"

"Yes."

"Well?"

"I'll call you tomorrow, Brian. I'm too confused to talk now."

"Okay, but promise me, please, that you won't just give up on us until we can talk again."

"Okay, I'll think about it. Good night, Brian."

"Good night and, Maggie . . . ?"

"What?"

"I care about you."

After Maggie hung up the phone, she thought about her children's contact with Brian that afternoon. What if something had happened when she was not looking?

When she opened the door to the children's room, both kids softly whispered, "Mom?"

"Yes," Maggie replied, as she sat down at the foot of Stacy's bed. "Did you two have a good time today?"

"Yeah," they replied enthusiastically.

"I like Brian; he's nice. Can we see him again?" Stacy pleaded.

Michael sat up in his bed eager to join in. "I like him too, Mom. He's cool. He can really play football."

"I'm glad you both like him. We'll see what happens, okay? But right now, you two need your sleep. I love you guys."

The children's voices rang out in unison, "We love you too, Mom."

The next day Maggie received flowers at work with a note written in Brian's handwriting. *I am sorry for the pain I have caused you. I will understand if you never want to see me again. Please enjoy these; they remind me of you.*

All day long Maggie had a terrible time concentrating. Thoughts of Brian occupied her attention, and she spent more time staring at the flowers than focusing on the stacks of papers that lay before her.

That night Maggie called Brian and told him that she would talk to him after their class the following evening.

Brian was elated. "I'm so glad you didn't shut the door on us, Maggie. I really am. I even told the guys at group tonight that I had met you and told you all about my offense. They are really supportive of me. Maggie, I'd like you to meet my therapist and have a chance to ask him any questions you'd like. I think you will feel a lot better after meeting him."

"That might be a good idea. Look, I have to go now; I had a rough day."

"So did I, that is, until you called. Thanks, Maggie. You've made me happy tonight."

The evening after their class, Brian and Maggie sat over mugs of coffee and talked. Brian told Maggie about his unhappy childhood. His sister had left the coop and married when she was barely out of her teens. His mother and father had always fought; and being the only child left in the home, he was given the role of arbitrator. He always took his mother's side, which further alienated him from his father. His father had sought solace in alcohol, and his mother had shut herself off from everyone. She suffered from terrible migraines that would banish her to bed for days. Young Brian would stand in front of the locked door and plead for her to come out.

"I'm not telling you all of this to make you feel sorry for me, Maggie. And I certainly don't want you to think that I am making excuses for my behavior. I just want you to know that I have always felt alone and abandoned by everyone."

"I know how you feel, Brian. I have felt alone, too. I was so in love with the father of my kids. I met him while I was only a freshman in high school; and since that time, my whole life was wrapped up in him. I didn't think about my own future, going to college, or what I was going to do; I just spent my energy worshiping the ground he walked on. But when our kids were born, he couldn't handle the responsibility. He said he was too young to have two kids hanging around his neck. When he left without warning, I was devastated. I couldn't get out of bed for a week. My parents had to come over, pack all of our stuff, and move us to their house. They saved my life, but now I feel so boxed in. I know that I owe them everything, but it's as if they are saying, 'We told you so.' Well, they were right, and I have certainly suffered the consequences of my bad decisions. But I feel that I have paid my dues; I want to get on with my life."

Brian nodded sympathetically as he reached over to take Maggie's hand. "I do too, believe me. We can have a life together if you just give it a try. Both of us have made mistakes, and we have paid dearly. But, hey, everyone deserves a second chance, don't they? Maybe we have just been given ours."

Maggie didn't take her hand away from the warmth of Brian's touch. As the tears streamed down her face, she acknowledged the strong connection she felt to Brian.

Together they made a plan. They agreed not to involve the children any further in their relationship, and that sexual intimacy would be put on hold until Maggie had a chance to talk to Brian's counselor. Maggie also told Brian that she was not going to tell her parents about his sexual offense because they would not understand. She also secretly feared that they would tell the children.

During the two weeks prior to their appointment with the counselor, Brian shared with Maggie the details of his treatment. He told her what he had learned during group sessions and let her read the materials he was given. She was given access to his journal, and he reviewed his homework assignments with her.

Maggie learned a great deal about offender treatment during this time; and the more she was exposed to the information about sexual offenders, the more anxious she became. She began to realize that Brian's treatment was not just for a limited period of time, but that it required a lifelong commitment—a commitment that would involve both of them if they stayed together. The fact that Brian was a sexual offender would follow them wherever they went, and there was a strong likelihood that her children would learn of Brian's offense.

The day of the scheduled appointment arrived, and Maggie was very nervous. As she sat next to Brian on the couch, with their knees touching and her hand clenched tightly in his, the counselor asked her how she felt about being there.

"Scared and confused. I'm afraid of what will happen, and I don't know if I can make a commitment to Brian at this time."

"That's understandable, Maggie. You need to find out all of the facts before you can do that."

"I want to ask something, but I don't want to hurt Brian's feelings."

"Brian should be ready to handle your questions. You shouldn't worry about hurting his feelings; and if you need information about his sexual offenses, you should feel free to ask it."

"Okay, here goes." Maggie paused to take in a breath as she looked directly at Brian's counselor. "I need to know your professional opinion. Do you think my children will be safe with Brian? Is there a chance that he could do this again?"

The counselor assumed a serious posture. "That is a difficult question but one that is necessary for you to ask. The truth is, Brian could reoffend. Once an individual has committed a sexual offense against a child, there is always the possibility that it can happen again. The men here learn that as part of their commitment to keeping children safe."

Maggie sank deeper into the couch, bearing the weight of his statement.

Brian's pleading startled her. "Maggie, I understand that you may not feel safe about me being with your children. But I promise you, I would never hurt your kids, never!"

"But what happens when they grow up, Brian; I mean, when Stacy becomes the age that your niece was when . . . you know what I mean?"

"I'm telling you that I would never hurt her. How could I ever have sexual feelings for your daughter, Maggie? I love you."

The counselor sat forward in his chair to emphasize his confrontation. "Can you really promise that, Brian? You know that a person convicted of child sexual assault may continue to be at risk around children. You always have a choice; but Brian, you can't be sure that feelings won't come up. You must make Maggie aware that you will do everything in your power to make sure that if you ever have any sexual feelings about her children, you will take the appropriate measures to deal with them."

There was silence in the room for a brief time as the clock ticked away the hour.

Maggie shifted her position on the couch to face Brian. "I just couldn't take the chance that my kids could be hurt, especially Stacy, who will be going through puberty in a few years. What if you develop an attraction for her like you did for your niece?"

"That won't happen. I've learned my lesson. I would never do that again and certainly not with you in my life. I wouldn't take the chance of losing you. When I had a sexual relationship with my niece, there was no one in my life that I cared about."

The counselor shook his head in disagreement. "Brian, you can't promise that and you know it. The most you can give to Maggie is your word that you will do everything in your power to avoid situations that will place you at high risk for offending; and that if you feel urges to offend, you will deal with them before you place anyone in danger."

"I'll do that," Brian conceded.

The counselor turned to Maggie. "There are things we can do to minimize the chance that Brian would offend against your children. But you will have to be involved in the treatment, and that doesn't mean for just another few years. This requires a commitment for as long as the two of you are together."

"Well, exactly what does this commitment involve?" Maggie asked.

"Well, first, the three of us will come up with a safety plan that we can implement immediately. We will also recommend that the two of you begin immediately with couples counseling. During these sessions, you can learn a great deal about Brian and his pattern of abuse. We would also suggest that you have individual therapy during this time so that you can talk about your feelings and reactions to being with Brian. Eventually, when the time is right, we will include the children in family counseling."

"I don't see why they have to be involved," Maggie complained. "They're only little kids; they won't understand. I'm worried that if Brian and I do stay together, they will always be afraid of him."

"Your family shouldn't have secrets. And more important, Brian's offense is not something he is supposed to keep from others. It is essential that your children know the truth and that they have their own safety plans when they are with Brian. Look, Maggie, Brian's offense is not going to be kept from others. He will need to inform landlords, employers, and register with the local authorities as a sex offender. You must be prepared for this."

"I've read that." Maggie's anxiety was escalating. "But my kids won't understand. They're never had to deal with anything like this before."

The counselor continued in a calm but firm manner. "I understand that; but children are remarkably resilient, and there are certain ways that this can be presented to them to minimize their fear. But they will need time to explore their feelings and talk about it. We can recommend you to counselors who specialize in children. But all of that is further down the road. Your children are safe right now as long as Brian doesn't violate his restraining order."

By now Maggie's apprehension had risen to genuine alarm. "What restraining order?"

"The one that prohibits Brian from having any unsupervised contact with children," explained the counselor.

"But he has already met the kids. We went on a picnic together before I knew about Brian's offense," Maggie cried.

The counselor faced Brian with a look of disappointment.

"This will have to be reported to your probation officer, Brian. You knew the rules. Why did you break them?"

"I tried to say no to Maggie when she asked if she could bring the kids to the park, but she was so insistent I couldn't refuse. Besides, she was there with us."

"Brian, that still is not within the mandates of your restraining order. Maggie is not an approved supervisor. But what I am most concerned about is that you're *blaming* this on Maggie. To inform her before you placed her or her children at risk was *your* responsibility and *yours* alone. This is something you should have told her when she first asked to bring the children. You should never have been in the park with them."

"You mean he can't be with my kids even if I am there?" Maggie cried.

"Not right now. Eventually we can present a plan to the courts to convince them that you are knowledgeable enough about sexual abuse to approve you as a supervisor for Brian."

Brian, who had been sullenly quiet up to this point, turned to Maggie for reassurance. "I know that this is a lot, Maggie. I don't know if I could do all of this for someone else; but I do know that we can make it work, and that I will do everything in my power to make sure that you and the children are happy."

The counselor looked concerned as he spoke to Brian. "You have to let Maggie make her own decision without making any unrealistic promises or bribes. Remember, Brian, you are good at seducing, and you have to respect the fact that Maggie has control over her own feelings and actions. I think that by pleading with her, you are pressuring her into a decision. Let it happen, Brian. Let her take the time to make the choice."

"I know . . . I know. It's just that I've never wanted anything so much, and I want a second chance." Brian tightened his grip on Maggie's hand. "I know that you're taking a risk being with me. I also know that I'm never supposed to say that I am cured, but that incident with my niece was a one-shot deal, and it will never happen again. I can't seem to make you all realize that I do *not* have a pattern of sexual offense. Deep in my heart, I know who I am and that what I did was wrong; but, Maggie, it was just a mistake."

The counselor had a look of exacerbation as he once again tried to make Brian see the danger in his assumptions. "That kind of thinking really worries me, Brian. I was under the impression that you had passed that stage of minimizing a long time ago. I've got to tell you that I'm hearing some very worrisome things coming from you. Presenting your sexual offenses as just a juvenile 'mistake' instead of a choice is not right. No matter how you rationalize it, you chose to abuse your niece. You also know that this was not a 'one-shot deal'; you have done this before."

"What do you mean he has 'done this before'? Brian told me he has only been convicted of sexual assault once on his niece. Were there others?" Maggie closed her eyes against the onslaught of the truth.

The counselor's voice pierced through her darkness. "I take it that Brian has not been totally honest with you about his other sexual offenses?"

Brian prepared for his defense. "Well, I did tell her about what I did when I was a kid, if that's what you mean, but that was different."

"No, it wasn't, Brian. You know that. Those kids you molested were younger than you were, and you coerced them into sexual acts. You weren't just playing games; you were sexually abusing them. We have been through this many times, Brian. Maggie has to know *all of this*; and unless you are ready to take responsibility for all of your abusive behaviors, *you are not ready to be in a relationship with a women who has children!*"

Maggie, who had continued to sit motionless next to Brian with her eyes closed, finally withdrew her hand. "I don't know what to say. I'm more confused than when I first came in here. I came for answers, and now I'm leaving with more questions."

"Maybe you need to talk about this with someone, Maggie, a professional who knows about sexual offenders. We can provide you with some names if you like."

"Yes, maybe that would help; but right now, I just need to think."

As Maggie and Brian left the office building, they stopped at the top of the steps to take a breath of the brisk fall air, relieved to be free from the suffocating confines of the therapist's office. Brian drove Maggie home in silence until they pulled up in her driveway. Brian then took Maggie's hand and once again pleaded with her.

"I know this is soon, but I think I'm in love with you, Maggie, and I don't want to lose you. I'm willing to do what it takes to make this work. I hope that you will give it a chance."

Maggie looked into the blue eyes of the man who sat next to her and felt sadness. "I care about you, too, Brian, and I would like nothing more than to have a life with someone; but I don't know if it can be you. I learned a lot in the session with your counselor. He told me things I needed to know, things you should have told me."

Brian moved closer to Maggie.

"No, Brian, stay where you are." Maggie turned to look out the car window. "I don't trust you. You were not totally honest with me. You told me that you had never molested anyone except your niece. You told me that the sexual things you did with those neighborhood kids was not abuse, that it was just kids' play."

"Maggie, you have to believe me; these treatment people think that every sexual contact you ever had in your life was abuse. The other incident he was referring to was just kids' play. Believe me, those kids were younger than I was, but not by that much. I swear, Maggie, it was nothing."

"And what about the restraining order? My God, Brian, you let me bring the kids to the park knowing that you were forbidden to be with them."

Brian placed his hands on Maggie's shoulders as he turned her around to face him. "Look at me, Maggie. You've had enough time to get to know me. Do you really see a sexual offender in front of you?"

"I really don't know who you are, Brian, and that scares me. You need to give me time. I feel like you are pressuring me, and I can't make a decision now."

"I understand, Maggie. Whatever you need, however long it takes, I'll wait. But remember, everyone deserves a second chance. We all make mistakes; even you admitted to making one with your ex-husband."

Watching Brian drive away, Maggie experienced a mixture of sadness and relief. The afternoon had been intense, and she decided to go inside for a quick nap before the children came home from school.

Unfortunately, once in her bedroom with the blinds shut, she was not able to get any rest. Questions kept nagging at her. Who could she share this with? Most people would tell her to run from this one, but maybe not. After all, Brian was a nice guy, and he seemed as if he had changed. But had he?

Maggie was unwilling to share her dilemma with her parents. They had always been judgmental of her, especially with her choice of boyfriends. She just couldn't bear right now to hear their condemnations of Brian and, more important, their criticism of her for allowing him to come into her life.

Without any close female friends to confide in, Maggie does not have the outside support she needs to help her make a decision. She may eventually choose to call one of the names the counselor gave her, but in the meantime, she needs someone to talk to.

Unless Maggie has read this book, she has not had the opportunity, like you, to understand the basic characteristics of sexual predators and their patterns of abuse. She may never have met a predator up close or become familiar with the components of offender treatment. So let's reach out to Maggie. You are in a good position, with the knowledge you have already gained about predators, to help Maggie resolve this critical dilemma.

Maggie actually has a great deal of information about Brian. He has talked to her about his offense and offered his explanations. She also had the opportunity to meet with the therapist from his sex offender treatment program. She has observed his behaviors, and all of this should tell her a great deal about Brian. But she is not clear as to where to put all of this information. So this is where we come in.

Let's start by reviewing what we learned in chapter 1 about the ten most common characteristics of a predator and determine whether we see any of these in Brian.

One of the most dangerous qualities in a predator is a *refusal to take responsibility for his or her actions*. In order for a predator to change, he or she must first acknowledge that the abuse was a personal choice. Brian blamed his abusive behaviors on outside influences, such as his terrible childhood, the traumatic circumstances of his mother's death, his father's alcoholism, and his niece's seductive nature. While these may be factors in predisposing Brian to choose to commit sexual abuse, they should never be offered as a reason. Brian should take full responsibility for his abusive behaviors.

Brian's claims that his niece was *flirtatious and that she seduced him into having sex with her* reflect serious distortions in his thinking; and contrary to what he may parrot to the counselors in his treatment program, Brian *blames others for his actions*.

We also saw evidence that Brian accuses the system for labeling him a sexual offender. He blatantly pointed a recriminating finger at the treatment professionals who labeled his "harmless kids' play" with the younger neighborhood children as "sexual abuse." Brian does not accept the fact that he *does* have a pattern of deviant sexual behavior and that he uses force, coercion, and manipulation to fulfill his libidinal desires. Unless Brian identifies his pattern of abuse and takes full responsibility for it, he is at high risk for reoffending.

Although Brian presented himself as accommodating and "willing to do whatever it takes" to make the relationship with Maggie work, Brian demonstrated a dangerous *sense of entitlement*. Brian feels sanctioned to make *a few mistakes* here and there, and he is pressuring Maggie to forgive him for these transgressions. Brian's belief that he is special was demonstrated in his demands to be exempt from the label of sexual offender because "deep in his heart" he believes he is not one. Brian sets himself apart from the other offenders, and this is dangerous because, in reality, Brian is not different. He is a sexual predator.

Brian has a need for power and control. This was demonstrated in Brian's repeated pleas for forgiveness, and his attempts to convince Maggie to stay with him. Maggie spoke of feeling pressured, which is another way of saying she felt controlled.

Brian never fully validated her feelings and concerns, particularly about her children, and instead focused on whether or not *Maggie* would forgive him. The conversations always came back to *his* losses, *his* mistakes, and what *he* wanted. This clearly illustrates his desire to occupy center stage, and his demand that others cater to his needs and desires.

Furthermore Brian did not demonstrate *empathy for his victims.* He minimized his sexual play with the children in his neighborhood, thus negating any harm that they may have suffered. And in his explanation of the sexual abuse of his niece, he focused only on himself and not on the impact that this certainly had on a twelve-year-old girl. This reflects problems in his ability to see the world through another's eyes. If Maggie decides to stay with Brian, his inability to empathize with others will create a serious threat to the emotional and physical well-being of her entire family.

Despite what Brian claims, he *does have a history of abusive behavior that most certainly reflects deviant sexual behaviors.* As an adult, he was convicted of sexual assault on a child, and it is very likely that his pattern of deviant sexual behaviors began early in his childhood, as evidenced by the coercion he used to engage other children in sexual acts. The fact that Brian does not identify his pattern of abuse will make him unwilling to modify these behaviors, and once again, this places him at high risk for reoffending.

The fact that Brian had a *troubled childhood* is not as critical a factor as the rest of the characteristics he displayed. Yet when it is combined with the other traits, it raises a red flag that should be taken seriously. Brian described to Maggie a lonely childhood characterized by an unavailable mother and an alcoholic father. His role models were certainly deficient, and unless Brian engages in counseling that will help him resolve his feelings of anger and betrayal, it is likely that he will continue to act out his unmet needs in inappropriate ways.

So what is our assessment of Brian up to this point? It is not favorable. He has displayed a number of characteristics that are commonly found in sexual predators, which should sound a clear and loud warning signal to Maggie. But let's look further and maybe we can gather more evidence that will strengthen our advice to her.

In chapter 2, we explored the stages of abuse that a predator uses to attract and snare his victims. What do we know of Brian's pattern of abuse? Are his behaviors indicative of a man who will identify his victims, approach them, set the stage for the abuse by gaining control of them, and then groom them for the final act of abuse?

Is it possible that Brian sensed Maggie's vulnerability and set out to win her affection in order to get close to her kids? It was clear from the start that Maggie shared a great deal about herself with Brian. When she met him, she was lonely, in need of companionship, and all too eager to have someone to talk to. And Brian was there to meet her needs. Yet initially Brian did not divulge much about himself. In most offender treatment programs, participants are taught to tell the person they are dating early on in the relationship that they are convicted sex offenders. For Brian, once the children became part of the picture, he felt "forced" into telling Maggie about his sexual offenses. It was then that the pace of the relationship accelerated. When Brian felt threatened by Maggie's withdrawal, he intensified his statements of affection toward her. It was too early in the relationship for Brian to claim that he was "in love with her" and that he wanted "to make her and the children happy." There is enough evidence that Brian used these statements to control Maggie and coerce her into staying in the relationship.

Does Brian remind you of any of the four predators you met in chapter 3? While he may not exude the charisma or have the accomplishment of the schoolteacher, Harvey, they do share certain characteristics. Brian can be charming and pleasant to be around; and, like Harvey, he had had a sexual relationship with an adolescent girl. They both evidenced a sense of entitlement in seeking a young girl to meet their needs, and they blame outside circumstances for their behaviors.

What about the other predators you met in chapter 3? While Brian certainly seems more responsible and mature than the perennial adolescent Andy, they both sought comfort in children. We don't know enough about Brian's sexual preferences to liken him to the pedophile Mitchell, and there is no indication that Brian is totally impervious to the feelings of others, like the antisocial Thomas. Yet there are indications that he, like Harvey, Andy, Mitchell, and Thomas, lacks the necessary empathy to prevent him from using children to gratify his needs.

Let us now apply the things we learned in this chapter about the treatment of sexual offenders to Brian's situation. Although Brian has been in offender treatment for the past eighteen months, he has a long way to go. His motivation for therapy appears minimal at best, and he is operating at a level where there is only partial compliance with the program's rules. Brian is not even close to the stage where he is motivated to change, and for this reason, like his counselor told him, he is not ready to be in a relationship with a woman who has children.

We have already noted that Brian does not fully acknowledge himself as a sexual offender, and he sets himself apart from the rest of the participants in the program. Therefore he believes himself exempt from the rules that govern the rest of the offenders. This was clearly evidenced when Brian played in the park with Stacy and Michael, thus breaking the rules of his probation that clearly prohibited him from contact with children.

Because Brian does not really believe he is a sexual offender, he has not begun to tackle the many issues that must be addressed in offender treatment. We have already discussed the problem with Brian's ability to empathize with his victims. In fact, Brian does not acknowledge that he has created any victims, and therefore he cannot begin the work that would be necessary for rehabilitation.

Even though Brian has been in offender treatment for a year, he continues to display a number of thought distortions that prevent him from accepting full responsibility for his actions. He clearly denies that his sexual behaviors as a child were abusive, thus negating his responsibility and the impact it had on his victims. He also justifies the sexual abuse he perpetrated on his niece by shifting the blame to his unfortunate circumstances at the time as well as his niece's seductiveness.

Brian also has the ability to distort his thoughts in order to minimize his sexual contact with his niece by referring to it as a "mistake." By repeatedly referring to his intentional acts of child abuse as mere "mistakes," Brian is able to deny the profound impact that his actions had on another.

He even goes so far as likening his error of judgment when he had sex with his twelve-year-old niece to the "mistake" that Maggie made in having children with her childhood sweetheart. These are definitely not comparable.

Brian also projected his own sexual desires onto his niece and claimed that it was she who wanted sexual contact with him. Under no circumstances should this ever be offered as an excuse for sexual contact with a minor. A minor is in no position to assess the detrimental effects of sexual contact with an older relative or to consent to behaviors that she does not clearly understand. Sex with a child is never consensual, and projecting sexual desires onto a child is merely a means in which the predator can justify his or her deviant behaviors.

So if we present this evidence to Maggie, should there be any question about what she should do? To protect her children, and to avoid the pain that she may endure if she emotionally attaches to him, Maggie should say good-bye to Brian.

It will certainly be hard, particularly if she allows Brian to once again plead his case. He is a master of manipulation; and if Maggie lets him play that game, he is likely to gain the upper hand. So instead, Maggie should inform Brian in a succinct and firm manner that she has decided that she no longer wants to continue their relationship. Maggie should present this decision as final with no possibility for reconsideration.

As you can see from Maggie's story, becoming involved with a predator is a risky decision. It also requires that you know all aspects of the offender's treatment and are integrally involved with the therapy. As Maggie learned, it requires a commitment for as long as you remain with the offender. To place children in this type of environment, you must always remain in charge of monitoring and supervising their interactions with the offender.

With the knowledge you have learned about sex offender treatment, you should now be able to discern behaviors that will indicate whether the offender is at a low risk for harm. Remember that taking full responsibility for his or her actions is probably the most critical factor in the rehabilitation process. Many factors, such as a traumatic childhood, substance abuse, isolation, and loss, may be discussed as preexisting conditions that led to a decision to abuse; however, ultimately, the individual must recognize that his or her abusive acts resulted from choice. It is also essential that the offender be committed to the process of therapy as an avenue for change. Continuing to put into place the critical elements of the treatment program throughout the offender's life is essential in preventing relapse. Such things as devising and revising safety plans, monitoring and correcting distorted thought processes, and continuing to develop skills in communication and problem solving should be an integral part of the offender's life. Open communication, support, and healthy intimacy are essential ingredients for success, and therefore it is critical that marital or family counseling should also be considered to strengthen the offender's family unit.

Many of us in the mental health field believe that change is possible, and therefore it is difficult to close the door on all sexual predators. There are those offenders who do heal and transform and, with the proper guidance, structure, and support, will never reoffend. However you must be aware that there will always be some risk involved when you expose your children to an individual who has sexually assaulted children, and to minimize this risk, the offender should recognize this as well.

You have learned a great deal about sexual predators, but a few questions remain. Namely, "How do I create an environment in my home that will minimize the risk that my children will engage in sexually abusive behaviors with other children?" Also, "How can I set the proper environment for my children to openly communicate with me about sexual issues?" In the next chapter, you will learn how to address these vital concerns.

Prevention at Home

In the preceding pages, you have met many sexual predators, men, women, and adolescents, who skillfully maneuvered their way into the homes, churches, schools, treatment centers, and the neighborhoods of unsuspecting families. Now that you understand more about their characteristics, their patterns of seduction, and their treatment, you may feel more confident about preventing one from gaining access to your child.

However, the foundation of safety begins at home. The bastion of protection must be firmly established in the confines of your own living room. Your family has the power and fortitude to lay the bricks of safety, mortar the cracks with security, and raise high the tower of defense against sexual predators.

The most critical defense against sexual abuse is open communication. *STOP IT* NOW!, a nonprofit organization that focuses on the prevention of child sex abuse, cautions parents about the pitfalls of silence. "When we don't take the keys from a drunk friend in order to prevent him or her from driving a car, we are risking the safety of our friend and other drivers on the road. When we don't question our children about sexual behaviors, we are risking the safety of our children." Parents must talk openly about sexuality with their children and, in particular, sexual abuse.

Be very clear with your children about what constitutes sexual abuse and that sexual abuse can involve touching and nontouching behaviors.

Sexually abusive touching behaviors include:

> Touching a child's genitals, including penis, testicles, vagina, breasts, or anus, using a hand or any other body part.
> Making a child touch someone else's genitals.
> Putting body parts, like the tongue, fingers, penis, or other objects, inside a child's genitals, mouth, or anus for sexual pleasure.

Sexually abusive nontouching behaviors include:

> Showing pornography to a child.
> Exposing a person's genitals to a child.
> Photographing a child in sexual poses.
> Encouraging a child to watch or hear sexual acts in person or on a video.
> Watching a child undress or use the bathroom, often without the child's knowledge.

PROTECTING YOUR CHILD FROM SEXUAL ABUSE

STOP IT NOW! suggests the following steps in protecting your child from sexual abuse:

> Adults must watch for the signs of abuse in their children because young children are often not able to put into words what has happened to them.
> Teach your child how to say, "No," and help your child put this into action. For example, if your child doesn't want to give Uncle Pete a kiss, encourage the child to voice this and give him or her alternative ways to show affection, such as a handshake. Practice various situations in which your child should say, "No," using dolls, puppets, or stuffed animals.
> Set rules for privacy within the family and respect others' privacy. All family members should have privacy when bathing, dressing, sleeping, and engaging in other personal activities.
> Speak up when you see any warning signs. Don't be afraid to interrupt

an adult whose behavior with your child is making you feel uncomfortable. Your child may need your help in stopping these behaviors.

➤ Report anything you know or suspect is sexual abuse. You don't have to be 100 percent sure for the police, social services, and other child advocacy agencies, who are responsible for determining if sexual abuse has occurred, will make that determination.

➤ Talk openly with your children about difficult issues. If you have open and honest communication in your home, your children will be less afraid to come to you when they are experiencing something painful or embarrassing. Remember to listen to everything that your child is saying before you make judgments or criticisms. It is critical that you provide a safe place for your child to talk.

➤ Teach children the proper names for body parts. Just as you teach your children the correct names for other body parts, such as the nose, ears, eyes, and feet, genitals should also be referred to by their proper names. By giving children silly names for these parts of their bodies, they learn that they are different in an embarrassing way. Also, children who don't have the proper names for their genitals may be unable to accurately report incidents of sexual abuse.

➤ Teach your children about when it is permissible to touch someone and when it isn't. Teach them to respect others' bodies, and remember to tell them that touching another child's genitals in certain situations can be *against the law*. Without frightening your children, give them the parameters in which sexual touching could be considered illegal. Most important, teach your children that *secret touching* is never okay, and that if someone touches their bodies and asks them to keep it a secret, they should tell you what happened.

➤ Teach your children about safe Internet use, and supervise their time on the computer.

➤ Visit the numerous web sites on the Internet designed for parents and children that teach families how to fight sexual abuse. Discuss them with your children. At www.childlures.com there is a program that informs children, parents, and teachers of safety issues regarding children. It also offers an Internet safety pact that your child can read and sign, and www.cyberangels.org promotes child safety and prevention methods.

➤ Design a safety plan that you and your children can follow in case they are exposed to sexual abuse. Keep the plan simple and easy to remember. Teach children about what to do if they are sexually threatened or molested by someone. Give them specific names of who they should contact if you are not available.

➤ Make a list of who you need to call for advice, information, or help when you suspect child abuse. Make sure you are aware of how to report abuse and what resources are available for your child if sexual abuse has occurred. An Internet site, www.officer.com, provides hundreds of links with a wide array of police agencies in every state in America. No matter where you live, you will find a police agency close to home.

What if you have done all of the above and, tragically, your child still becomes a victim of sexual abuse? It is impossible to monitor all of the situations in another person's life, no matter how hard parents try to structure a safe environment and inoculate their children against the perils of sex abuse. Sex abuse can still happen. So, in the unfortunate event that your child does become a victim of sex abuse, what can you do to minimize the impact of the abuse? Early detection is essential. The sooner that abuse is identified and stopped, the better your child's chances are for recovery. Remember that your child may not be developmentally or emotionally ready to tell you what has happened to him or her. Therefore, the following guidelines can help you determine what behaviors your child may exhibit if he or she has been abused.

COMMON BEHAVIORAL WARNING SIGNS IN SEXUALLY ABUSED CHILDREN

Along with direct allegations about sexual abuse, the following behavioral symptoms are often found in children who have been sexually abused. Take notice of sudden changes in your child's behavior, yet be aware that these symptoms *alone* do not necessarily indicate sexual abuse. They may appear during other stressful times, like the death of a parent, a friend, or a pet, a divorce, or when there are problems at school. Any one sign doesn't mean that your child was abused. However, the presence of several of these behaviors is a clear indicator that your child is in distress.

Infancy to Twelve Months

- Listlessness
- Loss of appetite
- Apathy
- Little eye contact
- Inability to be soothed
- Change in sleeping habits
- Startle response, which is a physical reaction to loud noise or unexpected movement that involves the infant's arms rising and legs stiffening

Twelve Months to Two Years

- Regression of developmental milestones, such as loss of speech, motor skills, and toilet training.
- Chronic stomachaches, fever, and pains when there are no medical explanations
- Biting others
- Increase in temper tantrums
- Night terrors
- Change in eating or sleeping patterns
- Separation anxiety that intensifies or has resurfaced
- Preoccupation with his or her own genitals and the genitals of others, even when the child is redirected to other play
- Uncontrollable crying
- Becomes nervous or jumpy when hearing a loud noise or is startled or jumps when unexpectedly touched

Two to Four Years

- Baby talk and other regressive behaviors
- Loss of toilet training
- Frequent or painful urination that has no medical explanation

- Preoccupation with genitals or feces
- Nightmares or night terrors
- Pervasive fear of separation
- Development of certain phobias, such as fear of snakes, water, etc.
- Startle response
- Hypervigilance
- Reacts negatively to any change in the environment
- A new fear of a person that the child has previously known
- Overly aggressive with other children, such as frequent biting

Four to Six Years

- Baby talk and other regressive behaviors
- Night terrors or nightmares
- Insistence on sleeping with parents
- Difficulty going to sleep
- Chronic stomachaches, headaches, and other somatic complaints that have no medical etiology
- Increased irritability and anger, including hitting or biting other people
- Uncontrollable bouts of crying
- Temper tantrums that involve destruction of property or damage to self and/or other people
- Refusal to talk
- Listlessness, loss of interest in activities
- Difficulty concentrating
- Inability to learn new tasks, such as reading or writing
- Increased masturbation
- Display of inappropriate sexual activity with peers or acted out with toys
- Rigid fears of certain people, things, or situations
- New words for genitals
- Refusing to talk about a "secret"
- Talking about a new older friend
- Having toys, money, candy, or new clothes that you didn't give your child

Six to Twelve Years

➤ Marked change in academic performance, such as a drop in grades
➤ Loss of concentration
➤ Premature focus on stereotyped roles of sexuality, such as a little girl who always wants to dress up, wear makeup, curl her hair, paint nails, etc.
➤ Inappropriate displays of sexuality or focus on opposite sex peers
➤ Increased masturbation, and masturbation involving the use of objects, rubbing up against objects such as furniture, or the insertion of objects in the vagina
➤ Inappropriate sex play with other children
➤ Increased displays of aggression toward others
➤ Destructiveness with toys and personal property
➤ Withdrawal, isolation, and periods of listlessness
➤ Loss of interest in previously enjoyed activities
➤ Change in eating or sleeping habits
➤ Noticeable weight loss or gain
➤ Wetting or soiling pants in the day or at night
➤ Poor self-esteem evidenced in statements such as, "I hate myself," or, "I wish I were dead"

Adolescence

➤ Failing grades
➤ Sudden onset of behavioral problems, such as drug use, lying, stealing, truancy, and running away
➤ Suicidal ideation
➤ Self-mutilation, such as excessive body piercing, tattoos, cutting one's body
➤ Drastic change in appearance manifested in type of clothes worn, hairstyle, etc.
➤ Withdrawal from family and/or friends

- Dressing in sexually provocative clothes
- Sexual promiscuity
- Increased sleeping
- Change in appetite
- Marked change in body weight
- Marked change in routines and daily behaviors
- Loss of interest in previously enjoyed activities
- Increased anger and irritability
- Persistence of fears or avoidance of certain foods, people, or situations
- Avoidance of opposite sex relations
- Sense of hopelessness

Physical Warning Signs in Sexually Abused Children

- Unexplained bruises, redness, or bleeding of the child's genitals, anus, or mouth
- Pain at the genitals, anus, or mouth
- Genital sores or milky fluids in the genital area
- The sudden onset of painful or frequent urination
- Frequent infections in the urinary tract and/or vagina

Remember that none of the above physical signs by themselves are exact indicators of sexual abuse; however, if any of them are present, bring your child to a pediatrician for further examination.

Many children who are sexually abused don't demonstrate physical injury because there was no force involved, the abuse didn't involve the child's genitals, or penetration may not have been accomplished. In many cases, when the child molester is caught, he or she will encourage investigators to have the child medically examined. They know, however, that there will not be physical signs of injury to substantiate the charge. However, the absence of physical signs of injury should never be the sole determinant of whether sexual abuse took place.

Conclusion

You have been given a great deal of information about preventing child sexual abuse, and you have met a variety of sexual predators up close, from the most nefarious adult pedophile to the curious adolescent who experimented with sex. You have been introduced to parents who naively allowed their children to have access to an abusive stepparent, babysitter, or school counselor. And you have traveled to neighborhoods where unsupervised children played among undetected child abusers. You have seen parents who relinquished control of their children to a sexual predator who was disguised as a coach, medical professional, psychiatric nurse, daycare worker, relative, camp counselor, or romantic partner. You have witnessed sex abuse travel into children's homes by way of the Internet and learned about those predators who were and weren't listed on the Sex Offender Registry.

For those of you who have chosen to read this book, it is obvious that you are already concerned and aware of the dangers of child sexual abuse and are searching for more ways to protect your children. Although it is hopeful that this book will make a significant impact by reducing the number of children who become victims of sexual abuse each year, it is certain that it will decrease *your* child's risk.

It may seem somewhat opportunistic to blatantly expose the tragic mistakes made by those parents you have met in this book, but I did so to make a point. While you may have found yourself judging a number of these parents, if you stop to think how many times you may have taken a chance with the safety of your child, your condemnations may become less harsh. I am acutely aware of the incredible fortitude required in raising a child. As we are aware, making errors is the price we pay for being human. Yet parenting demands the kind of sacrifice and discipline that, at times, appears superhuman. It is hard to find any other area of life where mistakes can have such a profound and permanent effect.

The challenge of raising a child can seem like an inherently daunting task. The formation of a child's personality begins in the home, and that enormous responsibility should always be at the forefront of a parent's attention. Not for one moment can parents assume that if they let down their guard and turn their attention in the other direction harm won't seep its way into their children's lives. And parenting requires that at times you place the needs of your child before your own or those of other adults in your life. And you must do this for as long as it takes to prepare your child to go out into the world as a healthy and secure individual.

Protective parenting also means reexamining the childhood dreams we have carried with us into adulthood. For these dreams, many of which were set long ago as antidotes for the pain and suffering in our own childhood, will only serve as decoys for the real tasks of life. Consider some of the single mothers you met in this book. Many of them were women who dreamed all their lives of meeting the perfect man who would erase years of hardship, loneliness, and pain. These dreams often clouded their judgment and caused them to rush into a relationship before they realized that their "ideal" man was, in actuality, a sexual predator who stalked, groomed, and abused vulnerable children.

Parents *must* take a major role in protecting their children; and now that you have the necessary information to do this, you can be a formidable agent in the fight against child abuse. Mark Gado, in his article, "Pedophiles and Child Molesters: The Slaughter of Innocence," emphasizes the important role that parents must play in fighting child sex abuse. He states: "It is up to us, the caretakers of children, guardians of their safety and their dreams, to assume control, cast off the ominous shadow of sexual abuse, and bring their nightmare to an end."

You must never fall asleep in your task. Although it may seem like a twenty-four-hour vigil, it is essential that you post the necessary securities throughout your home and your child's environment to ward off sexual predators. Hopefully, the information you have learned in this book will help you fortify your locks, batten down the hatches, steel plate the armor, and fine-tune your radar so that your children will grow up in an environment where they are loved, nurtured, and, most importantly, protected.

Appendix A: Resources for Child Sexual Abuse

➤ Parents For Megan's Law (PFML)
P.O. Box 145
Stoney Brook, New York 11790
Telephone: 631-689-2672
Web site: www.parentsformeganslaw.com

PFML is a nonprofit victim's rights organization dedicated to the prevention of childhood sexual abuse through education, advocacy, and legislative support services.

➤ The Jacob Wetterling Foundation
P.O. Box 639
St. Joseph, MN 56374
Telephone: 1-800-325-HOPE
Web site: www.jwf.org

This foundation works on a national level on the issues of nonfamily child abduction and gathers and provides information to families.

➤ KlaasKids Foundation
P.O. Box 925
Sausalito, CA 94966
Telephone: (415) 331-6867
Web site: www.klaaskids.org

This foundation focuses on parental awareness and child safety efforts, as well as laws to protect children from criminals.

➤ Rape Abuse and Incest National Network (RAINN)
635-B Pennsylvania Ave., SE
Washington, DC 20003
Telephone: 1-800-659-HOPE
Web site: www.rainn.org

This nonprofit organization operates a toll-free hot line for victims of sexual assault. Incoming calls are routed to the nearest rape center nationwide.

➤ Childhelp USA
15757 N. 78th Street
Scottsdale, AZ 85260
Telephone: 480-922-8212
Hot line: 1-800-4-A-CHILD
Web site: www.childhelpusa.org

Childhelp is dedicated to meeting the physical, emotional, educational, and spiritual needs of abused and neglected children.

➤ American Humane Association
63 Inverness Drive East
Englewood, CO 80112-5117
Telephone: 1-800-227-4645
Web site: www.amerhumane.org

This organization provides professionals and concerned citizens with facts, resources, and referrals needed to help children and families in crisis and to prevent child abuse in their own neighborhoods.

➤ National Clearinghouse on Child Abuse and Neglect
330 C St., SW
Washington, DC 20447
1-800-FYI-3366
Web site: www.calib.com/nccanch

This agency is a national resource and clearinghouse that collects, stores, organizes, and disseminates information on all aspects of child maltreatment.

➤ Prevent Child Abuse America
200 S. Michigan Avenue
17th Floor
Chicago, IL 60604-2404
Telephone: 312-663-3520
Web site: www.preventchildabuse.org

This agency provides information about child abuse prevention, programs, education, training, research, and advocacy directed toward reducing all forms of child abuse.

➤ National Victim Center
2111 Wilson Blvd., Suite 300
Arlington, VA 22201
Web site: www.nvc.org

The National Victim Center provides information and referrals to victims of crime. In addition, they offer information bulletins on various violent crimes and victim rights.

➤ The Safer Society Foundation Inc.
P.O. Box 340
Brandon, VT 05733
Telephone: 802-247-3132
Web site: www.safersociety.org

This agency is dedicated to the prevention and treatment of sexual abuse. Safer Society offers publications for professionals, families, victims, and offenders related to sexual abuse.

➤ *STOP IT NOW!*
P.O. Box 495
Haydenville, MA 01039
Telephone: 413-268-3096
Web site: www.stopitnow.com

This organization is based on the idea that adults, especially abusers and potential abusers, must stop sexual abuse. It works to help abusers seek help, to educate adults about the ways to stop sexual abuse, and to increase public awareness of the trauma of child sexual abuse.

CANADA

Canadian Society for the Investigation of Child Abuse (CSICA)
P.O. Box 42066
Acadia Postal Outlet, Calgary, Alberta
Canada T2J 7A6
Telephone: (403) 289-8385
Web site: www.csica.zener.com

Central Agencies Sexual Abuse Treatment (CASAT)
197 Euclid Avenue
Toronto, Ontario M6J 2J8
Telephone: (416) 216-0278/9
Web site: www.casat.on.ca.

Family Services of Greater Vancouver
1616 West 7th Ave.
Vancouver, BC V6J 1S5
Telephone: (604) 731-4951
E-Mail: irochielle@fsgv.bc.ca
Web site: fsgv.bd.ca

Appendix B: Sex Offender Registration and Community Notification Internet Access

The best source of information on the registered sex offenders in your community is quite often your local sheriff's office police department. If a web site does not represent your community, you should check with local law enforcement. The following is a list of the most recent updated on-line information regarding registered sex offenders.

Alabama: http://www.gsiweb.net/so_doc; shso_index_new.html

   Athens: http://www.athenspd.org/
   Calhoun County: http://www.calhouncountysheriff.org/html/calcosex.htm
   Huntsville: http://ci.huntsville.al.us/police/
   Russell County: http://www.rcso.org/

Alaska: http://www.dps.state.ak.us/nSorcr/asp/

   Anchorage: http://www.ci.anchorage.ak.us/apd/

Arizona: http://www.azsexoffender.com/

   Pima County: http://www.pimasheriff.org/
   Tempe: http://www.tempe.gov/police/
   Tucson: http://www.ci.tucson.az.us/police

Arkansas: http://www.acic.org/registration/registration-main.html (information only)

California:
Also: Child Molester Hotline Number-900-463-0400 ($10 per call). And 900-448-3000. CD Roms are also available at all sheriff's offices and police departments serving populations of more than 50,000

Fremont Sexual Offender Maps: http://www.fremontpolice.org/megan/megan.html
Pleasanton Sexual Offender Maps: http://www.ci.pleasantcon.ca.us/police_ml_01.html
Santa Rosa: http://www.santarosapd.com/

Colorado:http://cdpsweb.state.co.us/ (violent sexual predators only)

Connecticut: http://; www.state.ct.us/dps/

Waterford: http://www.waterfordpolice.org/

Delaware: http://www.state.de.us/dsp/sexoff/index.htm

Florida: http://www.fdle.state.fl.us/sexual_predators/index.asp 1-888-FL-PREDATOR 1-888-357-7332, or http://www.sexualpredators.com/index.html

Citrus County: http://www.sheriff.citrus.fl.us/
Escambia Counth: http://www.escambiaso.com/
Fort Lauderdale: http://ci.ftlaud.fl.us/police/contents.html
Highlands County: http://www.ct.net/%7Esheriff/
Hollywood: http://www.hollywoodfl.org/hpd/sexpred/sexpred.htm
Jacksonville: http://www.coj.net/jso/
Lake County: http://www.sundial.net/~lcso/top.htm
Manatee County: http://legal.firn.edu/sheriff/manatee/
Margate County: http://www.margatefl.com/police/
Martin County: http://www.martin.fl.us/GOVT/co/sher/
Okaloosa County: http://www.sheriff-okaloosa.org/
Orange County: http://myweb.magicnet.net/ocso/pg1.html
Orlando: http://ci.orlando.fl.us/departments/opd/predator.html
Osceola County: http://www.osceolasheriff.org/sexpred/Default.htm
Palm Beach County: http://www.pbso.org/
Pasco County: http://pascocounty.com/sheriff/Sheriffwp-index.htm
Pinellas County: http://www.co.pinellas.fl.us/sheriff/pcso.htm
Polk County: http: //polksheriff.org/wanted/
Royal Palm Beach: http://legal.firn.edu/muni/rpalmbch/offenders.html
St. Johns County: http://www.co.st-johns.fl.us/Const-Officers/Sheriff/predator.html

St. Lucie County: http://www.stluciesheriff.com/
Sarasota County: http://legal.firn.edu/sheriff/sarasota/
Suwannee County: http://www.alltel.net/~altonwms/
Seminole County: http://www.seminolesheriff.org/sex_offenders/
sex_offender_register.html
Tallahassee: http://www.state.fl.us/citytlh/tpd/cid/predator.html
Volusia County:http://volusia.org/sheriff/
Wilton Manors:http://legal.firn.edu/muni/wiltonmanors/

Georgia: http://www.ganet.org/gbi/sorsch.cgi

    Atlanta PD http://atlantapd.org/links.htm

Hawaii: http://www.ehawaiigov.org/HI_SOR/

Idaho: http://www.2.state.id.us/ag/forms/sor.htm

    Ida County: http://www.adasheriff.org/sexoffenders.htm#start

Illinois: http://samnet.isp.state.il.us/ispso2/sex_offenders/index.asp

    Belleville: http://www.bellevillepolice.org/
    Chicago: http://12.17.79.4/
    Cook County: http://www.cookcountysheriff.org/sex_offender
    DuPage County:http://www.dupageco.org/sheriff/
    Hoffman Estates: http://www.hoffmanestates.com/Police/alerts/
    Police_sex_offenders.htm
    Kane County:http://www.co.kane.il.us/sao/sexoff/sofind.html
    Kankakee County: http://www.keynet.net/_patrol/sexoffender.html
    Lake County: http://www.co.lake.il.us/sheriff/sexoffnd/index.htm
    McLean County: http://www.mclean.gov/sheriff/list.htm
    St. Clair County: http://www.sheriff.co.st-clair.il.us/megan.asp
    Wheaton: http://city.wheaton.lib.il.us/pd/sex_offender_listpicnew.html

Indiana: http://www.state.in.us/serv/cji_sor

    Indianapolis: http://www.ci.indianapolis.in.us/ipd/

Iowa: http://www.state.ia.us/government/dps/dci/isor/ (information only) and
http://www.iowasexoffenders.com

Kansas: http://www.ink.org/public/kbi/kbiregoffpage.html

Labette County: http://www.geocities.com/Heartland/Plains/3524/sex.html
Sedgwick County: http://www.sedgwick.ks.us/sheriff/index.html

Kentucky:http://kspsor.state.ky.us/

Louisiana: http://www.lasocpr.lsp.org/socpr/

Maryland: http://www.clpses.state.md.u/sor/

Michigan: http://www.mipsor.state.mi.us

Macomb County: http://www.jaye.org/MACPSOR.html
Muskegon County: http://www.mlive.com/news/crimes/faces.html

Minnesota: http://www.doc.state.mn.us/

St. Paul: http://www.stpaul.gov/police/sexoff.html

Mississippi: http://www.sor.mdps.state.ms.us/

Montana: http://svor2.doj.state.mt.us:8010/index.htm

Nebraska: http://www.nsp.state.ne.us/sor/find.cfm

New Jersey: http://www.state.nj.us/lps/dcj/megan/meghome.htm

New Mexico: http://www.nmsexoffender.com

New York:

http://criminaljustice.state.ny.us/nsor/index.htm
http://www.parentsformeganslaw.com/

North Carolina: http://sbi.jus.state.nc.us/sor/

Ohio: http://www.drc.state.oh.us/search2.htm

Butler County Sheriff: http://www.butlersheriff.org
Clermont County Sheriff: http://www.clermontsheriff.org
Fayette County Sheriff: http://www.faycoso.com
Franklin County: http://www.sheriff.franklin.oh.us/
Greene County: http://www.co.greene.oh.us/sxoffendr.htm
Hamilton County: http://www.hcso.org/records/offender.htm

Hamilton County Sheriff: http://www.hcso.org
Highland Co. Sheriff: http://www.highlandcoso.com
Licking County Sheriff: http://www.lickingcountysheriff.com
Montgomery County Sheriff: http://www.co.montgomery.oh.us/sheriff
Stark County: http://www.sheriff.co.stark.oh.us/pr01.htm
    University of Akron: http://www.uakron.edu/police/sexoff.htm

Oklahoma: http://www.tulsapolice.com/registry.html

Altus: http://www.intellisys.net/APD/
Bartlesville: http://www.cityofbartlesville.org/Police/sexual_offenders.htm
Bixby: http://www.bixby.com/police/offenders.htm
Blaine County: http://www.pldi.net/~blaineso/
blaine_county_sexual_predator_pa.htm
Broken Arrow: http://www.city.broken-arrow.ok.us/sex%20offenders.htm
Claremore: http://www.claremorepolice.com/offenders.html
Creek County: http://www.creekcountysheriff.com/CCSO/PAGES/
sexoff.htm
Custer County: http://www.geocities.com/capitolhill/senate/2189/sexreg.html
Granfield: http://www.law-enforcement.org/grandfieldpd/rso.html
Oklahoma County: http://www.oklahomacounty.org/sheriff/
registered_sex_offenders.htm
Perry: http://www.fullnet.net/np/perrypd/sexoff.html
Seminole County: http://www.geocities.com/CapitolHill/3831/sexoff.htm
Stillwater: http://www.stillwaterpolicedept.org/sex_offenders.htm
Tulsa: http://www.tulsapolice.org/sexreg/sexreg.html

Oregon:

Benton County: http://www.co.benton.or.us/sheriff/corrections/bccc/sonote/
Yamhill County: http://www.co.yamhill.or.us/correct/

Pennsylvania: http://www.meganslaw.state.pa.us

South Carolina: http://www.scattorneygeneral.com/public/registry.html

Tennessee: http://www.ticic.state.tn.us/sexofndr/searchshort.asp

Texas: http://www.records.txdps.state.tx.us/sexofndr/searchshort.asp

Collins County: http://www.co.collin.tx.us/sheriff/sxoffen.htm
Dallas: http://www.ci.dallas.tx.us/dpd/
Denton County: http://www.sheriff.co.denton.tx.us/sex_offenders/default.htm

Duncanville Police Department: http://www.ci.duncanville.tx.us/police
Farmers Branch: http://www.ci.farmers-branch.tx.us/police/sexoffend/
index.htm
Garland: http://www.ci.garland.tx.us/police/gpdsex.htm
Lubbock Police Department: http://www.lubbockpolice.com

Utah: http://www.udc.state.ut.us

Vermont: http://www.dps.state.vt.us/cjs/s_registry.htm (information only)

Virginia: http://sex-offender.vsp.state.va.us/cool-ICE/

Washington:

Bellevue: http://www.ci.bellevue.wa.us/police/sexoffenders/default.htm
Bellingham: http://www.cob.org/cobweb/police/sexoffr.htm
Clark County: http://www.co.clark.wa.us/sheriff/inter/comminfo/sexoffender/
sex.htm
Cowlitz County: http://www.cowlitzcounty.org/sheriff/rso/default.htm
Island County: http://www.islandcounty.net/sheriff/sex-map.htm
King County: http://www.metrokc.gov/sheriff/sosch.htm
Longview: http://www.ci.longview.wa.us/police/Services/notification.htm
Okanogan County: http://okanogancounty.org/Sheriff/soffend.htm
Pierce County: http://www.co.pierce.wa.us/abtus/ourorg/sheriff/default.htm
Renton: http://www.ci.renton.wa.us/police/sexlev13.htm
Tri Cities: http://www.tri-cityherald.com/sexoffenders/
Wahkiakum County: http://www.geocities.com/CapitolHill/Lobby/7649/
sexoffend.htm

Washington, D.C.: http://mpdc.gov/main.shtm

West Virginia: http://www.wvstatepolice.com

Wisconsin: Toll Free Access Line 1-800-398-2403

Appleton: http://appleton.org/police/sorp.htm
Kenosha: http://kenoshapolice.com/sex.htm
Madison: http://www.ci.madison.wi.us/police/sexoffend.html
Milwaukee: http://milw-police.org/RegSexOffenders.html

Wyoming: http://www.state.wy.us/~ag/dci/so/so_registration.html

Albany County: http://www.state.wy.us/~ag/dci/so/counties/so_albany.html
Big Horn County: http://www.state.wy.us/~ag/dci/so/counties/
so_bighorn.html
Converse County: http://www.state.wy.us/~ag/dci/so/counties/
so_converse.html
Crook County: http://www.state.wy.us/~ag/dci/so/counties/so_crook.html
Fremont County: http://www.state.wy.us/~ag/dci/so/counties/
so_fremont.html
Goshen County: http://www.state.wy.us/~ag/dci/so/counties/so_goshen.html
Johnson County: http://www.state.wy.us/~ag/dci/so/counties/
so_johnson.html
Laramie County: http://www.state.wy.us/~ag/dci/so/counties/so_laramie.html
Natrona County: http://www.state.wy.us/~ag/dci/so/counties/so_natrona.html
Park County: http://www.state.wy.us/~ag/dci/so/counties/so_park.html
Sheridan County: http://www.state.wy.us/~ag/dci/so/counties/
so_sheridan.html
Sublette County: http://www.state.wy.us/~ag/dci/so/counties/so_sublette.html
Uinta County: http://www.state.wy.us/~ag/dci/so/counties/so_uinta.html
Weston County: http://www.state.wy.us/~ag/dci/so/counties/so_weston.html

Index

About the Author

LEIGH BAKER earned a doctorate in clinical psychology and has worked with sexually abused children and their families for the past sixteen years. She is the director of the Trauma Treatment Center of Colorado, where she supervises and conducts research, training, and treatment of abused children and their families. She is the author of a handbook for parents whose children have been sexually abused and a manual for treatment providers. She has written numerous articles for parents and professionals in the area of trauma and abuse. She has also served as a forensic expert in childhood trauma and has lectured extensively in the area.